Inventive Negotiation

Inventive Negotiation
Getting Beyond Yes

John L. Graham, Lynda Lawrence, and
William Hernández Requejo

palgrave
macmillan

INVENTIVE NEGOTIATION

Copyright © John L. Graham, Lynda Lawrence, and William Hernández Requejo, 2014.

First published in 2014 by
PALGRAVE MACMILLAN®
in the United States—a division of St. Martin's Press LLC,
175 Fifth Avenue, New York, NY 10010.

Where this book is distributed in the UK, Europe and the rest of the world,
this is by Palgrave Macmillan, a division of Macmillan Publishers Limited,
registered in England, company number 785998, of Houndmills, Basingstoke,
Hampshire RG21 6XS.

Palgrave Macmillan is the global academic imprint of the above companies
and has companies and representatives throughout the world.

Palgrave® and Macmillan® are registered trademarks in the United States,
the United Kingdom, Europe and other countries.

ISBN: 978–1–137–37015–0

Library of Congress Cataloging-in-Publication Data

Graham, John L.
    Inventive negotiation : getting beyond yes / John L. Graham, Lynda
Lawrence, William Hernandez Requejo.
        pages cm
    ISBN 978–1–137–37015–0 (alk. paper)
        1. Negotiation in business. 2. Negotiation. 3. Business communication.
    4. Interpersonal communication. I. Lawrence, Lynda. II. Requejo, William
    Hernández. III. Title.

HD58.6.G697 2014
658.4'052—dc23   2013043935

A catalogue record of the book is available from the British Library.

Design by Newgen Knowledge Works (P) Ltd., Chennai, India.

First edition: May 2014

10 9 8 7 6 5 4 3 2 1

Printed in the United States of America.

John's—To the family I grew up in: Charlotte, John, Sherry, Mary Ellen, Steve, and Bill. They were my first teachers of negotiation.
Also, as I type these words of thanks I'm thinking of Anne Gallagher, founder of Seeds of Hope, driving me around Dublin and Belfast, showing me the paths to peace.

Lynda's—To Ruth, Lynn, and Tom for 156 years of love and support.

William's—To my family, Martha, William, and Marina for their creativity, thoughtfulness, and simplicity.

Contents

Exhibits and Table

Exhibits

Table

Preface

"AND?" When spoken with a rising tone, this simplest of sentences represents the essence of inventive negotiations in two fundamental ways. First, it recognizes that invention is a social activity involving you and me, and sometimes even Dick and Jane and Yoshi and Maria. Second, this simplest of questions asks "what's next" after an agreement and beyond that old "getting to yes." It also avoids the creativity killing "yeah, but..." It implies a long-term relationship among partners where synergy pertains. Our book (henceforward we'll just call it *Inventive Negotiation*) is about a new way of thinking about human exchange and about how to conduct inventive negotiations in all aspects of your life—personal, commercial, political, and global.

Acknowledgments

Thanks to all the members of the board of the University of California, Irvine, Center for Citizen Peacebuilding for their wonderful work and their influences on our writing. In particular, we appreciate the dedication to building peace and the good ideas from Paula Garb and Dulcie and Larry Kugelman. Eric Algreen-Petersen's tutelage was instrumental in building the team for the book. Laurie Harting, our editor at Palgrave Macmillan who saw a glimmer of opportunity that others had missed and profoundly affected the construction our book. And thanks to all our storytellers: Eli Simon, Bruce Money, Sudhir Venkatesh, Robert Nagourney, Marissa Arzate, Anthony Chang, Mary Robinson, Jan Sunoo, William Graham, Carol Holt, Matthew Alexander, Father Gregory Boyle, Amaury Gallais, Gregg Curly, Yoshihiro Sano, Mark Lam, David Obstfeld, Jorge Habetha, Mili Decompo Rama, Lawrence Burns, Geert Hofstede, Samantha Cross, Mary Gilly, John Gerretsen, Paul Ekman, Bernard Lafayette, Sharon Graham Niederhaus, Teresa Lavell, Paula Garb, Gwendolyn Oxenham, and Robert Cohen. The excellent cover was designed by Simone Beaudoin.

In memoriam: Miguel Alfonso Martinez, Anne Gallagher, Edward T. Hall, James Day Hodgson, and F. Sherwood Rowland.

Introduction: Bought a Car Lately?

The sale begins when the customer says yes.

—Harvey Mackay[1]

With hundreds of books and courses available on negotiation, why on earth would you need another one? The answer, in short, is that the world has changed in profound ways in the last decade, and techniques that worked in that world are not effective today—and certainly won't be tomorrow.

As a brief example, let's consider the one negotiation that almost everyone dreads: buying a new car. Each of us had that task this year, and our three experiences illustrate just how much the rules have changed.

John set out to help his daughter with her purchase. She'd already selected the model she wanted and had test driven it; their mission was simply to buy the car for the best price. The salesman was adamant—before talking about price, she just *had* to drive the car. It took John and his daughter ten minutes to explain several times that they had already done that—they just wanted to buy the car. Reluctant to relinquish this time-tested technique to soften up the customer, the salesman finally ushered father and daughter into his tiny office.

They asked about the price and terms. Following his script, the salesman wouldn't give them a price, and instead insisted that they tell him what John's daughter could afford to pay each month. They declined, asking the salesman again to tell them the price of the car. He refused and asked again what she wanted to pay. They asked again about the price. By this time, voices were raised, and John's daughter left in disgust. Ultimately she bought another brand.

Clearly, this salesman was following the negotiating strategy that has long been used in car sales. The test drive gives customers the physical feeling of the car, but more important, it helps them see themselves driving *this very car*, and they start to develop an emotional attachment to it. The salesman's next step is to get the customer to make the first offer and to commit to a price he or she is willing to pay. Typically, this takes the buyer down a path toward commitment, and the salesman can then jiggle the terms to match the price the buyer has already committed to. The salesman retains the power since he has all the information, and the buyer has already come more than halfway toward purchase. This strategy is typical of the competitive/transactional approach, where one person's gain is another person's loss. And this is a primary reason that people hate to buy cars, especially in the United States, where most other sales do not involve bargaining.

William took a different approach and sought the advice of a friend who had been the finance manager at a number of car dealerships. Trained as an attorney, William knew only too well that the selling of a car was one of the most highly choreographed commercial negotiations in the United States,[2] which is why he turned to his friend.

But even here, the friend (who in essence served as a broker/dealmaker) asked the same questions as John's salesman. Considering your status and needs, what kind of car do you see yourself in? How much are you willing to pay? Test-driving was not an option, and William's friend sent him carefully selected webpages. William drove the car virtually, and began establishing an emotional connection. Things such as status, personal needs, and certain auto features were quickly identified and put into the equation. Next came the price.

Just as in John's experience, the price was never discussed. Instead, what William was willing to pay became the critical point, now that the emotional connection was even stronger. In the end, William came away with almost exactly what he had sought: a Jeep Grand Cherokee 4x4 with all the bells and whistles. The lease price he had originally expected plus $30 per month for 36 months became the final agreement.

It had finally boiled down to whether William perceived the deal to be "fair." For the "fairness of the transaction" he trusted a friend who he knew understood the sales dance. In the end, William thought the price was fair, but then again, he did not determine—and did not necessarily want to invest the emotional energy necessary to find out—whether the deal was in fact "fair."

Lynda, who *really* hates car dealerships, took a third approach. For several days, she searched the Internet, looking at one-year-old, low-mileage cars for her daughter and comparing them with cars listed in newspaper ads. Since the new cars seemed to cost about the same as the used ones and came with warranties, she shifted her focus to new cars and checked out rankings for inexpensive, reliable, and gas-efficient ones. At the *U.S. News & World Report* site, she found a link that offered guaranteed pricing, clicked through, and filled out the details on the cars she wanted. Within minutes, she had price guarantees for the very cars she had selected from dealerships within 25 miles of her house, and all the prices were lower than the ones advertised for a model with fewer options.

Price negotiations, however, have another wild card: the trade-in value of your old car. The last time Lynda had been car shopping, that value was a closely guarded secret. The *Blue Book* was stored behind the salesman's desk; he paged around a bit and offered a price. Having all the knowledge about the new car's price and the old car's value, he was in a position of power.

Today, that information is available instantly, free. Thus, Lynda checked the *Kelley Blue Book* site, plugged in the details of her daughter's old car, and printed out the estimated value. Armed with this knowledge and some car buying tips she'd found on the Internet, they went to a nearby dealership early on the last Saturday of the month. Her daughter took the test-drive, and the negotiations began. It was simplicity itself.

They asked if the salesman would meet the price guaranteed on paper from a different dealership, 12 miles away. He did the obligatory check with his manager, decided that selling a car at a lower margin than he'd have preferred was better than no sale at all, and agreed to the price.

The trade-in was equally simple: he offered $500 less than the *Blue Book* price. They accepted $250 less, and they walked out within an hour. Everybody felt like a winner, and Lynda's family would recommend the salesman to their friends.

Three different approaches, three different outcomes. And yet, for the truly inventive buyer even more possibilities exist. Instead of pondering how to buy a car, you could reserve a car just for the hours you need it. With new services like Zipcar, there's no down payment, insurance, maintenance, gas, or storage. You can have an SUV when you need to haul stuff or a Smart car for crowded city parking. No negotiation necessary. If you live in a city, you can choose between various kinds of public transit (some of them as much fun as San Francisco's cable cars), cabs, or start-ups like Uber and Lyft.

In a world where information is available instantly wherever there's cell phone reception, the old rules no longer apply. Notice the prominence of networks in the last three examples—the old standby of William's friendship, Lynda's twenty-first-century information access, and Zipcar's social network enabled by the Internet and social media. Information symmetry changed the game for Lynda. The cultural importance of personal networks and relationships affected William's transaction.

In this century we've learned a lot about innovation processes. The smartest people in the room will use those techniques while the standard techniques will still yield gridlock. Negotiating today requires much more inventive techniques gathered from experts around the globe. We'll be sharing their stories of successful inventive negotiations in the pages to follow.

The Importance of Stories[3]

"Once upon a time . . . "

"In the beginning . . . "

"A long time ago in a galaxy far, far away . . . "

If you're human, you're already hooked by the time you get past the opening phrase. What is it that makes stories so compelling, and why are they integral to the idea of inventive negotiation?

Let's begin with a little history. Imagine, if you will, your long ago ancestors huddled around a campfire. That comforting flame itself is a new invention then. The world is a pretty scary place. Food is scarce, predators are numerous, and that nearby tribe is competing for your food and your women. Language is pretty new and survival skills are essential. To learn them, there's no teacher, no instruction manual, no YouTube videos to watch.

But your ancestors have discovered a wonderful tool for passing along vital information: It's the story—of how they outsmarted the lion or used the bark of a tree to reduce pain. The evolutionary history is clear: the tribes which successfully used those stories to pass along the information were the ones that survived long enough to produce offspring.

From a biological basis, storytelling may be derived from pattern recognition. Being able to spot something unusual in a landscape was critical if you wanted to see a lion moving through the tall grass. And from that innate skill of pattern recognition, humans began to assign meaning to otherwise random blots: There's a face on the man in the moon, a holy picture in a grilled cheese sandwich.

Our need to make sense of patterns often drives us to assign human emotions to inanimate objects. In a famous experiment done by psychologists Fritz Heider and Marianne Simmel in the 1940s,[4] subjects watched a crude animation of a box with a swinging flap, two triangles, and a circle that moved around a screen in fairly random patterns.

Asked after a viewing what they had seen, only 3 of the 114 subjects described the geometric shapes. The other 111 reported tales (that is, told stories) of heroism and bullies, love, and slamming doors, and a massive tantrum. (If you'd like to see for yourself, you can try it on YouTube: http://www.youtube.com/watch?v=VTNmLt7QX8E.)

This storytelling as information transfer is only one aspect of its use as a tool. Because of our tendency to pass all information through an emotional filter, the stories that had the most staying power were the ones with the most emotion: stories about damsels in distress, heroes and villains, wins and losses. At the core of each story there was some kind of trouble, and somebody solved the problem or failed. It's not a great leap from there to using stories to tell moral fables, the rules of how we live together. The good guys do this, the bad guys do that.

Every religion has these moral stories, easy ways for the tribe to remember the rules. Sometimes they explain behavior, sometimes they explain mysteries. It took us millennia to figure out where babies came from. So it's only natural that people would use stories to explain the greatest mystery: where do WE come from?

Hence the power of "once upon a time. . . ." That primordial form promises a story that will satisfy our curiosity and make us believe that we have a place in the scheme of things. It will create order out of chaos, sequence from random events, and a hope that the problem can be solved, the hero can win, and right will triumph in the end.

Indeed, it's in the nature of stories to create a beginning, a middle, and an end. Sometimes these narratives are long; the saga of Odysseus. Sometimes they're short: the punch line to a Country and Western song, or Ben Franklin's exhortation to deal with problems when they arise, "A stitch in time saves nine."

Because the early tales were easier to remember if they rhymed or if they were sung, research shows we believe in rhyming phrases even if they're not actually true. In the O. J. Simpson trial, jurors believed the phrase "If the glove doesn't fit, you must acquit." Good stories persuade us because they make us feel we understand the situation.

We trust our instincts, we let down our barriers, and we believe.

Some stories don't even have to have words to convey powerful emotions and pull us into a narrative. Imagine the famous Depression-era photograph by Dorothea Lange of the migrant mother and her children, turned away from the camera. In an instant, you feel her desperation, her will, her hopes, her fears, and you understand what the Depression had done to hard-working people like her.

So, why is this important in negotiation?

First, because everyone comes into a negotiation with her or his own story firmly in place. In a legal dispute, it's generally that I'm right and the other guy is wrong. Often there's a moral dimension: not only am I right, but I'm righteously right. The other guy is not only wrong, he's evil.

Second, it's because most of our stories throughout history are quite black and white. Only one of us can win. If you're St. George setting out to slay the dragon, either you cut off the dragon's head, or you're in for a fiery death.

Now, for an enlightened few, there might be a second scenario. For a few decades now, the theory of win-win has been in vogue: If we talk about what we really want, instead of dividing the orange, I'll get the juice, and you get the rind so you can grate it into your cake batter.

There are two problems with this approach. First, it doesn't have a long tradition in our stories. If Cinderella's foot fits the slipper, she and Prince Charming get to live happily ever after. But the stepsisters are still left nursing their grudges, and life tells us that they are not going to take this lying down.

The second problem is that the outcome is always finite. It's the same orange we're splitting, albeit differently. There's only one gal who can marry the prince. (And by the way, is he really such a prize? A guy who can't remember the woman he romanced last week without her trying on a shoe?)

No, the really successful negotiation is one where the outcome is much greater than we ever imagined. We don't just split one lousy pie, we build a pie factory together, and everybody gets to eat pie forever.

SIDEBAR I.1

The Most Common Negotiation Story Ever Told

Perhaps the most famous negotiation parable involves an argument over an orange. The simplest approach was to simply cut it in half so each person gets a fair share.

But when the negotiators began talking to each other, exchanging information about their interests, a better solution to the problem became obvious. The person wanting the orange for juice for breakfast took that part, and the person wanting the rind for making marmalade took that part. Both sides ended up with more. Neither agreement is particularly inventive.

The parable of the orange becomes a story about invention when both parties decide to cooperate in planting an orange tree.

So that's why we say it all begins with the story. The strongest story wins, often in surprising ways. In political circles, they call it framing or spinning: the first, most emotional stories set up the negotiation. For example, the notion that ObamaCare had death panels, although totally false, easily beat out the list of bullet points that proponents were selling. And the proponents have been on the defensive ever since for a program that most people actually agree with when they come to know the details.

Stories of successful inventive negotiations are the fundamental building blocks of our book. We know you're more likely to believe and remember our stories than a series of PowerPoint slides with bullet points or summaries of research findings. While the research is the foundation of this book, the stories will help you apply what you are learning to all the inventive negotiations you'll have in the future. And along the way, you may just learn how to become a compelling storyteller yourself.

CHAPTER 1

Going Forward to the Past: A Brief History of Negotiation

The further backward you look, the further forward you are likely to see.
—Winston Churchill

The word negotiation is derived from two Latin terms, *negare otium;* they translate literally as "to deny leisure." In French and Spanish, "deny leisure" becomes "business." Yet, while the word is Latin-derived, the behavior predates that culture by roughly 200,000 years, dating back to ever since *Homo sapiens* developed as a species.

During all those years, humans had four basic means to resolve disputes or solve problems. We have taken some creative liberties and call them the four M's—Might, Market, Mutual interests, and iMagination. Anthropologists think that for about 190,000 of those years we mostly used imagination. On the southeastern African savannahs, small migrating bands of hunter-gatherers sat around campfires and combined their imaginations to invent the best ways to survive. While they did not invent the fire that warmed them, cooked their food, and protected them, they did invent an impressive list of ways to use it. Around those campfires humans used their *collective imaginations* and their *long-term relationships* to survive and develop even better ways to live.

Yet, somehow we have lost these interaction skills that promoted our success as a species. Americans in particular are handicapped by our own culture when it comes to negotiating inventively. Consider your own approaches to negotiation in the twenty-first century.

Almost everything in your life depends on negotiation. Even before you could speak, you were negotiating what you would eat from your high chair tray—and tossing the losing items to the dog. From there, you graduated to bedtimes, TV viewing, homework, activities, and curfews.

As an adult, you still spend hours negotiating what's for dinner, where to go on vacation, and all those childhood issues with your own children. At work, you're negotiating which assignments you'll take, what hours you'll work, and maybe your salary.

Without realizing it, you're also negotiating all day on smaller issues: who is going to drop the kids off at school, how long you can stay at that meeting, who you want on your team, where you'll meet for lunch, when to schedule the conference call, which friends you'll see this weekend, which family you'll see on the holidays. In all these daily interactions, how often do the words *creativity* or *invention* come up?

You learned negotiation organically, mostly through unconscious imitation of your parents, siblings, and other role models. The techniques you honed in your youth are probably the same ones you use today, depending on your personal style: tantrums, charm, instant acquiescence, indecisiveness, procrastination, or nodding yes with no intent of doing what you've agreed to do.

Along the way, you may have had some formal training in conflict resolution or business negotiation. Chances are you've learned to "do your homework," state what you want, listen, even look for a deal that both sides find acceptable. There's some conventional wisdom that recommends you keep important information to yourself or start with an outrageous offer in order to "set an anchor" for the haggling. But nowhere have you learned how inventive negotiation can make everybody more successful, what the critical steps are in the process, and how to use the many tools you'll need along the way. How did we lose the inventive negotiation skills delivered to us during our evolution among the scattered shade trees on that arid plain?

The Way Forward Is in the Rearview Mirror

Among all the animals on the African savannah, the collaborators have always dominated. You cannot see their intricate social behavior in the zoos; modern cages don't accommodate herds, prides, and packs. But in a few hours on the savannah you immediately see the dominance of *groups* of animals. There are the lions, Cape buffalo, elephants, often in large extended families of twenty or so, commanded by the matrons among them.

Field biologists tracking Cape buffalo report an interesting behavior: they vote. During the long afternoons when the herd rests, the females will stand, shuffle around, and lay back down again. They end up facing the way in which each thinks the herd should move. After about an hour of this "voting," the herd will move in the decided direction. There's no hierarchy, no leader, just a democratic decision process that affects every member of the herd and everyone's chances for survival.

Of course, we human animals evolved in this same setting, and until relatively recent times we were organized pretty much the same way. Collaboration was the key to our species' success. Like most of the other big animals, humans have been genetically designed to work together in groups.

But simple collaboration is not what makes us a special species. Most lists of our distinctive characteristics include observable ones, such as our unusually complex and big brains (relative to body size) and our opposable thumbs. Abstract reasoning, language, introspection, problem solving, and culture are often on the list as well. But other large animals share at least some of these characteristics. Pods of orcas, other primates, and octopi all come to mind.

Scottish philosopher Adam Smith once opined: "Man is an animal that makes bargains—no other animal does this, no dog exchanges bones with another." Yes, humanness is most sharply delineated by the two activities in the title of our book: invention and negotiation. You can get a glimpse of this aboriginal approach to problem solving by streaming from Netflix the classic film *The Gods Must Be Crazy*. Those prehistoric Africans developed ways to collaborate among themselves and with those around them that have now evolved into the global trade of innovations that has yielded the incomparable progress of our species.

We know that even the most primitive tribes with no common language were able to exchange goods, sometimes without ever meeting face-to-face. Anthropologists point out instances of "silent trade" occurring well before the advent of common languages, writing, money, and the Internet intervened. Tribe A would leave a set of trade goods on a prominent riverbank, and signal tribe B that they had done so by smoke, drums, or gong. The people in Tribe B would take the goods they desired and leave a complimentary set of goods. If tribe A was dissatisfied with the amount, it would take nothing. Tribe B would then add to the goods. Once tribe A had taken the goods offered, the transaction was complete. Obviously, trust and long-term relationships were key aspects of this trade. Jared Diamond, *author of Guns, Germs, and Steel*[1] makes a similar point: "In traditional societies, you know everyone and you're going to be dealing with them for the next 50 years of your life. So, dispute resolution aims to achieve emotional closure."[2]

Humans by nature both negotiate and invent. Only by combining our imaginations can we get beyond the limits of our individual insight. And we all can use these tools of invention and negotiation every day. But inventive negotiation is also critical on the grandest and most formal stages of global commerce, international relations, and peacebuilding.[3]

From Might Back to iMagination

Only in the last 10,000 years has the dominance of imagination over might, markets, and mutual interests waned. While the minds and bodies of humans have remained pretty much the same, elements of culture have conspired to shift the balance of human interaction toward unhealthy inefficiencies. We've lost our natural abilities to negotiate inventively and have begun to rely more heavily on might, markets, and mutual interests to solve our problems.

Might

About 10,000 years ago, agriculture disrupted hunting and gathering behavior and the culture that went with it.[4] Instead of communally picking wild grain and moving on, some families stayed in one place for a season or two, delighting in the control they had over their future food source if they planted and nurtured crops. Of course, if they didn't want other wandering families or animals to eat that grain, they had to protect it with walls and spears. And they had to trade for the meat they could no longer chase while they were tending fields. The first intergroup negotiations were probably over water—give me access to your stream, and I'll give you part of my crop. Or maybe marry my daughter to your son.

This new system led to longer life spans, steep population growth, specialties like art and math, then cities and rulers, royalty, and social hierarchy. Not to mention the inevitable disputes over boundaries and fair prices, all of which increased the need for negotiation. When negotiation worked, it was wonderful. When it didn't, it was war. Genghis Khan and his raiders didn't do a lot of sitting around discussing options with their neighbors. Thus, agrarian societies adopted the sword and bludgeon and military coercion as persuasive tactics. Might prevailed over imagination.

Market-Based Competition

The cradle of ancient Western civilization was Greece in 500 BC. On a map, you see its prominent geographical feature is thousands of islands—and those islands are perfect breeding grounds for individualism. Indeed, the word "isolation" comes from the French *isola*, or "island." If you get mad at your neighbor, you can always move to another island, particularly when the seas are Aegean calm. You don't need your neighbor's help to cast your net. In fact, you can't fit many folks into your boat anyway. So personal freedom, individuality, objective thought, and even democracy have deep roots in this ancient island realm.[5] (Though those "voting" Cape buffaloes might disagree.)

When Adam Smith published *Wealth of Nations* in 1776, the concept of market competition really took hold. In that book, the Scottish philosopher created perhaps the most influential sentence ever written in English: "By pursuing his own interest he frequently[6] promotes that of the society more effectually than when he really intends to promote it." With a stroke of his pen Smith solved the age-old conundrum of group interests versus individual interests. And through his associates such as Benjamin Franklin, he inseminated that philosophy into the fundamental structure of the most dynamic social system ever devised by mankind. Thus, in no other country on the planet are individualism and competitiveness more highly valued than in the United States.

Moreover, throughout its history, America has been a nation influenced by its immigrants. Certainly, the continuous mixing of ideas and perspectives brought from across the seas has enriched all our experiences. Every newcomer has had to work hard to succeed—thus the powerful work ethic of America. Another quality of our immigrant forefathers was a fierce individualism and independence, characteristics necessary for the initial risk of immigration and for survival in the wide open spaces. Indeed, *The Declaration of Independence* both coincided with and defined our history and national identity.[7] But this fetish for independence does us a disservice at the negotiation table. Negotiation is by definition a situation of *inter*dependence, a situation that Americans have never handled well.

We have inherited more of this island/individualistic mentality from our frontier history. "Move out West where there's elbow room," ran the conventional wisdom of the first 150 years of our nation's existence. Americans as a group haven't had much practice negotiating because they have always been able to go elsewhere when conflicts arose.

SIDEBAR 1.1

Add a Dash of the Duke

Mix Adam Smith's philosophy and John Wayne's behavior, and you get this candid description from a very experienced American international negotiator in his sixties:

"You're always in some crappy little room, in some crappy little country. It's your duty to your company to get the best of all possible deals, so you walk in asking for way more than they'll give you. And you stay there just long enough to get what you want. With any luck, you've intimidated them so badly that they'll want to crawl back to the table the next time."

We asked, "How about the possibility of treating the other side like partners to establish a long-term profitable relationship?"

"Are you crazy? What are you, socialists?"

The long distances between people allowed a social system to develop with both fewer negotiations and shorter ones. A day-long horseback ride to the general store or stockyard didn't encourage long, drawn-out negotiations. It was important to settle things quickly and leave no loose ends to the bargain. "Tell me yes, or tell me no—but give me a straight answer." Candor, laying your cards on the table, was highly valued and expected in the Old West. Think of the John Wayne[8] role model so prominent in American male culture. And straight talk, not diplomacy, is still valued today in our boardrooms and classrooms.

Of course, our educational system also reflects Adam Smith's philosophy. And what goes on in the classrooms in our business and law schools, in turn, has a strong influence on our negotiation style. Throughout the American educational system, we are taught to compete, both academically and on the sporting field. Adversarial relationships and winning are essential themes of the American socialization process. But nowhere in the American educational system is competition and winning more important than in case discussions in our law and business school classrooms.[9] The students who make the best arguments, marshal the best evidence, or demolish the opponents' arguments win both the respect of classmates and high marks, not to mention jobs with prestigious consulting and law firms.

Such skills will be important at the negotiation table, but the most important negotiation skills aren't taught or, at best, are shamefully underemphasized in both business and legal training.[10] We don't teach our students how to ask questions, how to get information, how to listen, or how to use questioning as a powerful persuasive strategy. In fact, few of us realize that in most places in the world, the one who asks the questions controls the process of negotiation and thereby accomplishes more in bargaining situations. And where does creativity come in?

The bottom line is that Adam Smith and our "cowboy culture" justified a competitive approach to negotiation. Yes, market forces are better than the bludgeons and spears of kings, autocrats, and despots. Even Vladimir Putin recently agreed: "The authorities should explain to people in a clear and understandable way, not with truncheons and tear gas, but with discussion and dialogue."[11] Markets have conquered might, but with little emphasis on imagination and invention.

Mutual Interests and American Social Psychology

Jeffrey Rubin died climbing his hundredth of the 100 tallest peaks in New England. It was raining. He and his climbing partner had parted ways on the way up. Ironically, he died ignoring his own best advice: A cardinal rule of mountain climbing is never leave your buddy. Moreover, he was an expert on "psychological traps." Perhaps mountain climbing represents the ultimate case, where once you start on a path, it's hard to turn back. He was focused on reaching the top of that hundredth peak, when the responsible goal was reaching the bottom. Most climbers die on their way down.

Some two centuries after the epiphany of the invisible hand, we run into the third and final theory that prevents us from returning to the inventive negotiations of our ancestors' campfire discussions. Before World War II, negotiation was mostly studied by political scientists, and they focused on cases in diplomacy. This changed with the end of the war and the necessity of dealing with a powerful Soviet Union. In 1948 at MIT, under the tutelage of social psychologist Kurt Lewin, Morton Deutsch wrote his landmark dissertation on comparing cooperative and competitive groups. Deutsch moved on to Columbia University where he then supervised some 70 dissertations in the area of dispute resolution and social psychology.

By the time John Graham began his studies on international negotiations at Berkeley, the bible of negotiation,[12] *The Social Psychology of Bargaining and Negotiation*, had been produced by two of Deutsch's students. One of them, Jeffrey Z. Rubin, was the most central scholar in the area, on the faculty of Tufts, and a member of the nascent Harvard Program on Negotiation. In his 1975 book with Bert Brown summarizing the literature, neither "creativity" nor "invention" was mentioned in the table of contents or index. Rubin was also the first editor of the *Negotiation Journal*. In his initial editorial statement in 1985 he defined negotiation as, "the settlement of differences and the waging of conflict through verbal exchange."[13]

Three criticisms of the field, particularly at that time, were fair. First, it was criticized for its reductionism, for trying to study a complex process by breaking it into parts. Perhaps the most prominent example is the use of the prisoners' dilemma game-theory approach invented by Deutsch. Second, and perhaps worst, the field has been criticized for the need to quantify negotiation outcomes, which led directly to the field's fundamental omission of creativity and invention—how do we measure such mushy outcomes? Finally, the field has been criticized for its disregard for the ethnocentricity of its theories, findings, and implications. People in other countries and cultures negotiate differently and often do so inventively. Indeed, in the index of Rubin & Brown's bible, the word "culture" is absent, and "internationalism" is given a whole two pages in the text.

Lately, however, there has been increasing interest in international negotiations, and the concept of creativity is more frequently mentioned by important scholars in the field. In *Getting to Yes*,[14] the current bible of the field, chapter 4 is titled "*Invent* Options for Mutual Gain" [our italics]. We applaud Roger Fisher and William Ury for their quick discussion of the topic, and we appreciate their backgrounds in law and anthropology, respectfully. But the basis of their 7-million-copy-seller is the social psychology literature that dominated their field when the book was first written in 1983. Indeed, they even pay homage to the market in their definition of negotiation power: your best alternative to a negotiated agreement (BATNA). That is, if you are a sole seller with many buyers, you are in a strong position, and vice versa.

Other luminaries have mentioned invention, but have not elaborated on it. For example, Harvard Professor Howard Raiffa long advocated inventiveness in negotiations:

> The teams should think and plan together informally and do some joint brainstorming, which can be thought of as "dialoguing" or "pre-negotiating." The two sides make no tradeoffs, commitments, or arguments about how to divide the pie at this early stage.[15]

David Lax and James Sebenius, in *3-D Negotiation*,[16] go past getting to yes and talk about "creative agreements" and "great agreements." MIT Professor Lawrence Susskind[17] and his associates recommend "parallel informal negotiations" toward building creative negotiation outcomes. But at the end of the day, American social psychology has delivered only the concept of integrative bargaining. This is a further improvement over coercion and a step above competitive bargaining. But the integrative approach with its emphasis on mutual interests over positions still sees negotiation processes as transactions.

Finally, Jeffrey Rubin,[18] our mountain climber and negotiations expert, might explain the commonality of the two activities. Both reaching the top and getting to "yes" are only half the jobs. Getting back down the mountain and implementing agreements through good relationships are the more important goals.

iMagination: A Return to Inventive Negotiation

Our inventive approach to negotiations builds on all that work and adds proven concepts gleaned from a variety of disparate sources:

- Silicon Valley firms such as INTEL and IDEO[19]
- Open innovation[20]
- John Seely Brown's process networks and performance fabrics[21]
- David Obstfeld's description of *tertius iungens*[22] (the importance of the third party in innovation)
- Insights from the new brain science
- Virtual teams research
- Experimental economics
- Innovation processes perfected over 30 years of study and practice in advertising, creativity, and innovation
- Three decades of research on the best practices of negotiators around the world

Inventive negotiations also draw on practices typical in Japan and the Netherlands. The Japanese have developed a cultural ritual of collaborative negotiation that naturally uses tools of innovative processes in ways unfamiliar to most American bargainers.[23] Their *ringisho* bottom-up consensus approach yields excellent agreements, fast implementation, and lasting relationships. The Dutch are the world's experts in foreign languages, cultures, and openness to international commercial collaboration.

Our goal is to demonstrate how creativity and invention are keys to business negotiations. The field is still stuck in the past, talking about "making deals" and "solving problems." Even the use of terms like "win-win" exposes the vestiges of the old competitive thinking. Yet, business negotiation is not something that can be won or lost, and the metaphors of competition and problem solving limit creativity.

SIDEBAR 1.2

How Inventive Negotiation Works

1. Inventive negotiation is older than history, and more advanced than the future—and it's based on the most basic human talent: imagination.
2. It begins with a glimmer of hope, the vision that things can be better—even world-changing.
3. You have to find just the right partners and sell them on your vision.
4. Then you build relationships—with those on the other side.
5. You create the system that makes these relationships happen.
6. You add exactly the right people in specific situations, including facilitators.
7. You consider culture and encourage diversity.
8. You meet in the right places and the right spaces, at just the right pace.
9. You leverage emotion and overcome power and corruption.
10. You encourage changing roles.
11. You use tools of innovation.
12. And you use the tools of improvisation.
13. You keep improving the relationships in new ways.
14. And even when you think you've created the best outcome possible, you keep using these strategies to create an even better, longer-lasting, and more sustainable outcome.

Unfortunately, the social psychological approach,[24] including all its flaws, continues to dominate American thinking on the topic, particularly in business and law schools. Inventive processes in Japan and the Netherlands are almost always ignored in favor of the transactional approaches of competitive and integrative bargaining. Consider, for example, the Israeli/Palestinian conflict. Despite more than three decades of integrative bargaining (advice and practice), no progress has been made there. In the next chapter, we'll show you what an inventive negotiation might achieve.

CHAPTER 2

Spotting a Glimmer of Opportunity

If you want to build a ship, don't drum up people to collect wood and don't assign them tasks and work, but rather teach them to long for the endless immensity of the sea.

—Antoine de Saint-Exupéry

Our own use of the terms "problem solving" and "conflict resolution" in the previous chapters reflects an old, limiting way of thinking about negotiation processes. Inventive negotiation is not meant to solve problems or resolve conflicts. The purpose of inventive negotiation is to find and exploit opportunities. So the first step in the process is recognizing a glimmer of opportunity.

Our thinking leads to a definition of inventive negotiations. Indeed, the twentieth-century definitions, metaphors, and lexicon of negotiation are filled with words like these: problems, conflicts, disputes, dividing things, competitive games, military campaigns, even chess and poker. We use a different set of words (to see how different, take a look at Sidebar 2.1): *Inventive negotiation is the use of innovation processes to build long-term relationships for finding and exploiting extraordinary opportunities.* Yes, problems may be solved and conflicts resolved along the way, but the primary question of inventive negotiation is "What are the opportunities here?"

We had to laugh when we saw the *Harvard Business Review* table of contents for the March 2012 edition. We were initially excited—*HBR* was going to talk about new ideas, gracing the cover with "Reinventing America" and "Why the World Needs the U.S. to Bounce Back." Then we looked inside. The table of contents and the articles themselves were a glorious word fest about American *competitiveness*. "Special Report: Restoring US Competitiveness, Why US Competiveness Matters to All of US" are the first 13 words on the inside. Thank you, Adam Smith!

SIDEBAR 2.1

Negotiation Terms and Metaphors

Agreement, reaching
Arbitration
Auction
Bargaining
Barter
Battle of wits
Buying/selling
Campaign (military
  or political)
Chess
Competitive bargaining
Conflict resolution
Consensus building
Crossing rapids
Debate
Dickering
Diplomacy
Discussion
Dispute resolution
Dividing pies
Duel
Dutch auction
Exchange
Extreme negotiation
Game theory
Haggling
Horse trading

Integrative bargaining
Intercourse
Investigative negotiation
Joint decision making
Logrolling
Mediation
Meeting of minds
Mountain climbing
Negotiation
Parley
Peace talks
Poker
Prisoners' dilemma
Problem solving
Psychological trap
Sharing pies
Swap
Transaction
Tête-à-tête
Three-D negotiation
Tug-of-war
Wheeling and dealing
Yes, getting to

Creativity
Invention
Relationship building

In the twenty-first century the proper approach, the inventive negotiation approach, would have used article titles such as "Where are the Opportunities?" "Who around the World Will Make the Best Partners?" "How Can We Best Work with the Chinese, the Russians, and the Arabs to Promote Human Progress?" Indeed, that March 2012 *HBR* cover provides us with a glimmer of opportunity—yes, the US business system does indeed need a new way to think about negotiation, which is the fundamental business activity. We now turn to four stories about other glimmers of opportunity.

John Lasseter: To Infinity and Beyond

One of the most inventive negotiations in the history of entertainment began in the dark and only happened because of a series of failures.

The dark was inside the Wardman Movie Theater in Whittier in 1964, where seven-year-old John Lasseter had paid 49¢ to see Disney's *Sword in the Stone* and fell in love. By the time his mom picked him up, he knew he was destined to be an animator. And thanks to that passion and encouragement from a mom who was a high-school art teacher, a dozen years later he was studying with three Disney animators who taught part-time at the California Institute of the Arts. He even spent summers as captain of the Jungle Cruise in Disneyland. It was no surprise that he soon landed his dream job: a slot at the legendary Disney animation studio.

Yet, that vision and determination soon got him in trouble. Watching an early preview of *Tron* in 1982, he fell in love again, this time with computer generated imagery (CGI). He pushed hard for this new technology, insisting that it should change everything. At the world's most successful animation studio, that was not a message people wanted to hear. He was promptly fired for his enthusiasm about this new, disruptive technology.

Of course, there's much more to this story—and we'll get to it a bit later in the book. But the story started with Lasseter's recognition of glimmers of opportunity.

Eli Simon: Don't Sell the Show, Sell the Vision

Eli Simon teaches clowning in America, Korea, Italy, and Romania. He's written a book about it, and you can see him on YouTube demonstrating his techniques (http://www.youtube.com/watch?v=pZ57_prZ9e4). He wrote, directed, and produced a play combining traditional Korean dancing, Italian *commedia dell'arte* clowns, and masks. He has served as Head of Acting and Chair of Drama at University of California, Irvine. We figured he could tell us a little bit about using humor in negotiation. Instead, he told us a story that is a textbook case of a person seeing a glimmer of opportunity.

Eli Simon had a crazy idea. To be more precise, he had an insane idea that absolutely no one thought was possible: he wanted to build a portable Elizabethan theatre and perform Shakespeare in the huge green park that is in the center of the campus.

Even crazier, he had a plan to do it. Since the drama department had recently received a small pot of money, he figured he had enough funding to build a flexible mini-Elizabethan structure. With the partnership of his colleagues in the drama department and a strong relationship with Keith Bangs, head of the production studio, designing the theatre and paying for labor was next to nothing. And staging the plays—well, he'd been doing that for his entire professional career. He'd just donate his time.

And even though a major university is hardly an entrepreneurial setting, he just went and did it. The students and staff built the set—a 128-seat theatre in 15 one-ton sections. They hauled it into their performing space, staged *The Merchant of Venice*, and broke it back down to store. Now they just had to take it to the public. Piece of cake.

At this point, however, Simon bumped right into the wall that is typical in any bureaucratic structure. As soon as he started explaining his theatrical vision to anyone, they told him he couldn't do it. Too dangerous. Too much liability. Too expensive. No way, no how.

But, he protested, the theatre was already built. They just had to move it from the arts complex across the street to the park. Nope. Can't be done.

Now as it happens, Michael Drake, the Chancellor of the University is a pretty open guy, and he makes time to interact with students and professors. Simon had a meeting scheduled and he suggested they take a walk after lunch. They meandered around until they arrived at a particular vista on the campus. Along the way, Simon talked about how the department wanted much the same thing as the Chancellor did: to integrate the campus into the community, get everyone involved in collaborative projects, engage in efforts that would sustain meaningful interaction for generations. At exactly this point, Simon pulled out a gift-wrapped rectangle. (He's not a drama teacher for nothing.)

This is my vision, Simon said, as the chancellor opened his gift—a digital photo of the theatre superimposed on this lush green park before them.

The chancellor's response? "I wish we could have it tonight." And shortly thereafter, "What do you need?"

At this point, Simon didn't know, but he left it open. "I have no idea, but I am sure we will need your support sooner or later."

Just knowing that the Chancellor approved was enough to keep him going, knocking on the appropriate doors, and asking for support. There were technical issues: it turns out that 15 tons is a pretty heavy load for unreinforced grass, even before you add a couple of tons of people. The structure would have sunk straight down before the first performance. There were safety issues: an inspection that was enough inside the performing arts space wasn't sufficient for an outdoor space, where it could rain. In the alternative venue Simon found—a concrete plaza next to the library—there was no source of power except by borrowing electricity from the library, where there are lots of computers and a real possibility of power surges. Electricity had not been an issue prior to the move, but now it became a major hurdle.

The difficulties and the costs mounted, but Simon and his colleagues knew that they had to act now or never. If the festival wasn't launched that first summer, it would never happen. The theatre would be taken apart, and that would be that. Everything was over budget, but plans were already in place. Tickets had been sold. The project was morphing, growing into a monster, moving sideways, totally out of Simon's control.

Simon then used the classic bargaining chip, though he didn't know it at the time. He decided that the only responsible thing to do was to walk away. He didn't just threaten to stop the festival, he really meant it. His dream had become a nightmare and was further from reality than ever. "Get another artistic director/general manager/fundraiser/construction superintendent."

Of course, there was no such thing. It was Simon's baby, his passion; it had become his whole life. And if this had been a typical negotiation, the whole project would simply have failed. But it wasn't. Without realizing it, Simon had built the long-term relationships he needed. By now, the chancellor and the dean both felt it was too valuable a concept to abandon, so they used a little creativity, rounded up allies, found a little more money, and the first season of New Swan Shakespeare Festival sold out every seat in two weeks. It was an unprecedented success and received more press for the department and school than many other dramatic events all put together.

Yet, Simon's vision wasn't just for that season. It was to establish a summer tradition that would live on long past his tenure. But even a second season seemed out of reach without the funding that had jump-started the project, so Simon expanded on what he'd learned. His friend David Emmes, founder of South Coast Repertory Theatre, one of the most successful regional theatres in the country, told him, "Don't sell the show. Sell the vision."

Thus, Simon set out to sell that vision, not just to the people above him, but to everyone involved in the project. He started by stepping down from his chairmanship of his department, which allowed him to treat the theatre separately, both financially and legally. And made it possible for him to work totally without compensation from the theatre.

Instead of meeting with the facilities guys in the dim meeting rooms where they worked, he took them into the theatre. (We will talk about the importance of meeting in creative spaces in chapter 8.) He talked one-on-one, and he enlisted the other people in his community. He genuinely needed their help, and he asked for it. He explained that his was a start-up venture that needed all the creativity they could muster and would be working on a shoestring. And he got them laughing. (He does, after all, teach that laughter brings out everyone's creative, authentic self.) Soon the electricians and facilities managers were coming to him with suggestions, "I think I know how we can save some money and get this done."

He raised funds by sharing his vision with community leaders. Though he had never asked for money, when one of his buddies heard about the second season, he bought out a whole night's performance and brought his entire law firm. People at another legal firm across town thought that was such a great idea, they did the same.

Now the second season is a sell-out. He has a huge team of advocates and supporters and fans. And while there will always be difficulties to conquer, Simon has found that the easiest way to get more out of negotiation is to get everyone on his team in the first place. No kidding.

SIDEBAR 2.2

Rules for Persuasive Storytelling[1]

A story grows in the mind of your listener.

—Annette Simmons

1. Make people understand the need for change. Tap into their feelings of pain or frustration. Give them a personal reason to care.
2. Tell the truth. Don't sell more than you have to offer. The more people believe, the more they will buy in. If possible, let them experience it.
3. Make it simple. A single reason to believe, backed by a couple of proof points, is far more compelling than a laundry list. Tell too much and you'll end up sounding like a late-night infomercial.
4. Accentuate the positive. This will eliminate the pain AND make you feel better while you are changing the world.
5. Ask for the order. Join my team. Help us take this to the next step. See how different your life will be.

Amazon in Seattle

In an era when cities are fighting desperately to attract and keep major employers, the recent negotiation between Amazon and the city of Seattle is unique.

It's a very sweet deal for the city: the new headquarters will house about 12,000 of Amazon's 30,000 Seattle employees. That's roughly the size of the entire cities of Annapolis or Helena or Juneau. If you figure that at least half of these employees have spouses, significant others, or kids, that means enough highly paid taxpayers to fill the whole city of Olympia.

Amazon's new headquarters are located in a formerly low-rise, low-rent warehouse district, "South Lake Union was a place that people drove through, not to," according to Amazon's John Schoettler, director of global real estate and facilities. And Amazon is paying for a bike lane and a new streetcar for Seattle's light rail line, because the company encourages its employees to live near work and take alternative transportation.

This philosophy has prompted apartment developers to flock to the area—last year Seattle issued more residential building permits than at any other time in the past three decades. Other technology companies are seeking space nearby. Northeastern University set up a campus across the street, and dozens of food trucks are already tapping the demand that will lead to restaurants and service businesses.

So how did Amazon negotiate this deal? According to the *New York Times*,[2] "When Amazon executives showed up for the first meetings . . . city officials were taken aback. Not by the scope of the plan, but by the simplicity of the discussion."

"It was not a hard-boiled negotiation," said Marshall Foster, director of city planning. "They basically walked in and said, 'we think this is the site.'"

And what did they get in return? Huge multiyear tax breaks, the primary demand of any large employer anywhere? Amazon didn't even ask for them.

The secret is that Amazon had the same vision and goals as the city. Amazon attracts smart, highly educated engineers and managers, often young—the very people who want to live and work in a vibrant, urban setting. Thus, setting up shop in Seattle is a recruiting and retention tool for the company.

The city couldn't have had a better negotiating partner if they had selected the team themselves.

All the Kings' Horses...How about a Jerusalem Olympics?

We mentioned in the preceding chapter the great Gordian knot of international relations, that is, the Arab/Israeli conflict and a permanent peace in the Middle East among Jews, Muslims, and Christians. Every American presidents since 1948 has addressed this problem—Eisenhower, Kennedy, Johnson, Nixon, Ford, Carter, Reagan, Bush, Clinton, Bush, and now Obama—and nothing has changed. Roger Fisher and William Ury, the authors of *Getting to Yes*, have consulted on the negotiations, as have a variety of other integrative bargaining experts over the years. Most recently, however, a poll[3] in Israel indicates young people are less optimistic about peace than at any time in the past twenty years.

People in the Middle East are used to conflict and violence. Thus, simply negotiating peace there hasn't worked. It's time for a new way of thinking, for a more attractive goal than just peace. We can think of a glimmer of opportunity for the region. Instead of a war zone, imagine a prosperous, dynamic Middle East. Imagine peoples and countries that creatively and cooperatively take advantage of their natural and spiritual resources. A new focus on prosperity as the ultimate goal will yield peace along the way. Holding the Olympic Games in Jerusalem in 2024 or 2028 would be a useful first step. Here's what we posted on the topic for the *Harvard Business Review* blog network on July 7, 2011:

> The nearly complete destruction of the continental European economies by World War II seriously endangered the stability of Europe's social and political institutions. Europe's leaders knew that to rebuild from the ruins, it was essential to form new kinds of international institutions to ensure prosperity, stability, and peace in the region. The first of these institutions was the European Coal and Steel Community, established in 1952 to integrate the coal and steel industries of France, West Germany, Italy, Belgium, the Netherlands, and Luxembourg. Fifty years later, based on the success of this first small experiment in economic interdependence, we now see the European Union with 27 member nations and candidate countries hoping to join in the future. Except for the most recent economic doldrums the economies have burgeoned during the decades, but more important, peace has persisted.
>
> Might such an approach work in the war-torn Middle East?
>
> A new focus on prosperity as the ultimate goal will yield peace along the way. The key will be inventing a path for mutual benefit.
>
> The crux of the problem has been Jerusalem. The holy Old City is a matter of faith to so many. It is sacred to both Christians and Jews. For

Muslims, only Mecca and Medina are more important spiritual places. While the fighting over this religious real estate appears perpetual, Jerusalem can also be a solution.

Religious tourism already feeds the economies in Israel and Palestine as well as in the surrounding area. In 2000, before the most recent insanity of violence, tourism brought in $3.2 billion in revenues for Israel. Compare that with Disneyland in Orange County, California, which rakes in a comparable amount thanks to 10 million yearly visitors who spend about $150 each on tickets, food, and souvenirs—and also shell out for hotels and transportation.

And Jerusalem has more to offer more people than the Magic Kingdom (no offense to Mickey). Indeed, the potential gate is the 3.5 billion Christians, Muslims, and Jews around the world. The Church of the Holy Sepulcher (built over the tomb of Jesus) would draw Christians. The Wailing Wall is the most holy place for Jews. Muslims would flock to the Dome of the Rock. Many tourists would visit all three. And outside the Old City are Bethlehem, Hebron, Nazareth, Jericho, the Sea of Galilee, the Dead Sea, and the Red Sea, to name only the more obvious attractions. Our back-of-the-envelope estimate revealed $10 billion to $20 billion in annual revenues if things are done right—that's about 10 to 15 percent of the current GDP of Israel.

Does that sound crazy? We don't think so. Win-win agreements aren't good enough anymore. In the twenty-first-century global business environment, inventive negotiations are the keys to thriving in the new volatility. The distinction is between transactions and relationships, between trade-offs and sharing, between outside-the-box and open-systems thinking, and between acquiescence and creativity. Indeed, inventive negotiators transform bargaining into an innovation process, integrating the best practices of each.

What is needed in Israel and Palestine is a shared goal to kick off this process. How about Jerusalem as the site for the 2024 Olympic Games? Here's how we think it could work.

The principles of inventive negotiations suggest first forming a Jerusalem Olympics 2024 Committee including members from the key local constituencies—Israel and Palestine, and perhaps Jordan, Lebanon, and Syria. The committee initially would meet informally, at a neutral and comfortable location, and with international facilitation. The process of the initial meetings would be brainstorming, but the consequences of these meetings would be new ideas and positive interpersonal relationships.

The Olympics could bring in as much as $50 billion in revenues. And the spiritual symbolism of so many millions visiting the sources of their faith would be priceless.

But before the international investment dollars could flow, this little fantasy presumes a peaceful political division of Israel and Palestine along the lines reaffirmed in the Oslo Accords. It presumes a dropping of all commercial boycotts in the region. It presumes that Palestinians won't have to risk being shot while "hopping the fence" to work in Israel. It presumes that companies will be able to integrate the operations of their complementary plants in the area. It presumes that the United States and other countries will send to the region legions of tourists rather than boatloads of weapons. It presumes an open, international, and, most important, a whole Old City of Jerusalem. And it presumes free trade and travel among all nations in the region allowing all to prosper in new ways.

One small group of inventive thinkers we talked with recently came up with a surfeit of additional ideas: spreading the Olympic events not only at venues around Israel and Palestine (such as beach volleyball at Gaza or rowing on the Sea of Galilee) but also perhaps in close by Jordan, Lebanon, and Syria. Or use "bricks from the security walls" around the country to build the main stadium in Jerusalem. Why stop with the Olympics? The new tourism infrastructure for the games would also nicely support a World Cup competition, perhaps with preliminary games across the region as well.

Security is not as much of an obstacle as you might think. The death rate by violence in Israel (even during the dangerous middle of the past decade) is little different from that of the United States and one quarter of that in Brazil, where Rio de Janeiro is hosting the 2016 games. The Jerusalem Olympics would kick-start tourism to the area, get key regional players invested in working together, entice multinationals to invest in the region, and could even start the seeds of a broader Middle Eastern Commercial Union, just as the European Coal and Steel Community gave rise to the EU.

The Middle East was the cradle of Western civilization. It became so long ago because of innovation and trade in the region. One can only imagine what free trade in the area would produce now.

The commentary in response to our blog was, as you might imagine, all over the place. Some readers praised our inventive thinking. Others ranted and raged about our naiveté, our ignorance, our stupidity, and even worse. Most shocking was the way the commenters talked to one another. Several of those comments were deemed unprintable by the *HBR* referees. Unlike John Lasseter at Disney, we weren't fired; *HBR* continued with our series of blogs on inventive negotiation. While reading some of the comments was not fun, as we will describe in chapter 9, emotional venting can be useful in a number of ways. For more information on this topic you might also visit our website, www.JerusalemOlympics.org.

Thomas Edison and One of His Many
Glimmers of Opportunity

Thomas Edison[4] wasn't just an inventor. He was an inventive negotiator. Contemplate the array of companies he created—171 in all.
Fifty were in countries ranging from Argentina to Canada, from
Japan, China, and India to Italy, Germany, and France. He dabbled
with partners in electric cars, batteries, cement, chemicals, and office
machines. The creative teams he developed laid the foundations for
today's music, movie, and telecommunications industries. And we
haven't mentioned General Electric yet.

Historians list 22 inventors of incandescent lamps prior to Edison,
but his team's design improved on the others in three ways: better
incandescent material, a higher vacuum, and higher electrical resistance allowing power to be distributed from a centralized source. But
the better bulb by itself wasn't the reason for Edison's success. He
and his partners also developed the basic grid to bring the electricity
from a distant generator across the wires to the bulbs. Now GE makes
everything from toasters to turbo-machinery.

In 1878 when Edison began his serious work on the development
of the lightbulb, America was a wonderful potential market at about
60 million potential buyers. Yet on the horizon was an even greater
glimmer of opportunity, the 400 million potential buyers in the
Victorian British Empire. In the next chapter, we'll show you how
this inventive negotiator took the step to realize that ambition.

CHAPTER 3

Identifying and Creating Partners

In the progress of personality, first comes a declaration of independence, then a recognition of interdependence.

—Henry Van Dyke

By the time Thomas Edison applied for patent #223,898 for his version of the lightbulb, he had already formed the Edison Electric Light Company in New York City. He'd sold his vision: "We will make electricity so cheap that only the rich will burn candles," which helped him line up investors like the Vanderbilts and J. P. Morgan. And within a decade, he'd recruited dozens of the smartest engineers in the world and built the world's first industrial laboratory in Menlo Park, NJ.[1]

He owned the American market (some 60 million at the time), but his dreams were bigger: the entire British Empire (about 400 million). And one man stood in his way.

Joseph Swan held the British patent for pretty much the same technology, and he was suing Edison there. Where others would have seen this as an obstacle, Edison saw it as an opportunity. Soon he had persuaded Swan that partnership was a better idea than litigation—a move that would make both of them enormously wealthy.

So in 1883 the two partners created the Edison and Swan Electric Light Company (Ediswan) to manufacture and distribute the invention in Britain and its vast empire. Edison's gamble paid off handsomely, and he eventually bought out Swan.

The myth of the lone inventor is exactly that. Invention is, and always has been, a team sport.[2] We heard that same sentiment from UCI chemistry professor F. Sherwood Rowland in our MBA class as he described his Nobel Prize–winning work with collaborators on atmospheric chemistry, fluorocarbons, and ozone layer depletion.

SIDE BAR 3.1

"From Phoenicia to Hayek to the 'Cloud'"

Contrast the American cowboy talk from chapter 1 with *Wall Street Journal*'s columnist Matt Ridley:

> The crowd-sourced, wikinomic cloud is the new, new thing that all management consultants are now telling their clients to embrace. Yet the cloud is not a new thing at all. It has been the source of human invention all along. Human technological advancement depends not on individual intelligence but on collective idea sharing, and it has done so for tens of thousands of years. Human progress waxes and wanes according to how much people connect and exchange.[3]

Finding Partners

So how do you identify or create the best partners for developing that glimmer into an opportunity? We'll show you how some of the most inventive negotiators do it, in all sorts of circumstances, all over the globe. The first step is research.

In this Internet age, open source research has become much easier, and records for research are proliferating every day. In a millisecond, a Google search can tell you things about people that it once took a private investigator to find: affiliations, neighborhoods, political contributions, tax records, court records, and mentions in obscure publications. LinkedIn offers its own edited versions of career histories and glimpses of the people potential partners know. Following a career trajectory can explain background or offer mutual contacts. Depending on how carefully people use filters, Facebook will reveal way more about them than they intended to share about themselves.

Today a savvy young executive will follow a prospective partner on Twitter, so he can mention shared musical tastes in their first meeting. Instagram and Pinterest offer more opportunities for insight, and other social media sites are appearing so quickly that it's impossible to ever complete the list.

When it's so easy to learn about people from public records, it's tempting to skip old-fashioned human intelligence gathering—but that would be a major mistake. Only a former coworker can tell you the intimate details that will help you select a team member or brace for a conflict. Does he think of women as inferior beings? Did she renege on a verbal agreement? Does he pout or go into a rage when he doesn't get his way? Does she play nicely with others, does he hoard information, is she extremely well-connected or painfully shy?

You'll even learn a lot by things that people don't say about others. A conspicuous silence when you're discussing ambition or congeniality, follow-through or commitment will fill in gaps in a profile. As Carly Fiorino, former chair of HP says, "The goal is to turn data into information, and information into insight."

Of course, all that information isn't necessarily good information. Seemingly sacrosanct credit rating agencies are notorious for including bad data, mixing up social security numbers, confusing a female retiree with a young man. That online scandal could well have been manufactured by a spurned lover or a business rival. If considering the source was good advice in the last century, it's even more important today.

For organizations, you'll find good information in the CIA's *World Factbook*, the Economist Intelligence Unit and Oxford Analytica. Yet even in good sources, you need to be aware of the age of the data. Economic summaries from three months ago can be wildly inaccurate—it wasn't too long before its collapse that business magazines touted the brilliance of Enron.

Banker versus Internet?

Bruce Money is chairman of the Business Management Department at BYU. He was once included in an article in the *Wall Street Journal* about people whose names matched their professions—imagine taking classes in negotiation from a guy named Professor Money. He's a business school favorite, affable, quick witted, and tireless. In the fifty-year history of the Merage Business school, only two people have completed the PhD program in three years (the average is more like five), and he's one of them.

Two huge advantages for Bruce were the language and personal selling skills he acquired during two years as a Mormon missionary in Japan. While his choice to serve was voluntary, his location was assigned by the Church. (He does admit that young Mormon men who don't go on a mission couldn't get a date at BYU. This seems like a pretty strong incentive to us.)

Because of the skills acquired during their missions, much of America's international business is managed by Mormons. Indeed, in *Tribes,* Joel Kotkin lists five ethnic groups that exercise remarkable influence on the global business system: Jews, Japanese, Chinese, Indians, and Anglo-Saxons. He also predicts two upcoming tribes— Mormons and Armenians.

In one of his studies, Money used his Japanese skills to interview both Japanese and American managers on how they find industrial services. Here are two quotes from his report in the *Journal of Marketing:* [4]

"Don't laugh, but all the really important [business] services I have, I found in the *Yellow Pages*" (American manager of a small manufacturing company in the U.S.).

"When starting a new business, your bank means everything. Just about all my service vendors came from talking with my bank" (Japanese owner of a small cosmetics manufacturer in Tokyo) (83).

With copious empirical evidence, Professor Money describes this fundamental difference in the importance of referrals in the two countries. In Japan, and indeed in most countries around the world, people know the importance of referrals. But not so much in the United States. As a Japanese manager told Money:

"American managers don't understand the process [of how to select service providers]. The top executives of the two companies have known each other for many, many years. The decision is made at the top and things happen very quickly after that. Maybe things go slowly before. It's not just the price that makes the decision" (Japanese engineering services firm) (84).

Inventive negotiators, then, should learn to consider the way most companies around the world select their partners—a method that's a lot more established and productive than a Google search.

The Old-Fashioned Way

Once you've gathered all the information you can before you meet to negotiate, there's always more to learn. An inventive negotiator is skilled at observing and listening and pays attention to cultural indicators. Is the young woman arriving for a Chinese meeting in a shimmering white dress in mourning—or simply unaware of the cultural significance of her favorite summer frock? Is a man's loud voice an indication of anger or just his normal tone? Is the woman smiling behind her hand because she's embarrassed, or is she following her own cultural norms?

For example, a rookie football player walks into a locker room where the other team members have been playing together for years. As he circles the room shaking hands, he winks at one of the veteran players. Nonplussed, the veteran can't figure out how to respond. Is this a flirtatious move? An indication that the rookie thinks they share a secret? Who knows? So he just returns the handshake and continues to watch.

The rookie doesn't wink at the next player or the next. But at the third player, he winks again. Four handshakes later, another wink. Finally, the veteran sees the pattern and understands the meaning: there is none. The rookie has a facial tic that occurs at varying intervals.

Lesson one: while an inventive negotiator does his or her homework researching potential partners, it is almost impossible to collect all the information you need ahead of time.

Whether preparing in advance or observing on site, the best inventive negotiators are emotionally and socially intelligent, slow to come to conclusions, and quick to adjust to new information. The same skills you would bring to a prospective dating situation are just as handy when you apply them to everyone you meet in the long course of negotiations and particularly when selecting partners who will help your ideas thrive.

Sometimes They Find You

For Sudhir Venkatesh, doing his research nearly got him killed. And initiated his lifelong career.

As a young doctoral student in sociology at the University of Chicago, Venkatesh had long been interested in how people form their identities. A math major from Southern California, he was Indian-American and sported waist-length hair from his latest research project: following the Grateful Dead around the country.

Armed with a clipboard and 70 multiple-choice questions, he started his research in three 16-story buildings of a housing project on Lake Michigan. Because the project was condemned, families had pirated electricity and water, but there were no functioning elevators or lights. He figured it was an ideal place to study impoverished youth.

By the time he trudged up to the sixth floor, it was getting dark and he hadn't talked anyone into answering his questions. Then, according to Steven Levitt's *Freakonomics*, [5] "Suddenly, on the stairwell landing, he startled a group of teenagers shooting dice. They turned out to be a gang of junior-level crack dealers who operated out of the building, and they were not happy to see him."

The teens didn't know what to make of him. He was probably not a rival gang member, "certainly wasn't a cop. He wasn't black, wasn't white." They began arguing over his fate, as the crowd grew larger and louder. "Then an older gang member appeared. He snatched the clipboard from Venkatesh's hands, and, when he saw that it was a written questionnaire, looked puzzled. 'I can't read any of this shit.'"

So Venkatesh asked him the first printed question. A round of angry laughter ensued, and more discussions about his fate. "Just as things were looking their bleakest for Venkatesh, another man appeared." This was J. T., the gang's leader, who led a lively discussion about the terminology of the questionnaire. J. T. "had cooled down his subordinates, but he didn't seem to want to interfere directly with their catch. Darkness fell and J. T. left."

"'People here don't come out of here alive,' said the jittery teenager with the gun."

It was a very long night. Venkatesh's captors gave him a beer, and their leader dropped by a couple of times. Venkatesh tried to get his questions answered but got only laughter. "Daybreak came and then noon. Finally, nearly twenty-four hours after Venkatesh stumbled upon them, they set him free."

For most people, this would have been the end of the research, maybe even marked a change of career. But Venkatesh was hooked. He tried a new approach: attempting to imbed himself in the gang to truly understand their world. When he tracked down J. T., the gang leader "thought he was crazy, literally—a university student wanting to cozy up to a crack gang? But he also admired what Venkatesh was after. As it happened, J. T. was a college graduate himself, a business major." He'd worked briefly in marketing and knew the importance of data, and how to look for new business opportunities.

So for the next six years, Venkatesh studied the gang, first in that housing project and then in another project on the South Side. "Venkatesh would move from one family to the next, washing their dinner dishes and sleeping on the floor. He brought toys for their children: he once watched a woman use her baby's bib to sop up the blood of a teenaged drug dealer who was shot to death in front of him."

When the gang members finally came under indictment, one of them gave him a stack of spiral notebooks. Inside he found meticulous records of the gang's financial transactions: "sales, wages, dues, even the death benefits paid out to the families of murdered members." It was a priceless treasure, something no academic researcher could ever have been expected to acquire. It led, eventually, to a lifetime of study of the underground economy and the underclass.

Now, no one expects a participant in inventive negotiation to sleep on floors in impoverished housing projects. But Venkatesh's story illustrates exactly how important it is to select even the most unlikely of partners.

Obviously, when young Venkatesh set out to do his research, he had no idea he was entering a negotiating situation. Indeed, during that long first night, he felt like the hostage in a hostage negotiation—with no one negotiating on his behalf.

It was that second encounter when Venkatesh made a key strategic decision: he actively sought the young man who seemed to be in control, and he made an unusual offer—to become a part of J. T's gang.

In most negotiating situations, it isn't really possible to leap across the table and join the other side. Yet, that attitude of seeking the best partners from either side can result in extraordinary outcomes. It's a long-term approach, and it works even when the stakes are much higher than they were in Chicago.

Changing Partners

Selecting the right partners is always an important process—and sometimes it can be a matter of life and death.

One of William's clients, Rational Therapeutics, does chemosensitivity testing. Live tissue samples, also called assays, are shipped from all over the world to the company's headquarters in California. There, the scientists test various cancer drugs on that living tissue, thus sparing patients the agony of testing each drug in their bodies while creating a personalized cancer treatment regimen.

When Rational Therapeutics wanted to expand, the managers looked south to Brazil—a nearly perfect new market because it's growing and has a level of health care that can support this sophisticated testing.

It seemed like it would be easy. Chemosensitivity testing is a relatively small field, with only a handful of experts capable of working with ex vivo programmed cell death. Yet all of them know one another, and they are fiercely competitive. To court one would be to snub another.

The CEO of Rational Therapeutics, Dr. Robert Nagourney, reached out to an ideal partner, a friend he'd made at international medical conferences. As an MD and PhD, Dr. Ismael Dale knew the science, and more importantly, knew the professional landscape of Brazil's largest city, São Paulo. He recommended a local lab that already did HIV testing, and Dr. Nagourney traveled to Brazil to meet the owners of the lab.

Next, he started due diligence for this alliance—a process that normally takes 9–18 months. At first, things went quickly: the lab had the technical capabilities, and the principals and staff could integrate seamlessly. Soon, however, they discovered that the two firms had different visions, and the talks stalled over intellectual property, profit sharing, documentation, and transaction tempo. After five frustrating months, Dr. Nagourney called off the talks.

Yet, the vision of expansion into South America remained. And the talks had helped Dr. Nagourney realize that he needed a partner who was established enough to engage with a US firm but not large enough to overwhelm his company. The pool of candidates was growing smaller.

In Brazil, there are only three or four "superoncologists" with elite concierge practices. They've been trained at top facilities in the United States, such as MD Anderson and Sloan Kettering, or at top Brazilian medical centers. They treat heads of state, celebrities, and international CEOs. By selecting one of them as a partner, Dr. Nagourney would immediately gain access to their patients, which would virtually guarantee success. And this would immediately alienate the other "superoncs."

Dr. Nagourney began reaching out. One oncologist, affiliated with São Paulo's top hospital, simply didn't believe in Rational Therapeutics process. Another wanted complete control, possibly so he could co-opt the technology and start his own lab.

Nothing was working, and Dr. Nagourney didn't want to damage his relationship with Dr. Dale, who had made all those introductions. Then, as word of the partner search got out, Dr. Nise Yamaguchi emerged as a prime candidate.

A friend of Dr. Dale's, Dr. Yamaguchi was already a big fan of Rational Therapeutics. Several of her dying patients had reacted well to the creative drug treatments she designed, well outside standard protocols but recommended by Rational's test results. One small boy with little chance of survival was still in remission due to Rational Therapeutics' personalized testing. And she had reported these results throughout Brazil.

Now Dr. Nagourney had to reexamine his whole approach. Perhaps a traditional strategic alliance with another lab wasn't the right answer.

Based on Dr. Dale's relationships, Dr. Nagourney began to create another idea—an integrated strategic alliance. Now the team could take advantage of Dr. Dale's affiliation with the Federal University of São Paulo and its labs as well as of Dr. Yamaguchi's clinical practice and entry into two top hospitals. Together, they created the opportunity for collaborative research for top medical students, a nonexclusive vendor agreement with Hospital Albert Einstein, all while preserving Dr. Nagourney's intellectual property. As the first chemosensitivity testing firm now operating in Brazil, Rational Therapeutics is ideally positioned to succeed. The company's flexibility in changing partners, its sensitivity to the relationships of its Brazilian friend, and its open attitude toward a different structure has given Rational Therapeutics first-mover advantage.

Converting Enemies into Partners

Nelson Mandela once said, "If you want to make peace with your enemy, you have to work with your enemy. Then he becomes your partner." Do the same principles apply in a David and Goliath situation—say a single teenager and a huge international conglomerate?

Because she wasn't yet 18 when she left for college, Marissa couldn't qualify for her own cell phone plan and so she piggybacked on a friend's family plan. For almost a year, she faithfully sent a check for her share. In the first week of her summer break, however, she was deeply involved in an internship at a local hospital when her cell phone service was cut off. With a schedule that changed daily, sometimes hourly, she couldn't afford to be without her phone.

When Marissa checked with the carrier, she found that the master bill was seriously in arrears. According to the haughty service rep, the only way she could get off that plan and begin paying her own bills was to pay the master bill in full (more than $650) and a $250 service termination charge.

Stunned, she got off the call and began brainstorming about other ways to get phone service—but all the alternatives she could think of involved sums nearly as high. And then she enlisted the carrier to help her.

Her next phone call was fielded by a different rep. "I'm just 18 and this is my first experience with a cell-phone carrier. I'm hoping you can help me." Like a submissive wolf, Marissa bared her belly to the alpha dog.

Once she had explained her situation, including her perfect history of payments that had gone astray before reaching the company, she asked the rep to help her explore different ways to solve the problem.

Soon the rep spotted a loophole—while the bill had mounted, it wasn't officially past due until the next day—seven hours away. All that had to be paid today was a lingering $50 from the previous month's bill. Within a minute, she paid that bill, and was then cleared to open a new plan in her own name. Without the $250 termination charge.

Presto, like magic, both sides had an outcome that was better than expectations. The carrier got a new and loyal customer, something companies spend millions of dollars to achieve, and Marissa got the service she needed. Sometimes your best ally can be your original opponent, once you believe that every negotiation represents an opportunity.

Affecting Your Partner's Team

Japanese managers don't get mad, and they certainly don't pound on negotiation tables. At least that's the conventional wisdom. Yet Shigeru Hashimura, general manager of marketing and sales for the space communications division of one of Japan's largest *kieretsu* conglomerates, was genuinely mad. When he heard his American vendor's proposals to produce a multimillion dollar communications satellite, the pounding began. Usually a response like this from the Japanese side could mean only one thing: the deal is dead.

How had it come to this? The trading company arm of the Japanese firm had represented the American company in Japan for more than twenty years. At the beginning of that relationship, Hashimura had been assigned to work at the American firm's offices in Southern California as a trainee. Thus, he knew the executives well and described his relationship with them as "almost family." During that time, the relationship between the two companies had been quite positive, resulting in sales of eight satellites to the Japanese National Space Development Agency (NASDA), Japan's equivalent of NASA.

With the deregulation of the space industry in Japan the trading company asked its American partner to submit a proposal for a new, privately owned communications satellite. The American firm was preselected as the sole supplier for four reasons:

1. The long and personal relationship
2. The American firm had been reliable and had the required experience
3. The proposal process could be handled more efficiently
4. "We expected them to be fair"

The proposal the vendor delivered was quite different from what Hashimura had expected. It included a 45-month delivery schedule (twelve months longer than a competitor's) and a price tag 30 to

40 percent higher. Hashimura felt the company's American partner was taking advantage of its position as the sole source. Still, Hashimura had signed the Authorization to Proceed (ATP), including a down payment in excess of $1 million, because he didn't want to delay the launch date any further.

Then came the February meeting. The American team was headed by a project manager, and included Chris Masterson, a project engineer, and several others. The Japanese side was represented by Hashimura and others from the trading company's local offices in Southern California. First, he learned that the work had not been done on the project despite the ATP, and Hashimura began to get upset. The American position was that substantial work could not begin because the specifications and requirements for the satellite had not yet been clearly defined. Then the Americans refused to budge on the price and delivery schedule and offered no alternatives. At that point Hashimura blew up and walked out of the meeting.

Soon thereafter, Hashimura called Robert Delaney, a vice president at the America firm and director of its space systems operations. Delaney, with fifteen years of experience with the Japanese, had already heard about Hashimura's behavior at the meeting. Hashimura asked Delaney to replace the entire American project management team.

Delaney promptly complied with the demand, but he put Masterson in charge of cleaning up the mess. Fortunately, Masterson spoke some Japanese and had a good understanding of the Japanese business system's nuances. Production of the satellite proceeded, and Masterson's relationship management skills came into play once again. When his team later encountered delays, he carefully kept Hashimura informed. Hashimura ultimately paid the early delivery premiums "because of the good relationship with Masterson."

It's not often you can replace the whole team on the other side of a negotiation. Yet, if the ultimate goal is working together, you may have more leverage than you think.

A Final, Untold Story about Partnering

Walk down any street in Shanghai and you'll see kids in T-shirts that say things like "Toy Snory" and "Mickey Louse." Thus, one of Americans' biggest complaints about China is its theft of intellectual property. And the dispute (or opportunity) is more important than T-shirts. Billions, or even trillions, of dollars are at stake.

You hear the horror stories because journalists and their editors like horror stories. The stories you don't hear, though, involve successful

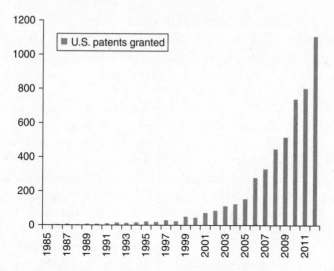

Exhibit 3.1 US patents granted to invention teams that include both American and Chinese citizens.

Source: patft.uspto.gov.

collaborations between American and Chinese enterprises. Consider, for example, your iPhone. It's assembled in China, including parts and technology from China, Japan, Germany, Taiwan, South Korea, several other countries, and the United States. In fact, Apple and Honhai/Foxxcon are involved in one of the most fruitful partnerships the world has ever seen.

The part you haven't heard before is based on our original research: today US patents filed by joint American and Chinese teams are the fastest growing segment of patents, increasing exponentially even as you read this page. The first US/Chinese invention team to be awarded a patent included Patricia C. Wang (from Shanghai), Robert Wingard (Palo Alto), and Leonard Bunes (San Carlos) for their work on a "Process for preparing orange polymeric colorants" (#4,258,189, March 24, 1981). From that humble beginning, the numbers have burgeoned: 45 US patents granted to US/China teams in 2000, 156 in 2005, 742 in 2010, and 1,109 in 2012 (see Exhibit 3.1 and http://merage.uci.edu/longinstitute/NewsAndArticles.aspx for more details). There is also growing evidence that such international cooperation leads to more important (more frequently cited) research papers.[6] Moreover, as American and Chinese inventors continue to work together, we believe the Chinese will become very interested in protecting intellectual property protocols. And those enemies could become our very strongest allies.

CHAPTER 4

Building Personal Relationships

All change in America begins at the dinner table.

—Ronald Reagan

In a highly classified document released just this year, the world finally learned about a secret meeting to build the alliance between Winston Churchill and Joseph Stalin, a meeting held in Moscow during World War II. According to Richard Norton-Taylor's story in *The Guardian*, Sir Alexander Cadogan,[1] a top official from the foreign office, described the meeting in a letter: "Nothing can be imagined more awful than a Kremlin banquet, but it has to be endured."

Frustrated, Churchill asked for a private meeting to be held the next evening. Cadogan describes it, "Winston and Stalin...sitting with a heavily laden board between them: food of all kinds crowned by a suckling pig and innumerable bottles.

"What Stalin made me drink seemed pretty savage: Winston, who by that time was complaining of a slight headache, seemed wisely to be confining himself to a comparatively innocuous effervescent Caucasian red wine. Everything seemed to be merry as a marriage bell. The party broke up at 3 a.m."

Non-Task Sounding

Now, let's fast-forward to June 2013. Relationships between China and the United States have been troubled for decades. Each side denounces the other routinely. Then, with absolutely no fanfare, President Barack Obama and Chinese President Xi Jinping have an informal meeting at Sunnylands in California. Another example of the press ignoring good news about the US/China relationship? Perhaps.

According to Fareed Zakaria in *Time*,[2] the summit was the result of months of preparation. There were eight hours of informal meetings, with no set talking points, no list of complaints; in itself this was a complete break from the past.

In the middle of the first night's dinner, the Chinese delegates, much to their host's surprise, brought out Moutai, the famous (or infamous) sorghum-based liquor, for a special toast. Perhaps they thought it would grease the summit: Henry Kissinger is said to have told China's former supreme leader Deng Xiaoping, "I think if we drink enough Moutai, we can solve anything." The casual talk continued.

The highlight of the summit, however, was a one-on-one between the two presidents. They talked about poverty, describing their childhoods during the Cultural Revolution and during Obama's years in Indonesia. They talked about their dreams for their countries and the opportunities that lay ahead for both.

Neither side expected any substantive agreements, though there was a distinct change in attitudes about North Korea. What this summit did accomplish, however, was a critical step in long-term negotiations.

It wasn't the food and drink, though both summits had that in common. Instead, this element is a throwaway line in Cadogan's old classified letter: Churchill "engaged the company in irreverent and irresponsible discourse."

That irreverent discourse, or small talk, is part of a little-appreciated aspect of inventive negotiation we call non-task sounding. The term "sounding" is a nautical term to describe testing the depth of water, and here it applies to any probe of the people and environment for useful information.

At this writing we are seeing some positive consequences from the Obama/Xi meeting at Sunnylands: a continuing thaw between the two Koreas and, perhaps most surprising, the commander of the People's Liberation Navy visiting the US Navy Chief of Naval Operations at the Washington, DC, Navy Yard. Chinese Admiral Wu explained the purposes for the visit were: "to have a close look at the U.S. Navy. And the other is for friends from the US Navy to get to know us up close." Joint fleet exercises off the coast of California coincided with the visit. We don't know what the admirals had to drink.

So often what seems to task-oriented Americans a total waste of time is to most relationship-oriented cultures the entire point of the first meeting or perhaps of the first dozen: the non-task sounding.

Take, for example, the typical way Americans get started:

1. You send a letter explaining your business purpose. You might drop a name or two if possible.

2. You place a follow-up call for an appointment.
3. During the appointment, you engage in five minutes of small talk across her desk (this is the non-task sounding).
4. You talk business. There might be a few more steps to the dance in Asia, Latin America, Southern Europe, India, and Africa, but those just seem like unnecessary stalling from the American point of view.

There are several reasons why the rest of the world sees this stage differently. The first two are legal and cultural: In the United States we tend to trust until given reason not to. And if things end up in a mess down the line, we have a phalanx of attorneys who can come to the rescue.

Most folks on the planet, however, are loath to use their attorneys and courts to clean things up if the business goes sour. Some of them don't even *have* strong court systems for backup. And no one on the planet has a legal system like the United States. Please see exhibit 14.1 on page 202 for more information.

Instead, most people depend on strong and trusting relationships to mitigate conflicts down the road. Time and money are *invested* in building those relationships *before* getting down to business. Thus, five minutes of non-task sounding in the United States can translate into five days, weeks, or even months of non-task sounding in Shanghai, Lagos, or Rio de Janeiro. There is no other way.

In the relationship-oriented[3] cultures of Asia, Africa, Latin America, and Southern Europe, suspicion and distrust characterize all meetings with strangers. There it is difficult to earn trust, yet business will not even begin without it. In these cultures, trust must be transmitted via personal connections or intermediaries: a trusted business associate of yours must pass you along to one of his trusted business associates and so on. Thus, the key first step in non-task sounding in many countries is finding the personal links to your target organization and/or executive.

Those links can be ties to hometown, family, school, or previous businesses. In some places the links can be institutional—as in Japan where your banker can do the introductions. In China or India, the links must be based on personal experience. For example, you call your former classmate and ask him to set up a dinner meeting with his friend. Expensive meals at nice places are key to demonstrating that you understand the value of strategic personal relationships. (Notice the food and drink appear again.) If things go well, your classmate's friend accepts the role of your intermediary and in turn sets up a meeting with your potential client or business partner whom he knows quite well.

Often, your intermediary will then arrange a lunch or dinner the night before a visit to the client's offices. The intermediary will attend both. Your intermediary will insist that you spend big bucks on the meal: This is extremely important because your sincerity will be gauged by the size of the check. Now, for someone who grabs a sandwich for lunch and sits hunched over a computer to eat it, this ritual meal will seem inefficient. Yet, experts know that this $500 meal may in fact be the best investment you could make in most places around the world.

The talk at these initial meetings will range widely, even inanely so from the American perspective. Even though your intermediary has "blessed" the relationship, your foreign partner will still endeavor to sound you out in the broadest sense—your trustworthiness, sincerity, integrity, and competence. Your counterpart will be looking for feelings of interpersonal harmony and connection. And there is simply no rushing this process. While this "empty questioning" may test your own patience, even your endurance, you should take it as a sign of progress—your counterpart is interested.

At some point when you have "passed" the total-you test, the client or the intermediary will bring up business. This signals the end to non-task sounding in relationship cultures. Only the client or intermediary can give this signal. We repeat, only the client or intermediary can give this signal, *not you*! And even then, after brief discussion of business, your foreign client may lapse back into more non-task sounding.

Most Americans make it through the dinner, but at the client's offices the next day they can't keep from making proposals. This is incredibly rude from the foreign perspective. Even when they've been told by their own experienced staff to continue the small talk until the client broaches business, most high-powered Americans can't stand the "delays."

For example, we talked with a group of American executives developing a business relationship with Spanish counterparts. The Americans' complaint was that every time they went to Madrid, the trip was exhausting because the Spaniards insisted they eat and drink late into the night. Combined with jet lag, that left absolutely no energy for discussions during the days. We recommended they invite the Spaniards to Houston to continue the work. The Texans responded, "We've tried that. But even in Houston, they still party late into the night—and there we have to contend with our families!"

The implications are clear: In foreign countries, and often also in the United States, always, *always*, let the client or intermediary bring up business.

Non-task Sounding for Top Executives

The role of top executives in negotiations internationally is often ceremonial. By ceremonial, we do *not* mean unimportant. Ordinarily, these executives are brought into negotiations only to sign the agreement after all the issues have been settled by lower-level executives. On occasion, top executives are included earlier in the talks to communicate commitment to and importance of the negotiations. In either case, the executives' main activity is non-task sounding. Only vague statements should be made about the potential for a strong, long-lasting business relationship. Specifics must be left up to managers and staff.

Getting top American executives to understand the importance of non-task sounding and to make these adjustments in their behavior may be difficult. One successful way has been to supply task-oriented executives with a task: memorizing a list of appropriate questions to ask during the initial meetings with their high-level counterparts. Soccer's a good topic almost everywhere, but a little knowledge about cricket will go a long way in Sydney. Ask your local representatives or intermediaries what topics are appropriate and do a little studying ahead of time.

Because most businesses and organizations have a hierarchical structure, most people assume that the culture of the leader is the culture of the organization. Thus, these soundings at the highest level are critical indicators of trustworthiness, compatibility, and sincerity. Rushing through the motions can destroy years of lower-level negotiations.

Note that while the talk may seem small, a variety of small nonverbal nuances could be especially important in this critical phase. They, too, are a part of non-task sounding.

It begins at the airport. Top level executives, especially from Asian cultures, will expect to be met with a limousine to take them from the airport to a luxury hotel and from there to your meeting. Dining should take place at a fine, and preferably famous, restaurant. Business card presentation, while subject to strict cultural rules at the lower level, is not generally done at all at the executive level. You should have learned all about your counterparts long before these meetings take place, and they will expect to be recognized on sight.

The setting of your meeting also plays a role. First meetings should never take place across a huge boardroom table or from two chairs across the expanse of an executive desk. Just as you entertain your friends across a tiny restaurant table or relaxed on sofas in your living room, an inventive negotiator will arrange for non-task soundings to occur in non-task locations.

Then let the small talk begin. And continue. And continue.

SIDEBAR 4.1

Dr. Chang

When CHOC Children's Hospital of Orange County, CA (CHOC), needed to step up its cardiology program, the executives tried to recruit a hot young physician who had trained and taught in the country's leading pediatric cardiology programs— Johns Hopkins, Harvard, Boston Children's, LA Children's. Just at the height of his success, working in a world-class setting at Texas Children's, a tenured professor at Baylor, he had no desire to jump ship.

At first, Dr. Anthony Chang recalls he had about " a one percent interest" in taking the position. But CHOC's pediatrician in chief, Dr. Nick Anas, was persistent. He kept calling, learning more about Chang and what motivated him. They spoke of their shared experiences in Texas and their shared dreams of pediatric innovation. At the end of each call, Dr. Anas asked about the interest level, and Chang would respond with a slightly higher fraction, "maybe 1.3 percent."

By the time they'd had a dozen calls over the course of a year, that percentage was still below 20. Still Anas kept calling, talking about Chang's interests and the hospital's commitment to becoming a leader in the field.

Today, Chang leads CHOC's Pediatric Heart Institute, has a successful practice, has acquired two additional graduate degrees in public health and biomedical informatics, and is editor in chief of the textbook, on *Pediatric Cardiac Intensive Care*. A member of the National Institute of Health's grant review committee, he is on editorial boards of every major journal in his specialty. He teaches public health, global health, and biomedical informatics at UCLA and runs international conferences.

How did this superstar land there? It took nearly two years and at least 50 phone calls and visits. By the time he finally agreed to come, he had formed a firm friendship with Anas and a good relationship with the hospital's CEO. Not exactly a typical negotiation, but one that has led to a productive long-term affiliation. Few hospital administrators would have taken the time or learned so much about a potential recruit, particular when his interest level was down in the tiny fractions. For Chang and the hospital, the process has been well worth it.

Long-Term Personal Relationships
Are the Grail

Of course, the initial non-tasking sounding and relationship building is just the beginning. The most successful relationships are built on years, even decades, of working together. And this process becomes even more complex when there are more people and more organizations involved in the project. Here's where an inventive negotiator can really make a difference.

Mary Robinson has a warm, engaging smile, and takes the time to chat with each student, professor, and community leader in the long, long line turned out to honor her with the UCI Citizen Peacebuilding Award. Former President of Ireland, UN High Commissioner of Human Rights, recipient of the US Medal of Freedom and Amnesty International's Ambassador of Conscience Award, professor at Columbia University and University of Pretoria, Chancellor of the University of Dublin—her resume has enough highlights for any six high-achieving people.

Perhaps more important, her work has changed the lives of millions of people in countries around the world, through some of the most inventive negotiations imaginable.

When Robinson was elected as the first female president of Ireland in 1990 at age 46, she had already racked up an impressive number of achievements. After legal degrees from Trinity College and Harvard, she'd juggled a career as a barrister, represented women in international courts, taught law at Trinity, and served as a Senator—all while having three children.

It was not an easy time to lead the country. Poverty was endemic, and Northern Ireland had been suffering for nearly 30 years from a civil war known as The Troubles. Since Ireland's independence from England in 1922, the region had been torn by conflicts both political and religious. Belfast was so dangerous that people could not travel from one side of the city to the other.

Robinson approached the conflict in Northern Ireland in stages, each unexpected and unprecedented. First, in her inaugural address, she extended the hand of friendship and love to both sides. Perhaps only a woman could have used the word "love" and gotten away with it.

Then she installed a light in the kitchen window of the President's house, an Irish tradition that signals to any weary traveler that there is hospitality within. And while this was largely a symbolic act, it set the stage for the actions to come.

Next, she went to a very unlikely place: Buckingham Palace. To understand why this was so significant, you need to know that the

President of Ireland is forbidden by the Constitution to leave the country. She must ask permission of the legislature before going anywhere, and in the seven decades after independence, no President had overcome the remaining enmity enough to travel across the Irish Sea.

She'd been invited to deliver the Dimbelby Lecture. Denied. Meetings with Irish communities in London. Denied. A dozen other invitations. Denied. An honorary degree from Cambridge University and a meeting with Vaclav Havel of Czechoslovakia—finally, after all these submissions, the Irish government consented. During her day in Cambridge, she met Prince Phillip, Chancellor of the University. Their visit was so pleasant that two years later she received an invitation from Queen Elizabeth. By this time, the government caved in, though it was neither a "state visit" nor an "official visit." After a brief tea, there was a photo taken. Not a world event, just, as she describes it in her book, *Everybody Matters*, "the President of Ireland and the Queen of England, two women, heads held high."

Three years later, there was an official visit, with Prime Minister John Major, and ultimately in 2011 Queen Elizabeth actually traveled to Ireland.

Again, these meetings were not a direct approach to the conflict in Northern Ireland, but they served an important purpose. They showed that hundreds of years of conflict could be forgiven between the Irish and their neighbors. And they connected Robinson with a number of powerful allies.

Unlike in most countries, the president of Ireland is supposed to be apolitical. Robinson ran as an independent. Her background was Catholic, her family was descended from important conservative Irish figures, but she had worked for gay rights and women's rights to contraceptives and remarriage.

Her next step was to work with another disenfranchised group—the women of Northern Ireland. While their sons and husbands and brothers were shooting one another and setting off bombs, these women were working hard to try to create a peaceful place where their families could break out of poverty.

From the beginning of her term, she had invited community groups, particularly cross-community groups, to visit Aras an Uachtarain, the president's house, and many of those invited were women. Thus in 1992 Robinson accepted an invitation from a coalition of women's groups from the most disadvantaged areas. They in turn invited elected officials and other dignitaries to meet with her at a reception. It was the first working visit by an Irish president to Northern Ireland but not the most controversial. That came a year later.

In her own words:[4]

> It is virtually impossible to describe the intensity of that occasion without understanding the context. There was no cease-fire and no peace process at that stage, and the violence was escalating. The situation was at an impasse, framed in terms of "win or lose." The British government was determined that it would "win the war," but the IRA would never concede "losing it."
>
> There was no room to bring any other perspective to the situation, such as urging that a human rights framework could facilitate a dialogue without blame being attributed.

Yet, Robinson was determined to go to West Belfast to meet with these community groups, and that meant she would have to meet the local elected representatives there, including Gerry Adams, leader of Sinn Fein, the "political wing" of the IRA.

> Nobody was going into West Belfast, and nobody was meeting with Gerry Adams...it was illegal to broadcast his voice on radio or television. This community in West Belfast felt completely isolated: in its view, it was not a part of Britain. No money was going in from anywhere...it was a no-go area for the police. Yet it had a vibrant community; it was full of good people working hard to counter the lack of facilities and resources and the discrimination they suffered. That was what I wanted to honour.

When the British government heard about the proposed visit, Robinson was informed that the visit must be cancelled. Robinson's own Irish government was discouraging the visit, though it couldn't forbid her travel, since her destination was still part of Ireland. She decided to go ahead anyway.

At the border Robinson was escorted by special security guards, but by the time she arrived at her first scheduled location, she was greeted by crowds of schoolchildren waving tricolored flags, the St. Agnes Choral Society was singing, pipes were being played, and there was Irish dancing. Out of sight of the cameras, she shook hands with Gerry Adams and then met with teachers, trade unionists, musicians, schoolchildren, IRA leaders, local councilors, and the women of the community.

She arrived home safely, having respected and honored the people in West Belfast, and a week later 75 percent of the Irish people thought she'd done the right thing to shake Adams's hand. Her popularity soared to 93 percent, and the impasse was broken.

That visit was an important part of the negotiations that eventually led to the 1998 Good Friday agreement that ended The Troubles.

And the visit is a good example of several of the principles of inventive negotiation. First, Robinson believed it was possible to find a solution, though decades had gone by without one. She managed to bring the right people to the table, people whose lives were being destroyed by the daily battles, many of them women. She was willing to take risks—including endangering the new and tentative relationship she'd formed with the British government. Instead of focusing on winning or losing, she focused on building trust and then relationships.

Using Innovation Processes to Build Relationships[5]

Looking for new sources of energy always seems to generate—well—lots of energy. With all the controversy about oil pipelines, deep sea drilling, and fracking, you'd think that tapping natural heat from the earth would be a slam dunk. But you'd be wrong.

Consider a project first proposed two decades ago in Bend, Oregon, certainly one of the most eco-friendly environments in the United States. The customer-owned power company in Eugene, Oregon (EWEB), and Cal Energy wanted to use local geothermal sources to create electricity. The technology had been around forever: Romans used hot springs to create public baths and underfloor heating in England in the first century, and the Chinese had used geothermal energy three hundred years earlier. The French were heating whole districts this way by the fourteenth century, and the Italians were using the technology for industry in the early 1800s. By 1892, geothermal energy was heating Boise, Idaho, and eight years later it was working in Iceland, Tuscany, and even in Klamath Falls, Oregon. Today, geothermal plants operate successfully in 24 countries.

Geothermal energy is cost-effective, reliable, sustainable, and environmentally friendly—a perfect fit. Unfortunately, wells need to be drilled; there are some emissions (though much less than by any other form of plant), and it can be expensive.

Thus, the energy companies began to enlist allies long before they began to negotiate with local governments. They put together an organization called the Central Oregon Geothermal Working Group and invited many of the stakeholders to take part. The working group's goal: to advise the project sponsors on the planning of an environmentally responsible pilot geothermal project. They didn't agree to support the project, just to learn about it.

The team began by selecting a local facilitator, JoAn Mann. According to her, "Bend was still a very small community at the time (about 17,000), so you'd see these folks in the store, at the kids' soccer games."

Then they convened a weekend retreat. Mann used a personality test to learn more about each participant and to head off potential problems. By the end of the weekend, the participants had reached consensus on rules of conduct and procedures, avoiding some of the battles that might have loomed ahead.

The next step was scheduling community meetings, held once a week on the first Thursday of every month for two years. *The Bend Bulletin* ran a notice every Sunday night, and everyone in town was urged to attend. Then the group arranged field trips so residents could see other plants in operation and visit their proposed site.

These were all pretty standard steps in a thoughtful process. But Mann went further, arranging cozy premeeting dinners with groups who had similar interests. Since all the members had busy working and family lives, these caucuses gave them a unique opportunity to talk about issues in an informal setting.

Mann sat in on them all. "Everyone had the opportunity to meet with me to clarify or air their views. I'd say that during the course of the two years, everyone did meet with me individually. If they asked me to bring something to the whole group, I followed through. If I was asked to keep something confidential, I did. I think I had a good reputation prior to the session for 'not speaking out of school' and I didn't abuse that."

Aside from the townsfolk, there were two other groups that met frequently: the project sponsors and an ex officio group of representatives from federal agencies. These federal agency people began with a pro-project attitude and determined before every meeting that no laws were being violated. When questions came up in meetings, they had the answers, and those answers were generally that the issue was not going to be a problem. Even with that attitude, however, they also made sure that the community members had a say in the project design.

The project sponsors also had a standing role: to supply technical expertise and outside experts to educate everyone involved and answer specific questions. According to Mann, "The group was asked to help 'fill in the experts' if they knew of someone when the sponsors didn't. Both Cal Energy and EWEB were very open to having a different source or expert. Questions were always taken. I don't remember even a single time where a question was 'redirected.'"

As a result, all the stakeholders had a voice; they felt respected, and the meetings were always civil. (Contrast that with your local city council meeting.) If something came up that couldn't be resolved, the issue was moved to the next meeting, and the group would find more experts to inform them. When they reached an impasse at a meeting, Mann used a five-finger straw poll to gauge the sentiment in the room. Five fingers was full agreement. Three meant partial agreement but concurrence. One meant serious reservations but eventual agreement. No hand meant no dice. By taking this nuanced approach instead of a simple hand count, Mann felt that important issues were raised and addressed. Ultimately, this approach resulted in greater understanding and more durable agreements.

Since the plant location had already been determined, the working group was able to address landscaping, location of access roads, steam plume visibility, stack design, routing and appearance of power transmission lines, and even general facility design. All these issues could have derailed the project if the group hadn't participated in all those informal meetings.

At the end of the two-year project, they produced a document with their recommendations and had a formal signing ceremony. Their recommendations and agreements became part of the plan and were key to going forward.

By selecting a local facilitator, engaging every possible stakeholder, and taking the time to get to know one another outside the meeting room, the group took all the hard negotiating off the table before the work even began. From an array of possible adversaries, the group members forged a team of respectful colleagues. And those people are still working together two decades later. Indeed, in 2013, after a variety of financial delays, the project is again proceeding with demonstration wells.

Never Negotiate with a Terrorist?

In 2006 being a military interrogator in Iraq was among the world's most difficult assignments. Every day, suicide bombers were blowing up mosques and markets, killing hundreds of innocents. The citizens of Iraq, displaced and impoverished and missing family members, were hardly inclined to share information with the U.S. military. Yet, without that information, there was no way to stop the bombers, the bomb makers, or the leaders who were ordering the attacks.

Traditional adversarial approaches simply weren't working. Abu Graib had just made headlines around the world, and if anything these revelations made captured prisoners even more reluctant to talk.

As a former criminal investigator, Matthew Alexander knew that the only way to get good information from a hostile witness was to establish a relationship and trust—an assumption of collaboration and shared goals.[6]

SIDEBAR 4.2

Carol Holt & Strengths

At her biomedical manufacturing firm, Carol Holt was a one-woman SWAT team. Trouble with getting nurses to buy a new product? Call Carol. The new website needs to work internationally? Carol can do that.

She even solved the accounts receivable problem that plagued her industry: collecting payments from huge hospital chains took months and months. Even with dedicated, knowledgeable people in accounts receivable, her firm was averaging 120 days to collection, so millions of dollars in inventory was being used long before it was paid for. Every call, every month, was a mini-negotiation.

The reason Carol had excelled at all her tasks, however, was that she was a people person. A former nurse, she had a great deal of empathy, and she spent the time to build solid relationships with staff, clients, doctors, vendors—everyone she met. But Carol couldn't personally make all the collection calls, and she needed the system to work when she'd moved on to the next emergency.

So she trained the staff in a simple personality test that measured preferred forms of motivation and had them post the results on their doors or cubicles. Some people loved learning new things; others liked familiarity and routine. Some loved meeting new people; others would rather have a root canal than enter a cocktail party. These reps then asked their counterparts at the client hospitals to take an online version of the test "because it's fun," and Carol's company paid the fee.

Suddenly every rep knew exactly how to relate to every client. Conversations got warmer as the reps appealed to the individuals on the other end of the phone. There were no overt requests to speed up payments, but somehow their invoices rose to the top of the pile. Within a few months, collections were completed in half the time—besting the industry average by two to three months. And those monthly calls became relationship builders, not plea bargains, assuring that even when staff moved to other hospitals, Carol's company would always be paid first.

The "negotiation" setting was far from ideal—a bare six-by-six-foot room with plywood walls and plastic chairs. After weeks of interrogation by specialists, an important prisoner named Abu Haydar had revealed nothing. Yet Alexander suspected that he had the key to finding Zarqawi, al-Qaida's second in command. In less than six hours, Abu Haydar would be transferred to Abu Graib, his secret knowledge intact.

Alexander decided to make one last, unauthorized, attempt. According to his book, *How to Break a Terrorist*,[7] he only had time to rehearse his tone and opening lines in the few minutes before Abu Haydar arrived and the black hood was pulled off his face. Instead of threatening, trying to persuade, or bribe the prisoner, Alexander began his discussion by treating him as an ally—a respected, learned man who might share a common goal.

They spoke at length about the intricacies of Abu Haydar's religious beliefs, with Alexander using his own copy of the Koran to ask questions. They talked about their favorite Ultimate Fighting champions. Alexander commiserated with Abu Haydar about the chaos that had been unleashed by Shia death squads after the fall of Saddam and the political consequences of a Sunni-Shia regional war. Abu Haydar was surprised but curious. There were only minutes left before his transfer.

Alexander was honest. "I'm going to be straight with you because we don't have much time." He spoke as one intelligent, studious man to another. Two more bits of honesty: "We need strong capable leaders whom we can trust and work with closely as equal allies. I think you are one."

And then: "Before I can offer this to you. I need to know I can trust you." And he asked for a name. After long moments of silence, Abu Haydar produced it: Al Masri. Just one link away from the man Alexander had been seeking for months. In short order, he described the man accurately and where they'd met. This moment of truth from Abu Haydar was key. The interview was over, time was up, and Abu Haydar stood to shake Alexander's hand.

Alexander halted the transfer, arranged for Abu Haydar to receive the Harry Potter book he'd requested, and ultimately got the information he needed to take out the al-Qaida leader. Respect, relationship, and trust: if you start with them, even an enemy can become an ally in negotiation.

CHAPTER 5

Designing Systems for Success

The wise man looks into space and he knows there are no limited dimensions.
—Lao Tzu

He looks exactly like a member of the real-beard Santa Club in his crisp Oxford shirt, white beard, and ruddy complexion. Yet, the gift Father Gregory Boyle brings is a belief in people abandoned by society long ago. And to make that belief reality, he negotiates hundreds of times every single day.

We interview him in his office in Los Angeles, a couple of blocks from the huge tower that is the LA County jail, a convenient spot since the vast bulk of his employees were gang members revolving through the prison system. Next door, the HomeGirl Café is still serving lunch to a clientele of office workers: salmon pesto tacos and cucumber drinks, brought to tables by women covered in tattoos. For these waitresses, hostesses, and cooks, this is their first real job. The café and bakery is one of three locations, including one added last year at LA International Airport. A sleek bakery case holds fancy cakes and the chocolate coconut macaroons are to die for.

That is perhaps an unfortunate phrase, because death is what gave birth to Homeboy Industries, the rapidly expanding organization led by this Jesuit priest. When he arrived 25 years ago, his parish spanned the two largest and poorest housing projects west of the Mississippi. The death toll was staggering: he was burying several of his young parishioners from rival gangs every week. He began by trying to negotiate truces and cease fires, but those efforts seemed to strengthen the solidarity of the gangs, giving them the status of nation-states arguing over conflicts. He soon came to realize that gang conflicts certainly had violence, but there wasn't actually any conflict to fight over. These young men derived all their identity from hating people in the other gangs. The real cause of their behavior was, as he says so succinctly, "a lethal absence of hope."

And no wonder. This was a generation of fatherless boys, sometimes motherless too. There were no adult role models, no good jobs available, no reasons to stay in school. When the boys set out into other gang territories, they fully expected to die. Drugs, gunshot wounds, prison—all just way stations leading to their inevitable fate.

Father Boyle decided to address that underlying hopelessness by supplying one thing nobody else was providing: jobs. It was far from easy: ex-convicts and current gang members are not high on anyone's list of ideal employees. While he could place some young men with sympathetic adults who had somehow escaped and outgrown the gang life themselves, he needed more than a job here and there.

He knew one thing: Nothing stops a bullet like a job.

He found donors who were willing to invest in an abandoned bakery, and he began hiring. The jobs paid minimum wage; they were hard physical work, but each was a legitimate job, the very first one for many of his workers.

There was only one requirement: you had to show up and work with your coworkers. And those coworkers were likely to be your sworn enemies. This was the one rule on which there could be no negotiation whatsoever: if you didn't want to work under those conditions, there was somebody standing in line who did.

And something about that work forged new bonds and created a community that none of these young men had ever experienced. "Women relate face-to-face," Boyle says, "men shoulder-to-shoulder." Standing side-by-side, kneading dough, sliding fresh loaves out of the oven, those enemies slowly turned into allies without a single word being spoken.

With the success of the Homeboy Industries bakery, Boyle and his sponsors added more businesses: screen printing, then HomeGirl Café. Some of their attempts were not successful. Boyle describes his plan to teach his employees the plumbing trade: while they learned well, there wasn't much of a market for their services. "Who knew that suburban men would not want 6-foot, heavily tattooed ex-cons in their kitchens, alone with their wives?"

Jobs are just one part of the mix. One day an ex-con came in to talk about his difficulty finding work. Across his forehead, covering every centimeter of space from eyebrows to hairline, was a prison tattoo that read "Fuck The World." Could it be that this wasn't exactly the image a fast-food chain wanted? "Do you want fries with that?" as moms took their terrified toddlers straight back to the parking lot.

Boyle found a sympathetic doctor who agreed to remove the offensive tattoo. And other ex-cons quickly came in with the same request.

Before long, there were 30 volunteer doctors using two lasers to remove some 40,000 tattoos a year.

It was easy for these young men to find their way into gangs. For young women, it was another ugly path. Almost all of them are victims of sexual abuse; many are also victims of physical abuse and criminal neglect. A few therapists came on board, then more were needed as the stigma of seeking help began to fade for both sexes. Now 40 carefully screened licensed psychologists and psychiatrists offer help in the main office or in their private offices nearby.

There's also a high school in the old headquarters. "To say these kids are difficult to teach would be totally wrong. They're *impossible*. They've dropped out years ago, and they were probably way behind then." Boyle's eyes mist up. "We just graduated 37 seniors. Thirty seven high-school graduates."

When we ask him how they did it, he says, "Because every one of those teachers cares. That's it. They care, and the boys learn because someone finally cares."

What Boyle has built is a community in a place where none had been. "You can't talk people into understanding that a gang is an empty place. You have to let them live in a community where people actually care about them before they can see the difference."

We're in his office: three walls covered with photos and drawings, with a floor to ceiling glass wall facing the lobby of HomeBoy Industries. It's a modern, open plan, with concrete floors, people filling out job applications, heading up the stairs to offices, next door to the bakery or the gift shop, waiting to see Boyle. Every two minutes, he is gesturing over our heads to someone in the waiting room, performing a silent triage as people vie for his attention, and he fends off phone calls for a few minutes. Several young men come in politely to request his keys: the only parking in the neighborhood has strict two-hour limits, and they want to move his car before he gets a ticket.

At one point, he interrupts our interview for something he has to deal with immediately. And in those four minutes, we can see his highly perfected art of inventive negotiation at work.

A young man and young woman enter the room. Boyle greets them, stands up from his desk, and draws near. It seems the young man has an ongoing medical problem, and his coworkers are pressuring him to go to the hospital for an opinion. They've made arrangements, but the young man doesn't want to go until 8 at night, which means he'll probably not go at all. He has a family history that has made him afraid of needles, of doctors, of hospitals. He believes that if he goes there, he will die.

Boyle begins, "I understand you don't want to go to the hospital until 8. Can you tell me why?"

The young man looks down. "I'm at work. I don't want to leave work."

"Listen," Boyle says softly. The young man looks up. "I am your boss, and I am telling you that this is your job today. I am paying you to be a healthy productive worker, and this is your most important job today."

Boyle gives him a minute for that to sink in and turns to the young woman. "Can you drive him there and stay with him?" She nods.

Then he takes the young man gently by the shoulders and looks at him directly. "Son," he says. "The only thing to be afraid of is not dealing with this. And I know you are strong enough to do this."

The young man is fighting his emotions, and Boyle turns again to the young woman. "You'll stick with him all the way through this, right?" She says yes eagerly.

"She can take you and stay with you, no matter what it takes. And we are blessed to have her on our team. So, can you go right now?"

The young man nods. There's another minute of discussion about insurance cards, and then the two leave the room.

Boyle returns to his desk. "I bet you thought she was his case worker, huh?" he smiles. We nod. "No," he says, "she just works in the clock room. She spotted the problem and has been bugging him to get it fixed."

When you analyze this interaction, you can see many of the elements of inventive negotiation and a big dose of how Boyle builds the relationships of this community. First, the conversation:

Boyle started by framing the decision in a small chunk the young man could handle. "I understand you don't want to go to the hospital until 8." Not a confrontation, not even verbally acknowledging the past or his fears. The question has moved from *whether* he's going to get treatment to *when*. Then he stands back, gives the young man the floor, and listens carefully to his answer. The young man plays an important role here—he is an adult, and he may have perfectly good reasons to delay until 8.

Then Boyle rationally removes the objection. "I am your boss, and I am telling you this is your job today." He gives him a reason to agree—"I am paying you to be a healthy, productive worker." So now, by going to the hospital, the young man is actually doing his job.

Next Boyle gives him a little space to absorb this different perspective. Boyle asks for some buy-in from the young woman. He's enlisting a third-party ally. See? Both of us really want you to do this.

And he still gives the young man a choice and a chance to commit to the outcome. "Can you go right now?"

Boyle rewards him for that choice, while simultaneously trusting the young woman to care for him. By the time the two young people leave, both are more firmly a part of the community, both know that they play a bigger role in that community—by healing each other, they are strengthening the whole.

For the young woman, the unexpected outcome is much bigger than she could have imagined. Often Homeboy Industries' new employees start in her position. Making sure people punch in and out of the time clocks doesn't require much skill, but it does give every current employee a chance to meet the newest ones, so when the new ones enter the rest of the workforce, they have made some friends and know their coworkers. She's now gone from newcomer to vital community member.

We point out one element that Boyle himself had missed: the moment when he held the young man's shoulders and called him "Son."

Boyle shrugs. "He's a fatherless boy."

There are many lessons about inventive negotiation in the story of Father Boyle: The speed of an effective negotiation. The beauty of building long-term relationships. The emotional commitment. His improvisation and quick change of roles (from employer to father figure). But Father Boyle demonstrates the importance of systems design in two different and subtle ways.

Systems Design: The Third Dimension

In "3-D Negotiation" in the *Harvard Business Review*, David Lax and James Sebenius[1] reviewed hundreds of negotiations and found that most negotiators only pay attention to two dimensions of the job—negotiation tactics and deal design (what ends up in the contract). Both occur primarily at the negotiation table. Yet, very few actually planned for the far more important "third dimension," designing the system.

Consider the HomeBoy story. Father Boyle's original intent was to stop the killings in his parish. He tried the peace negotiations approach. It didn't work. So he expanded the horizon of the talks by bringing in a third party—potential employers.

According to Lax and Sebenius, "3-D negotiators reshape the scope and sequence of the game itself to achieve the desired outcome. Acting entrepreneurially, away from the table, they ensure that the right parties are approached in the right order to deal with the right issues, by the right means, at the right time, under the right set of expectations, and facing the right no-deal options."

Certainly Father Boyle has done all of this right: There's his entrepreneurship of thriving businesses in half a dozen different industries. And the people he has brought into the fight against violence—employers, donors, his vendors, his customers, tattoo removal doctors, LA International airport, therapists, high school teachers, volunteers, and of course both male and female parolees and potential gang members. Indeed, he gathered a whole community working toward peace—proof that nothing stops a bullet like a job.

At another level, Father Boyle demonstrates principles of systems design physically, in his office. We've visited many CEO offices over the years, many with what they call an open-door policy. Bill Gates was perhaps the most famous example of a guy without a door, just a cubicle. But Father Boyle's design is unique and particularly fitted to his goals. You could call it a fishbowl. But then you wonder who is the fish—he or his community? He can sit behind his desk and give an interview, all while observing his gang over the interviewers' shoulders. He judges moods and emotions by the movements and facial expressions he sees outside. He'll interrupt a meeting to take care of another person, based on the need, not the status. His community can witness his egalitarian toil into the night, an example for the entire organization.

If we asked Father Boyle if he had planned it this way, he'd probably say, "No, God made it happen this way." Or maybe he'd say, "Nope, and none of this is really important. What is important is simply the 'utter mutuality' of our work together." And maybe he'd be right.

Systems Design and Inventive Negotiation

In the late 1960s, as a college student, John delivered produce around the San Francisco Bay Area. One of his stops was the cafeteria at the then-new General Motors assembly plant in Fremont, California. It was the size of 88 football fields. (And today it hosts a collaboration between Tesla Motors and Toyota.)

From 1984 to 2010, the plant was the site of one of the most successful international joint ventures in history. The NUMMI (New United Motor Manufacturing, Inc.) plant was co-owned by General Motors and Toyota, two fierce international competitors. GM was motivated to learn about Japanese lean manufacturing methods, while Toyota needed a manufacturing foot in the door in the United States as trade sanctions loomed in an angry Washington, DC. The quarter-century venture included all kinds of joint manufacturing and design awards, while the two companies produced cars under both brands, including the Chevy Nova and the Toyota Corolla.

Stephen Weiss, now at the Schulich School of Business in Toronto, wrote perhaps the most complete case analysis ever of a major international business negotiation in the GM-Toyota negotiations for NUMMI (see exhibit 5.1). The central square in the exhibit lists the key "actors" in the negotiation, and in the outer squares Weiss lists the multitude of "audience" members. In this case, he also presented the list of important meetings between the actors and described the process of the negotiations in some detail. Notice that he gives credit to Jay Chai, the facilitator (or in Japanese, the *chukai-sha*). Most of the

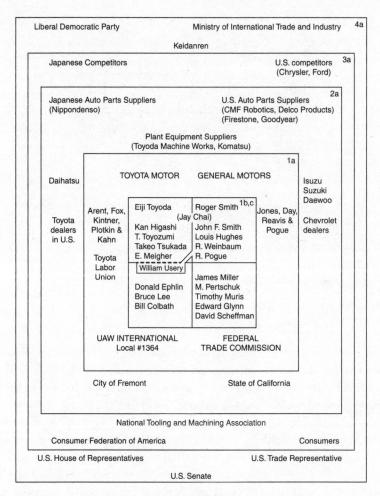

Exhibit 5.1 Actors and audiences in the GM-Toyota negotiations.

Notes: This structure was suggested by Ian Wise.

Larger rectangles (rings) represent diminishing degrees of involvement: 1–primary actors; 2–affiliates, network members, and supporting audiences; 3–industry and market actors (opponents); 4–environmental (political) actors. *Letters* designate levels of behavioral analysis: a–organizations; b–groups; c–individuals. With the exception of the FTC, Boxes 1b, c contain negotiating teams (excluding CEO's Toyoda and Smith) as well as primary individual players.

Source: Stephen Weiss, "Creating the GM/Toyota Joint Venture: A Case in Complex Negotiation," *Columbia Journal of World Business* (Summer 1987): 23–35.

rest of the details are not important here—but the representation of the negotiation is. It's an early attempt at describing systems design.

Weiss' map of the NUMMI negotiations provides the sort of "map" to which David Lax and James Sebenius might apply their idea of "A 'negotiation campaign,'" which may take months or even years, involves identifying the relevant parties and grouping them into fronts; determining if the fronts can be combined; figuring out the order in which you will

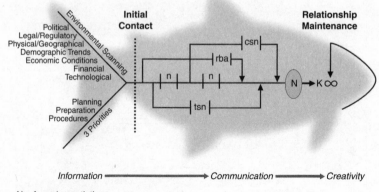

Information ——————————→ *Communication* ————→ *Creativity*

N = formal negotiations
n = information negotiations
K = contract/definitive agreement
rba = relationship building activities
tsn = technical side bar negotiations
csn = creative side bar negotiations

Exhibit 5.2   The global negotiation process

engage the fronts; and assessing how much information to share among the parties—and with your opponents."[2] Of course, we do not like their use of a military/competitive lexicon in their explanation, but we do appreciate the guide to planning for complex and huge-ticket negotiations.

In William's and John's latest book, *Global Negotiation: The New Rules*, the authors describe a different systems design model (see exhibit 5.2): A protocol, or road map for global negotiations... the integrated use of knowledge, communication, and creativity toward building commercial arrangements that deliver mutual prosperity around the world. The blueprint for this process resembles the skeleton of a fish.

Here's how this works: Like a fish's tail, the *knowledge* gained through environmental scanning, planning, and preparations powers the entire process. The main body of the fish consists of the *communications* among partners. Finally, the head of the fish includes the *creativity* (or *invention*) of agreement, the vision reflected in the contract, and the view of the future in the ongoing relationship.

The fish illustration identifies key areas of research, preparation, planning, and procedures. It establishes the critical time line and the initial point of contact. Then it distinguishes between formal and informal, cultural, and technical sidebar negotiations as they lead to the contract. Finally, it projects into the future with relationship maintenance.

The fish introduces the novice negotiator to the various stages and issues in global negotiations and organizes multidisciplinary tasks into manageable working units. Yet the fish diagram depicts only two negotiation parties and ignores third parties and other audiences.

Try to imagine using these diagrams to analyze the Homeboy negotiation processes. Yikes! There'd be boxes and arrows going everywhere. There's simply no way to capture the structure and processes in any two-dimensional diagram.

A better analogy might be an information cloud—think three dimensions with access open to all. Or perhaps a solar system? Think of the central sun (the fundamental relationship) encircled by planets and their moons (assets) with crossing orbits, all attracted by a mutual gravity that holds the three-dimensional system together. Think of Father Boyle and his homeboys as the fundamental relationship that attracts other assets—people (their ideas, time, and sweat), capital resources (money, real estate, brand equity), and the subtle, incalculable value of community and "utter mutuality." And like a solar system, inventive negotiations are open systems that also encourage input from outside sources. The universe is infinite.

Since no two-dimensional chart can adequately describe the complex processes of inventive negotiation, we'll just demonstrate the elements and let you combine them in your own unique systems designs.

How Design Improves Knowledge Flows

The key to inventive negotiations is learning as much as possible about the other parties. Particular people, certain personal relationships, meeting places, times, and communication channels stimulate truthful communications. Others prevent open communication and rich knowledge flows. And it's your job to maximize these flows.

Several years ago, in one of our corporate seminars at Boeing, we discovered that the engineers in the group had already begun to "diagram" the negotiation process in their own familiar way: a Gantt chart. For a forthcoming negotiation with a parts vendor for an aircraft tail structure, the diagram considered each step with a remarkable level of detail and sophistication. We encouraged the engineers, but then asked them to include factors and variables that were not easily quantifiable. The procedures quickly began to fall apart. Unexpected forces simply do not show up within a perfectly reverse-engineered project management chart.

Here the *science* of negotiations met up with the *art* of negotiations for the first time. The engineers came to realize that the vendor wanted a good price but also wanted "other things": a long-term relationship with Boeing, the ability to provide other products, and referrals to other Boeing departments. These factors did not fit well within the initial cost/benefit analysis.

No matter how much structure you put into the environmental scan, and into negotiation planning, preparation, and process design, you always need to integrate those unknown and immeasurable factors. The fluidity of the process and the improvisational nature of the art permit inventive negotiations.

The next step is manipulating the negotiation to maximize knowledge flows. While some of these factors may seem trivial, they are all keys to successful systems design:

1. Number of parties
2. Number of individual participants
3. Audiences (news media, etc.)
4. Communication channels

In chapter 8, we'll discuss three others—the place, space, and pace of negotiations. All seven factors are ordinarily set before formal negotiations begin, and any one factor can make the difference between success and failure.

Number of Parties

In many negotiations, more than two companies are involved. In addition to a buyer and a seller, there are often other suppliers, engineering consulting firms, banks, trading companies, and government officials. Generally, the more parties involved, the greater the opportunities for inventive outcomes, but also the more complex and the more difficult the negotiations. Unfortunately, our American impatience often leads us to try to get everyone together and quickly "hammer out" an agreement. This almost always ends in frustration.

Instead, we recommend that initial negotiations include as few parties as possible—maybe only representatives of the two primary companies. If more than one other party is involved, we might recommend a lobbying approach, meeting with the separate parties individually before calling everyone together. In *Dolphins and Sharks,* Peter Shikerev notes the different approach to lobbying in Russia. Rather than meeting with everyone separately, coalitions are "accumulated": You meet with one other party. When you agree, you call in a third party. When the three of you agree, then the three of you call in a fourth party.

After you've reached an agreement with your partners, after you have "gotten to yes," we recommend one additional step with everyone included. The idea here is to maximize the creativity of the business agreement by going beyond "getting to yes." At this final meeting, the focal questions should be, "Is there some way to make this relationship better for everyone? In particular, is there something we haven't considered?" The more parties are involved, the more new ideas you can generate.

Number of Individual Participants

In negotiations, Americans are almost always outnumbered, which can be a serious disadvantage. It's vital to learn who is coming from the other side and then put your team together in response. Don't hesitate to include additional members, including financial or technical experts. The extra expense may be a wise investment.

Audiences

In any deal, there might be several audiences that exercise influence on the outcomes. DP World is a good example. In the wake of 9/11 and the subsequent negative responses of Americans to all Middle Eastern countries, this Dubai-owned firm made a bid to acquire several US port operations. Consider their audiences:

1. Other suitors and competitors, even Chinese firms
2. Governmental agencies: FTC (antitrust), Congress (trade barrier saber rattling), State Department, Commerce Department, and the US Trade Representative, plus a variety of security agencies
3. George Bush's donors
4. The American public
5. Dock workers' unions
5. The local and international media
6. Other Middle Eastern firms considering other American acquisitions

Now consider how the company might have manipulated these various audiences to its advantage. All of the audiences had a stake in how the DP World talks continued, and certainly some were manipulated through selective leaking of information. Yet, ultimately Democrats in Congress and the antipathy of the American public worked together to kill the deal despite Bush's veto threat. As business people, the company executives had figured out all the rational justifications, but they weren't prepared for the emotional reactions.

Or consider Telenor, a Norwegian cell phone company that accused its Russian business partner, Altimo, of buying Ukrainian press coverage of their disputes over assets. This is not the first time information has been deliberately leaked to the news media to pressure the other side to agree to the terms of a proposal. It's difficult for the other party to say no to an already publicized agreement. Yet, it's a risky tactic: it frequently results in mistrust and a breakdown in the negotiations. Trying to influence negotiations through leaking information to a foreign press (that is, Americans in a foreign country or vice versa) is even riskier.

Often international clients or partners will manipulate audiences to their advantage, particularly their local audiences, including local governments. You may be able to do the same, especially when you envision some audience members as partners.

SIDEBAR 5.1

Feeding the Beast

As Captain D (that's what her men called her) walked to the negotiating site at Camp Pendleton, she used one technique that is too often neglected: The power of the press.

In this case, the press included the actual press, the hostile hijab-clad woman who was the local reporter and her aggressive cameraman. The Captain took time to stop and talk with them, answering all their questions, deliberately feeding them information that would cast the Marines as good guys coming to help and the local participants as very important people indeed whose opinions were highly regarded.

She also used the more informal network, talking to people who accosted her and who were likely leaders within their own small subcommunities. She knew only too well the maxim that one of her own senior officers had taught her.

The press is a beast. It must be fed, tidbits of information at frequent intervals, or it will stay hungry. And it will devour you.

Channels of Communication

You can communicate via a vast number of channels: face-to-face, through an intermediary, through the press, telephone, conference call, fax, e-mail, instant messaging, text messaging, teleconferencing, videoconferencing, Skype, Twitter, Vine, YouTube, Instagram—even more that haven't been invented yet. It's hard to imagine how communication technologies will evolve as the bandwidth widens. Today's

$400,000 HDTV "telepresence" systems could be superseded to even more convincing faux reality.

The conventional wisdom is that it's always best to meet face-to-face. There all channels are open, verbal and nonverbal. People can touch, smell, even taste one another—kissing is appropriate in some cultures. You can easily measure attention and comprehension by facial expressions and postures.[3]

This is especially true with clients from relationship-oriented cultures. Other channels of communication that might be used in the United States are simply not effective or acceptable. For example, the Japanese social system is built on almost continuous face-to-face contact. Too much of the important, subtly transmitted information can't be communicated in a letter, memo, fax, e-mail, telephone call, or even by teleconferencing. Written communications also leave a record of interactions that may not be ideal in some circumstances. And it is much harder for Japanese bargainers to say no in face-to-face situations. The social pressure and interpersonal harmony preclude negative responses, and these pressures are not as strong over the phone or e-mail.

There are, however, some distinct advantages to electronic contact. Information can flow more smoothly and conveniently over the Internet. When we compared transcripts of face-to-face negotiations with email negotiations, we found that in person there can be miscommunication, missed messages, error correction, and repetition. It is actually hard to listen carefully when you are thinking about what you are going to say next. E-mail, on the other hand, gives you time to read carefully and even to consult others on specific messages. E-mail also allows time for careful responses. In fact, e-mail works somewhat like talking on the golf course—there you talk on the tee, then while you're chasing your errant shots in separate directions, you have time to carefully consider the information received and your response.

There are two basic lessons here: (1) Ask about preferences in communication channels, and (2) design communication systems that maximize knowledge flows to build creativity.

On Paper It Couldn't Be Done

Like Father Boyle, the US Marine Corps Civil Affairs Group (CAG) in Afghanistan had as its primary goal saving lives—both those of their fellow marines and the local good guys. But sometimes the lines of authority make that tough to do.

About halfway between Kabul and Kandahar it's hot as hell. In Nawa District in Afghanistan the average temperature in July is 103 degrees. Opium poppies grow well in the heat, irrigated with water from the Helmand River. So did the Taliban, until 2009, when the United States Marine Corps undertook Operation Strike of the Sword and the "surge." By 2010, Nawa was the poster child for military success in that God-forsaken war. By 2010, it was an island of security surrounded by dangerous regions controlled by the Taliban.

Remember Omar Sharif shooting a water thief in *Lawrence of Arabia*? This act makes perfect sense to folks in Nawa. In a place where water is life, the marines' brown camouflage uniforms are an exact match for the arid terrain.

Nawa, for all of its successes since the surge, had to solve the problem of the desert people if the district wanted to ensure its future prosperity. Along the banks of the Helmand River, Nawa's communities were stable, secure, void of insurgent elements, and enjoyed a growing economy. Four miles west of the river, however, where fields were no longer easily irrigated by the free-flowing water, lived the disenfranchised people of Shoshurak, also referred to as "the desert people" by the locals from the greener regions. As a result of its marginalized status, Shoshurak was a potential hotbed for instability, where poppy was still being grown and with a significant potential to put in jeopardy the stability Nawa had enjoyed in recent years. The US Marine battalion commander overseeing the district had to solve this precarious problem of the desert people if he wanted to ensure the stability of his assigned battle space and building wells seemed like a logical option given his dwindling resources as a result of the US military's rapid drawdown. He turned the problem over to his Civil Affairs advisors.

Captain Gregg Curley and Captain Amaury Gallais are marines, wiry and whip smart. As Civil Affairs (CA) officers, they were to support public works projects in Nawa, and they served under the colonel in charge of all CA activities in the region. The colonel (who wrote their fitness reports) had assigned them to work directly for the battalion commander in the Nawa District. The battalion commander had only bullets to use in his work, but the addition of CAG added another "weapon" to his arsenal, their friendship-inducing public works.

Given the scarcity of water, Curley and Gallais favored the tactic of paying to drill some wells to earn the goodwill of the locals. Their battalion commander was all for it. Drilling wells had become a preferred device for battalion commanders and their CA advisers on the ground across Helmand Province due to their relative ease, low costs, and popularity among the Afghans.

But the CAG chain of command at headquarters had ordered the end to all well drilling in the area. The CAG staff's studies had shown that water from these wells was usually of such poor quality that over time the locals would be angrier with it than without it. Additionally, the wells had a disruptive impact on the local economy, putting the locals who had been making money by fetching and distributing water to villagers out of work. This could create some very unhappy unemployed locals who might then have a reason to find work with insurgent groups. Moreover, there was reason to believe that such wells would support opium production or lower the water table. And the CAG wrote the checks.

Things were no less complicated on the Afghan side. Drilling wells in any particular spot might cause increasing animosity among the local leaders. It bears repeating—water is life, and therefore, water is power, and water is money. Controlling access to a US-built well meant changes in authority and influence that might impact the natural pecking order of the tribal communities.

In Shoshurak, Curley and Gallais carefully considered the location for the two wells the battalion commander insisted on building. Placing one well near a mosque was a possibility, assuming greed would not motivate a religious leader. Another location that might work was just outside a base of the Afghan National Army (ANA), the least corrupt and most respected security force, and this would ensure indiscriminate and safe access to the water. But the locals don't much like the Tajiks (Persian speakers) from up north who largely make up the army's ranks. A third option was on the centrally located compound of a very popular local elder who had built excellent relationships with the US Marine detachment posted nearby and had been working hard to bring Shoshurak under the fold of the government of the Islamic Republic of Afghanistan.

So the CAG team's problem was overlaying a sensible negotiation systems design on top of a dangerous can of worms. The battalion commander was relatively close to Shoshurak, but Camp Leatherneck and the CAG headquarters were more than 50 miles away. Face-to-face meetings involving all marine parties weren't in the cards. That difficult communication link was dramatically improved when Captain Gallais was assigned to work on the CAG staff at Leatherneck.

The meeting rooms at the battalion command post were not exactly luxurious, but at least you could take off your body armor "inside the wire" (the marines' term for inside the fortified areas). Visiting the locals was another matter. Just getting there meant being in harm's way from snipers and roadside bombs. Captain Curley described it to us:

> You show up for a meeting with weapon in hand and body armor on. They're on their own time schedule. They had cell phones, vehicles for some, TVs for the rich, but they harvest wheat with a sickle. Some have electricity, but generally the sun dictates the schedule. The grind ages them faster here—guys in their 30s have white beards. The smarter individuals, like the district governor, often tend to be pro-American. But they know we're here for six-month tours. As soon as one team leaves, another shows up and hears about all the promises made by the last team. They know our timetable. They are primitive, but not stupid.
>
> I didn't lie to them—told them when we were stopping projects and what we were doing. They went through this with the Russians and knew what we were going to do. Most wanted us to leave, except the people we were paying rent to. Anyone at a high enough level to even engage with us culturally was smart enough to realize that we aren't here for the long haul. We engaged with individuals on a daily basis but were trying to disengage on a macro level. Still, they saw us as the best available source of funds.
>
> We attended a Shura, their word for a town hall meeting. I was there with Matt Duncan, the local political officer from the State Department. He was the local expert on governance and he and his predecessors were a large reason for Nawa's success. The elected head of this district community council was the focus of the group until we walked in, and then everyone turned in our direction. This is exactly what we didn't want—nobody's interests were served if the Americans became the focal point of local governance. I tried to play the role of an observant reporter.
>
> Gold 1970s couches lined the walls. The floor was extremely old industrial carpet with a rug on top of it. A GI desk, people sitting on couches and cross-legged on the floor drinking tea, flies everywhere, spitting on the floor, very hot, a single light bulb hanging from the ceiling. Broken windows, a view of the walled compound next door. No cultivated plants. High grasses in cracks—the gardens outside seemed to be for show. Totally disgusting by our standards.
>
> Senior guys got to the meetings first—they don't work in the fields. So they got the couches, latecomers got the floor. The head of the council chaired the meeting, but Triple H (our nickname for Haji Hamedaullah Helmandi, the senior elder who held the most influence in the informal/tribal power structure) had put the younger man in

charge. When two or three others started talking, everyone else shut up. Our two dedicated interpreters were kids from Kabul who had been given a crash course in English and been hired on to work with US ground military units. The fact that they were outsiders sometimes created tensions with the locals who had a deep resentment for their ethnicity.

Not exactly a recipe for prolonged negotiation, and keeping the information flowing at a Shura was no easy task. But it was Captain Curley's task, and he prevailed.

Eventually they built a single well, just outside the US Marine Patrol Base, which was to be turned over to the Afghan National Army (ANA). The funding for the well came from the Commander's Emergency Response Program (CERP)—a source of development funds that could be used for one-time quick-impact spending. The CAG team specifically tapped the CERP small-scale quick impact projects funds, which were designed for anything under $5,000. As long as the well was less than $5,000, the battalion commander was the approval authority, and not the CAG colonel who opposed the well project. The CERP funds also allowed for quick disbursement with a streamlined bidding process. Captain Curley considered three contractors and chose one based on price, reputation, his membership in the district community council, and his concurrent contract building a school.

The precarious security situation in Shoshurak added yet another problem for the team because the locals from Nawa's green zone and elsewhere would be taking a significant risk by going to work in this remote region. Thus the contractors they knew weren't willing to go to Shoshurak unless a cost-prohibitive "security premium" was paid by the marines.

Captain Curley then turned to Governor Manaf, the district governor of Nawa, whom he considered to be a very effective ally and a competent administrator. The governor knew a company from Lashkar Gah, Helmand Province's capital, that agreed to build a single well in Shoshurak within the $5,000 budget. The CAG team never determined with certainty why this particular company was able/willing to build the well so cheaply. They suspected, but were never able to confirm, that there may have been an additional back door deal done by the governor, who probably asked for a kickback from the company in exchange for arranging its security. It is also possible that the company was willing to assume additional risk and complete this first project on the cheap in the hopes that the Americans would award it additional contracts later on.

Once the Marines received photographic proof, confirmation from two independent sources, and conducted a visit, the contractor was paid. The CA advisor who replaced Curley reported that the well had the desired effects: it made good on the battalion commander's representations, provided potable water for the local population, and provided the confidence and incentive for the Shoshurak people to participate in local governance. While the well accomplished the Marines' end-state, it wasn't a complete success because some of the locals complained that the well water wasn't sweet, as had been predicted by the CAG headquarters staff.

Ultimately, the battalion commander's intent was fulfilled—to provide a new water source for Shoshurak. This enabled the corps to earn political buy-in in Shoshurak, the center of potential instability in southern Nawa. The ultimate location advanced two secondary coalition interests as well. While primarily for civilians, the ANA post would be able to utilize the nearby water source, mitigating a logistics concern. Since the well was within the line of sight of the ANA post, free security to the site and its patrons was inherently part of the deal—indefinitely and free of charge.

Guns, body armor, working through translators, grass-roots diplomacy, overly complex regulations, dangerous driving distances, and competing factions; yet attracting assets and cooperation from diverse interests. All this is systems design for inventive negotiation at its best.

CHAPTER 6

Getting the Team Right

Humanity needs practical men . . . But humanity also needs dreamers.
—Marie Curie

Shanghaied in Shanghai

The name of only one city in the world has the distinction of also being used as a verb. It is, however, an unflattering distinction:

> Shang·hai: To put aboard a ship by force, often with the help of liquor or a drug. From the former widespread use of this method to secure sailors for voyages to the Orient.

Today, the term is used any time when you are tricked into an undesirable position, particularly in a high-level negotiation. And the word reveals a lot about the difficulty many negotiators face when they encounter a foreign culture.

Back in 1995, Jim Paulsen figured he was in the driver's seat. As the first-ever president of Ford of China, he was ready to negotiate a joint venture with Shanghai Automotive Industry Corporation. And Ford had an advantage: Henry Ford had been selling cars there in the 1930s. Henry Ford II was one of the first American executives who met with Deng Xiaoping after China reopened its economic doors in 1978. And by the 1990s, the company already had three parts-related joint ventures working and another was scheduled to begin.

On the other side of the table, Shanghai Automotive was the largest, most profitable of Chinese automakers, with a Shanghai plant already slated to produce 100,000 Audi sedans and 200,000 vans a year in a joint venture with Volkswagen.

Ford and Shanghai Auto had been in secret talks for some time when suddenly the Clinton administration announced trade sanctions that would slap 100 percent tariffs on more than a billion dollars' worth of imports from China. Beijing responded with tariffs of its own and threatened to cease all joint ventures with American automakers. The deadline on this threat was February 26.

Twelve days ahead of the deadline, the president of Shanghai Automotive, Lu Jian, announced that both contenders for the contract, Ford and GM, would need to submit their final bids by the end of the month—and if those bids weren't to his liking, Toyota was standing in the wings.

Still, Paulsen felt he had the advantage. Talks were going well, and Paulsen had met with the US Trade Representative and the Commerce and State departments in Washington, DC. As an added precaution, he detoured to the Merage School of Business at UC Irvine for some cross-cultural training, and that is where we met him.

Though we had trained more than 2,000 Ford executives in Japanese culture, for this foray into Chinese culture we had partnered with Katherine Xin, a native of Beijing who is now the Associate Dean and Bayer Chair of Global Leadership at the China Europe International Business School in Shanghai.

To our surprise, we realized that despite working on plant-related issues in Mexico, the Czech Republic, Poland, and France, and traveling back and forth to China for 18 months, Paulsen had never lived outside the United States. A bright and affable Midwestern engineer, he was a career Ford man, but he was woefully unprepared for Chinese negotiations.

Meanwhile, the trade war deadline was off—both countries decided that the rhetoric earned them more political clout than actually staging that war. But the competition was still on.

Ford played a new card: announcing a program to research environmentally friendly engines with the Chinese Academy of Science. The announcement came complete with a set of keys to a Ford Taurus that ran on gas and methanol—a gift to the Science and Technology Minister of China.

GM countered with its own announcements about technology transfers, complete with a one-million yuan grant to Tsinghua University in Beijing (not coincidentally, the alma mater of most high-ranking Chinese officials). It was to be the first stage in creating a GM-China Technology Institute with even more research labs and technical centers.

Back in the United States, Paulsen persuaded Ford to make some design changes in the Taurus, extending the leg room in the rear, since most Chinese buyers at the time were driven by chauffeurs.

GM Changes the Game

At this point, GM upped the stakes again by, of all things, adding a woman to its crew. Shirley Young had been working as a consultant and then a vice president since 1983, and her list of US credentials was impressive: board member at major firms, nominating committee of the New York Stock Exchange, US State Department for International Development, trustee of Philips Academy Andover, Wellesley College, and Interlochen Center for the Arts. Board member of the Associates of the Harvard Business School. Woman of the Year for American Advertising Federation and the Chinese American Planning Council. Not to mention chairing the Committee of 100, a Chinese-American leadership group, and being on the board of the Shanghai Symphony Orchestra (with a $125,000 donation funded by GM.)

But if Young was well-connected in the United States, her Chinese *guanxi* was even better. Her father was a hero in both China and Taiwan because he'd been killed by the Japanese when he was China's consul general in the Philippines during World War II. Her stepfather had been China's ambassador to the United States, the United Kingdom, and France. Born in Shanghai, Young spoke fluent Mandarin and had many relatives throughout China.

Her job was to promote technology transfer, and she worked directly for GM's VP in charge of China operations. Yet, her credentials were only the beginning. She personally organized Chinese executives and dignitaries on their fact-finding trips to Detroit. While they were in town, she recruited GM's 1,000 plus Chinese-American employees to greet them. In return, she delivered GM's top executives to Shanghai, escorting the CEO for three trips, and five of GM's seven top executives through the early fall—an unprecedented showing in GM's history of international relations. There was even a junket to Rio for Shanghai Auto executives, ostensibly to visit GM's successful operations there.

While she was busy connecting, Ford was unfortunately doing the opposite. After 19 months of shuttling back and forth, head negotiator Paulsen retired. In late August, he was replaced by Vaughn Koshdarian, a 33-year Ford veteran with international experience in Japan and Europe. Koshdarian spoke not a word of Mandarin and had not a shred of experience in China.

By this time, Ford and GM had each invested or committed tens of millions of dollars, establishing technology institutes and parts manufacturing plants. GM had also thrown in technology from its Hughes Electronics and Electronic Data Systems divisions. All Ford had to offer was the slight resizing of the backseat of the Taurus.[1]

As Paulsen later described the situation in *Time* magazine, "We didn't have enough Chinese-speaking people to establish close contact with the officials in Shanghai. We were playing catch up with fewer resources."

It should not come as a surprise that on October 31, Shanghai Auto inked a deal with GM to produce 100,000 Buick Regals in a new billion-dollar assembly plant in Shanghai. Minivans were soon to follow.

Too Little, Way Too Late

After their loss, Ford officials blamed their "too modern" engineering. The real loss occurred, though, much earlier in Detroit. They had shanghaied their own efforts with the guy they *didn't* send.

Dr. Larry Wong was another 32-year Ford veteran with a very different résumé. An aerospace engineer, he had technology in spades and had been president of Ford of Taiwan for eleven years, leading it to become the dominant player there. A native speaker of Mandarin and Cantonese, Wong had been named Taiwan Businessman of the Year just the year before.

Ford's selection of Paulsen, then, was truly baffling. Especially when you look at where Wong went from there: a year later he was the first ethnic Chinese to head the Hong Kong Jockey Club, a tiny enterprise that earns $12 *billion* a year and returns $1.5 billion to what was then a British colony. That was 11 percent of Hong Kong's tax base, with enough left over to fund the $300 million Hong Kong University of Science and Technology.

In the decades since then, Ford has still not recovered from that single bad personnel decision. The company finally hired an ethnic Chinese, who was able to complete a deal with China's third largest car company six years later. By 2005, GM was outselling Ford-produced cars three to one. By 2012, the numbers were GM 2.8 million, Ford 627,000. And even today, Ford's current CEO Alan Mulally is refocusing on China, still trying to catch up.

The lesson is pretty simple. The real heroes in inventive negotiation start early, maybe even before birth. They understand all the cultures involved, and they strive for long-term collaborative relationships. With perhaps decades of business ahead of them, they use all the resources they need to establish those relationships. Because nobody does international negotiation—it's always people-to-people negotiation.

Selecting Your Team

An important part of systems design is selecting negotiation team members. Negotiators come from all ranks, depending on the size of the firms involved and the size and importance of the transaction. Choosing the best representatives can make or break a business relationship, as the story about Ford in China illustrates.

SIDEBAR 6.1

A Fine Balance, Chemistry Counts

Olympic rowing. Ergometer machines, legs, backs, arms, abs, Gatorade, cold mornings, dawn alarms, exhaustion, and expectations for four years. The US men 8-man rowing team had won a record three consecutive world championships from 1997–1999. The 2000 Olympic gold was up next. The American men hadn't won an Olympic gold medal in rowing since 1964.

Coach Mike Tepi talked all about the importance of team chemistry, trust, and emotions during the months of preparations for the Sydney Games. Then he got suckered by the numbers. There's one truly objective metric for a rower's abilities—the ability to pull on an ergometer. Brown University sophomore Dave Simon won the US championship in 2000 with a score of 531, the second highest ever recorded. Tepi handed him his medal at the event, a big honor for the youngster.

Enamored with Simon's numbers, Tepi gave him a seat in the Olympic Eights. That meant dropping team-favorite Michael Wherley, who had won gold medals at all three World Championships with the American Eights. At Sydney, the American Eights finished a disappointing fifth. Brad Alan Lewis's *A Fine Balance*, a documentary about these events, is a strong testament to the importance of team chemistry.

By the way, we do notice the irony of using a competitive sports metaphor to make a point about the importance of negotiation team chemistry. But in both contexts trust and emotions are essential to successful teams.

We all have our own ideas about what makes a good negotiator. Sir Francis Bacon advised using "bold men for expostulation, fair-spoken men for persuasion, crafty men for inquiry and observation." Some people extoll persistence, extroversion, a nimble tongue, a quick wit, or an friendly demeanor. While these characteristics may sound good, do they really make a difference in negotiations?

Key Bargainer Characteristics

Through our continuing research, our interviews with experienced bargainers, our reviews of the literature, and our own experiences as negotiators in commercial transactions, we've identified seven characteristics as key for negotiators:

1. Listening ability
2. Social intelligence
3. Willingness to use team assistance
4. Self-confidence
5. High aspirations
6. Influence at headquarters
7. Language skills

Whether you're looking for temporary or permanent negotiators or for long-term relationship managers, you'll need people with several of these interrelated skills.

Listening ability. Since negotiation is by one definition joint decision making and those decisions should be made with as much information as possible, listening skills are critical. In order to achieve the most inventive outcomes, bargainers must be alert to even the most subtle indications of clients' real interests.

Good listening is also the initial step in both persuasion and invention. Before trying to change the minds of those across the bargaining table, you need to ask good questions to learn what they need to know. In international transactions, your listening abilities are really tested—you must ascertain meaning from less-than-fluent English and different nonverbal vocabularies. The bottom line? Good listeners maximize the flow of information.

Social intelligence. Particularly in relationship-oriented cultures, the social aspects of business meetings are critical to success. Social intelligence, the ability to get along with other people, not only smoothes the social contact points but also encourages the flow of information and ideas. In turn, you can make more informed and creative decisions.

Daniel Goleman in his book *Social Intelligence: The New Science of Human Relationships*[2] defines social intelligence this way:

Social Awareness—Social awareness refers to a spectrum that runs from instantaneously sensing another's inner state, to understanding her feelings and thoughts, to "getting" complicated social situations. It includes:

- Primal empathy: Feeling with others; sensing nonverbal emotional signals.
- Attunement:[3] Listening with full receptivity; attuning to a person.
- Emphatic accuracy (emotional intelligence):[4] Understanding another person's thoughts, feelings, and intentions.
- Social cognition: Knowing how the social world works.

Social Facility—Simply sensing how another feels, or knowing what they think or intend, does not guarantee fruitful interactions. Social facility builds on social awareness to allow smooth, effective interactions. The spectrum of social facility includes:

- Synchrony: interacting smoothly at the nonverbal level
- Self-presentation: presenting ourselves effectively
- Influence: shaping the outcome of social interactions
- Concern: caring about others' needs and acting accordingly

Willingness to Use Team Assistance. Even the most skilled American executive can't be an expert in technical details, finances, cultural considerations, and relationship maintenance. Application engineers, financial analysts, interpreters, and foreign agents are vital to a good negotiating team, and they are well worth the investment. Add junior members whenever possible to observe—they add another set of eyes and ears, new perspectives, and vital links for long-term relationship building.

Self-confidence. Bridging the gap between companies and cultures can be exhausting work for the key representative. For example, negotiations are being conducted with clients and with the home office. Clients question your company's policies. Financial managers question the time and money you invest in building personal relationships. To work in situations where your role is ambiguous, you need to believe in yourself and your ideas.

SIDEBAR 6.2

Pencil Diplomacy, Bringing in an Expert

Susan is a master teacher, a professional who teaches other teachers and who is remembered by hundreds of students as their favorite teacher ever. Her first-grade classroom is a hum of activity, children working together, reading in a corner, asking questions. Because they are so engaged, they rarely cause disruptions when they step over to the alcove to sharpen their broken pencils.

But children today must take dozens of standardized tests, sitting for long periods in assigned seats, without getting up for any purpose. To train them for that discipline and to help them learn to plan ahead, Susan made a new rule: everyone has two pencils, and they can only be sharpened at the end of a lesson, right before recess.

With 22 children rushing to recess, the crowd around the pencil sharpener was unruly at best. Not-so-gentle pushing and well-placed elbows led to harsh words and a few bruises. Enter an expert, well-versed in the native culture. Jeremy, a shy kid who rarely spoke, offered Susan a solution: Make it like the carpool pick-up line. One at a time, one per square tile, groups assigned their order each day based on their group behavior during the lessons.

Susan made the plan even better, incorporating games based on adding and subtracting places in line—real world math problems while the children learned the patience they needed. All it took was a six-year-old expert with a fresh insight to eliminate the need for dispute resolution altogether—no negotiation required.

High aspirations. One of the basic lessons in hundreds of bargaining studies is that bargainers who ask for more in the beginning end up getting more. Thus, given two otherwise equal executives, the one with higher aspirations is the better one to send. Negotiators with higher aspirations will not be satisfied with just getting to yes; they will be more interested in truly inventive outcomes.

Influence at headquarters. Particularly in international business negotiations, most often the toughest part is selling the agreement to headquarters. It can be dangerous to present the other side's point of view too well—your own management might trust you less. The more connected your representative, the better your chances for success.

Language skills. No bargainer characteristic is more important in international negotiations, yet more ignored, than the right language skills. When executives recruit business students, they look for good communication skills—writing great letters and reports, then presenting them. So in our business schools, we emphasize these skills with instructions, practice, and feedback.

Now comes the paradox. As American companies continue to expand globally, there is still little payoff for fluency in Chinese or Spanish. In fact, the lockstep curricula in almost all business schools in the United States almost preclude those key tools that make things happen in other countries.

And that gap can be devastating.

Ford in Vietnam

Imagine a country that is, in theory, Communist. After decades of stagnation with state-run enterprises, the government has decided to encourage some capitalism, as it watches nearby countries leap ahead economically. The stakes are high and so are the hurdles.

Enter Jan Jung-Min Sunoo, a 30-year veteran of the US Federal Mediation and Conciliation Service (FMCS). He's an expert in transforming labor/management disputes into labor/management relationships. In 2003, he accepted a three-year assignment (that was later extended to six) with the International Labor Organization, an agency of the United Nations, to improve labor relations in new capitalist enterprises in Vietnam.

Oddly enough, the legacy of communism had left two gifts to Vietnam's new private and foreign firms: a largely literate workforce and a mandate that all firms with more than 20 workers required unions. These particular conditions are unique among communist countries and gave Sunoo a running start. His job was to build on that foundation, and he decided to use aspects of inventive negotiation as both subject and method.

Work began in the seven most industrialized provinces. Ten medium-sized firms, all with active unions, were identified in each province, for a total of 70 new clients. Some were state-owned enterprises, some were privatized or in the process of becoming so, and several were owned by a variety of firms in Asia, Europe, and the United States. The most interesting client was Ford Motor Company, which had agreed to a 75/25 joint-venture assembly plant with Song Cong Diesel Company in 1997 in Hai Duong, about 40 miles outside of

Hanoi. The firm was slated to assemble five Ford models for domestic and export markets.

Some of the key principles of good labor relationships FMCS advocates are:

1. Respect for all parties and their roles in the workplace
2. Ongoing two-way communication
3. Copious information sharing
4. Building people-to-people relationships

Lawrence Susskind's list of consensus building principles that we will review in a few pages, and ours in our book, *Global Negotiations*, are similar to FMCS's recommendations.

In the United States, joint training programs for company managers and union officials include building capabilities in social dialogue and communication, interest-based collective bargaining, and mediation skills. Ideally, training is scheduled well before the end of labor contracts, but training programs are even more critical at the beginning of the toughest mediation assignments. In effective programs: (1) Both sides learn the techniques of inventive negotiations, and (2) managers and union leaders build personal relationships.

The key to success is training, and for Ford this training began in an unusual spot: a beach resort on spectacular Ha Long Bay. Tens of thousands of years ago, ancient cultures began here, on a bay containing almost 2,000 limestone islets of incredible shapes and sizes. Five hundred years ago, Nguyen Trai praised it in a poem that was an ode to the" rock wonder in the sky." Today the place is a UNESCO World Heritage site and a must-see on any itinerary of world travel.

Ford, along with the other nine firms from that province, was invited to a three-day training session. Some of the content was pretty standard—formal lectures with introductory materials. This part was supplemented with role-playing exercises and then team building. Perhaps more important, there was plenty of time for informal meetings, dinners with entertainment, and walks on the beach. By the time the participants got to brainstorming sessions, they knew and liked each other.

The geography played a role: research shows that walks near trees and water stimulate creativity. The neutral—indeed gorgeous—location leveled any power issues that may have been lurking back at the plant. And this training had another key ingredient: an experienced facilitator.

How It Worked: The Details

1. **The people.** In this case, Sunoo gathered key HR managers and union stewards long before their labor contract negotiations were to take place and taught them how to be collaborative partners rather than adversaries. They got to know and understand one another as people before issues were on the table. And they got the support of their peers, putting the Vietnamese partners and the foreign ones on equal footing.

2. **The goals.** By working together so early, the integrated teams had the opportunity to create the same goals. They began to see a future in their shared enterprises.

3. **The teams.** Sunoo's teams had a number of characteristics that are proven to increase creative solutions. For example:

   - They were the right size: eight per enterprise, which falls in the sweet spot of 5–12[5]
   - They included people with different personalities and experience[6]
   - They were culturally diverse[7]
   - They included some women[8]
   - They had some experts[9] and some nonexperts[10]

The size of the entire retreat group was also ideal—80 participants were enough to reinforce the teams' shared goals, and well within the 150 outer limit of group size that can still feel like a community.

4. **The timing.** Three days were the optimum length for off-site training for several reasons:

   - The timing enabled the group to learn in several different ways—formal lectures, hands-on exercises, and informal discussions during breaks. Since different people have different learning styles, everyone could share the knowledge.
   - The timing imposed a real deadline. Unlike discussions in most workplaces, a difficult discussion could not be tabled until next week or next month. There was a built-in incentive to get issues solved.[11]
   - There were nine meal opportunities, plus the same number of break times when participants could do something entirely different.[12]
   - There were two nights for participants to sleep on their ideas, giving their unconscious minds time to improve on the ideas.[13]

Ford now manufactures in 21 countries around the world, from Germany and Japan to Brazil, Russia, India, China, Romania, Venezuela, and Vietnam. While the diversity of labor laws and work environments in all these countries is challenging, Ford takes pride in its current global reputation for its positive labor relations. Ford's collaborative practices in Vietnam are reflected in its early participation in the FMCS workshops and its success in operating in that daunting labor environment for 16 years without a strike.

Notice the key lessons from Jan's design of the FMCS programs in Vietnam: Context is crucial. Good personal relationships must be built before inventive negotiations can hold sway. The offsite location is key (trees and water). And the informal meetings all are designed to stimulate inventive thinking that goes beyond simple problem solving. Finally, Jan and the FMCS play the pollinating role of facilitator.

Negotiator Training and the Importance of Facilitators

Many companies in the United States provide employees with negotiations training. But Jan Sunoo's work during the past three decades has been extraordinarily successful in mitigating strikes because of his proactive approach to building communication and problem-solving skills.

Teaching both labor and management the principles of "interests-based bargaining" has also been an important priority of FMCS. This process emphasizes trading information about interests toward building a *new set of options* and *trusting relationships*—exactly what we call inventive negotiation—or building pie factories.

Jan's story also demonstrates the crucial role that facilitators can play: If you're not familiar with modern social networks analysis theory, then "nodes" probably sounds like something you'd find on another planet. But nodes are simply the network nerds' term for people (although nodes can also be other entities such as germs, cows, organizations, companies, or countries). Nodes that have "centrality" are people who connect people in the sense that bees help flowers have sex.

David Obstfeld earned his PhD at the University of Michigan by observing and analyzing patterns of interaction among nodes at a major automaker's engineering center for more than a year. He concluded that third parties were crucial in the innovation processes. In his award winning *Administrative Science Quarterly* article,[14] he called them *tertius iungens* (Latin for those who join, or "nodes") and described them as much more than mere brokers or Malcolm

SIDEBAR 6.3

Lessons from Pamplona

The risks are high. The sounds of the crowds and the hooves are deafening. The possibility of death is ever present. Yet for centuries, young men from all over the world have gathered for the Encierro, to spend three or four terrifying minutes running ahead of the bulls as they race from their corral outside the village to the bullring.

Every year some of them are gored. Some years runners die. Over the years, people have designed safeguards to reduce those injuries. The first safeguard is a 3,000-part fence to separate the spectators from the runners. There are strict guidelines in place—runners must not drink, take a rest during the running, turn toward the bulls or harass them. Their *faja* and *panuelo*— traditional red sashes and neckerchiefs—must be tied in slipknots.

There are experienced professionals who play vital roles: first the *pastores*, or shepherds, who are placed along the run with sticks to keep the odd bull from straying (or the odd human from doing something stupid). The *dobladores*, often former bull fighters with deep understanding of the bulls, then use their capes to help the runners fan out to the sides as they enter the ring and the bulls to run directly to the corral.

The personalities that really help the bulls negotiate the street, however, are not human. In the center are the *toros bravos*, those Spanish bulls bred to fight. And while all livestock have learned to stampede away from danger, heads down, these bulls are much more likely to deal with threats from the side by turning their heads and thrusting upwards. They will separate from the herd and attack a predator, even turn back as a lone bull, a *suelto* or loose one, will trade his fear for anger.

In the narrow streets thronged with chanting people, these bulls could easily get distracted and attack. The reason they don't is that two sets of cooler heads prevail. The first six fighting bulls are accompanied by *mansos*, larger bullocks with more placid personalities to guide the bulls forward. Two minutes after all the bulls have left the corral, a set of smaller, slower *mansos* follow, guiding any possible strays back to the herd.

In a typical negotiation, some of the parties may well be like those *toros bravos*, all alpha males, conditioned to fight or run roughshod over any obstacles. That's why it's so important that successful teams include some characters like the *mansos*, more deliberative people, some with experience and existing relationships to guide the strays back to the main topic and keep anger in check.

Gladwell's "connectors." [15] These nodes both introduced unconnected individuals *and* facilitated new coordination. This richer role more closely resembles the Japanese *chukai-sha*,[16] and also the Chinese *zhongjian ren*.[17] Closer to home, just ask any empty nester about the last kid leaving the dinner table and the loss of both a mediator and a witness. Third parties add dramatically to inventive processes.

Energy/environmental executive William Graham,[18] working with Lawrence Susskind to study four international energy projects in the United States, reports that using professional facilitators shortened negotiation times and yielded more durable agreements in three of the four energy projects he studied (see chapter 4.)

All four US negotiations involved at least ten different parties each—agencies of the federal and local governments, politicians, commercial developers and investors, power companies, environmental NGOs, local community groups, adjacent land owners, and Native American tribes (which makes the negotiations "international" in both the legal and cultural senses). All four projects required multiyear negotiations. Yet, in one of them, Calpine has spent millions of dollars over 20 years, and their Medicine Lake project is still languishing in litigation in the US Ninth District Court.

Graham is convinced that the professional facilitators hired in the other three cases made the difference. According to one participant, "Everyone had an equal voice, but not necessarily equal power. By definition, some entities with mandatory conditioning authority or the project applicant have bigger hammers. Some things were done separately. For example, the [Native American] tribes met separately with PGE [the local power company] on culturally confidential issues." In all three successful negotiations the third-party facilitators managed an approach of "building consensus" that created an egalitarian and trusting atmosphere, which then yielded inventive alternatives and led to durable agreements. Contrast this to participants in the failed Medicine Lake negotiations: their meetings were "raucous and emotional," and the government representatives were neither neutral nor in favor of the geothermal energy.

Lawrence Susskind[19] and his associates have set the standards for consensus-building processes: Facilitators must oversee three core elements of a negotiation: substance (what underlies the conflict), relationships (who is in conflict), and process (how stakeholders will work out their differences). Professionals agree on these concepts, derived from the science of innovation processes and Susskind's consensus building:

1. Participants must be free to explore ideas safely and have equal voices in process development.
2. Cross-cultural differences and customs must be considered and observed.
3. Several forms of intervention can include: work groups, plenary sessions, caucuses, and one-on-one sessions to clarify interests, foster cooperation, and generate options.
4. Separate inventing from committing.
5. Strive to invent options for mutual gain.
6. Emphasize packaging ideas together.
7. Test options by playing the "what if" game.
8. Avoid attribution and individual authorship.
9. Brainstorm without criticism.
10. Plan two-day off-site meetings allowing sleeping on the ideas.
11. Mediate subcommittee, teleconference, and face-to-face meetings.

The process of selecting mediators is crucial. Participants in the successful Crane Valley Hydroelectric relicensing project in California said, "We, the regulatory agencies, knew PG&E was serious when Jim Holeman (PG&E's project manager) asked us to participate in the vendor interview process and help select a facilitator we could all work with. This added a sense of credibility that had been missing and allowed us to move ahead as a group with greater confidence in the process."

Not surprisingly, facilitators are best if they are brought in at beginning. Yet, in the successful Bend geothermal project described in chapter 4, the mediator was brought in after an impasse was reached. In that case, the US Forest Service facilitator was able to conduct consensus process training before restarting the substantive talks. She was then able to refocus discussion on interests rather than arguments about positions. Ultimately, she was happy to report, "The strength in the consensus developed by the community is clearly what held the proposal together through the legislative process. It is also what baffled and frustrated legislators and staffers who were used to position-based bargaining and compromise."

In this one area of commerce, "consensus building" is well established as the gold standard. Virtually all of the energy/environmental executives interviewed by Graham were well aware of the concepts of inventive negotiation and its advantages. Indeed, for more than a decade the Federal Energy Regulatory Commission (FERC), which oversees the licensing of hydroelectric projects in the United States, has officially encouraged neutral facilitation and consensus-building processes in new license issuances.

Lawrence Susskind developed the theory and practice of consensus building and parallel informal negotiations, and these approaches are widely used today, particularly in multiparty international disputes. He and his colleagues acknowledge some inspiration: "Japan has been successful at consensus building, and that success has contributed to Japan's postwar economic triumphs." According to anthropologist John Pfeiffer, Japanese society is the most civilized of all. The Japanese have lived in big cities longer than anyone else on the planet, and through the millennia they've developed social processes that created one of the safest and wealthiest countries in the world in an area with virtually no natural resources.

Crips/Bloods in Northern Ireland, Odd Facilitators

Sometimes your best facilitators come from places you would never expect.

After decades of The Troubles in Northern Ireland, grassroots efforts were connecting mothers on each side who had lost sons to the violence. Yet while the mothers were seeking peace, their remaining sons were still at war, sworn to avenge those earlier deaths.

Meanwhile, in Los Angeles, gang rivals from the Crips and Bloods were engaged in ceaseless drive-by shootings.

So it made sense to get them all together in Belfast.

The first morning, eight wary and hostile young men from each country entered the room. For those from Los Angeles, it was the first time they'd left their neighborhoods, flown on a plane, been to another country. For those from Belfast, it was their first exposure to African Americans.

All were reluctant to speak, and the first few hours resulted in very little true dialogue. When they did speak, all that emerged was anger—at lives cut short, families broken, children exposed to unimaginable scenes.

After lunch, the topics were slightly altered. Now they were asked more specifically about how their mothers felt, their sisters, and their younger siblings. Here the stories began to change: they could very clearly describe the pain, the grief, the hopelessness their relatives felt.

Over dinner another layer was peeled back. Now the young men were talking about their own pain, masked by anger and refueled every time there was another death. To their surprise, the names of the streets were different, but their experiences were exactly the same.

By the second day, the young men began to talk about their own hopes and dashed dreams, their own fears and regrets. Somehow, listening to the same stories in different accents helped overcome their reluctance to listen to their own rivals.

Then someone asked a single question: How could you change it? The lads from Belfast suggested ideas for the Los Angeles street gangs. They, in turn, suggested things that could work in Northern Ireland. All of the suggestions were solutions they'd heard before— but they hadn't been able to imagine them through the layers of pain and anger, from perspectives across a single street.

By the time the Crips and Bloods departed on the third day, all four warring parties had developed concrete plans, with lists of people they could enlist, specific goals, tasks and deadlines. Because they were all influential—not in any conventional sense, but within their own peer groups—the plans were feasible.

The plans were not an immediate win. There are still flare-ups in Belfast and drive-by shootings in Los Angeles. But those numbers have decreased significantly, starting with the actions from that core group of very unlikely facilitators.

CHAPTER 7

Leveraging Diversity

The diversity of the phenomena of nature is so great, and the treasures hidden in the heavens so rich, precisely in order that the human mind shall never be lacking in fresh nourishment.

—Johannes Kepler

Why is it that a tiny country (about the size of the state of Maryland), with virtually no natural resources, threatened every year by rising sea levels, is home to some of the world's most innovative negotiators?

How does a country with a population that's more than 80 percent native and speaks a language spoken by no one else in the world perfect the art of tapping diversity? The answer is based on fish and flowers.

Back in 1579, after centuries of being conquered and overrun, the Dutch United Provinces declared their independence from Spain. For the next couple of hundred years, they became a leader in world trade, exporting their agricultural products to colonies around the globe, and bringing New World novelties back to Europe. With their location on the North Sea, the provinces' major export, not surprisingly, was fish; though perhaps it's a bit more surprising that they were expert in growing flowers in this cold climate.

And unlike, say, silk or gold, fish and flowers have a short shelf life. Thus Dutch traders had to be very, very good at making deals very, very quickly. Their language barrier also proved to be a boon. Unlike the Spanish and English, who were powers big enough to demand that traders speak their language, the Dutch simply learned everybody else's.

And both imperatives made long-term relationships critical.

By 1815, after a couple of decades of French occupation, these skilled traders emerged as the Kingdom of the Netherlands, with their expertise in languages and negotiation intact. Indeed, this cultural sensitivity has always been so acute that the first researcher to define different cultural characteristics in a scientific framework was Geert Hofstede.[1]

Born in Haarlem and attending school in The Hague, Professor Hofstede spent the years of World War II under Nazi occupation. When he fell in love with an English girl and visited her there, he experienced another culture shock and then an entirely different one when he sailed to Indonesia as a ship's engineer. By 1981, he had gathered enough data as a researcher at IBM to create a documented theory: people from different cultures respond to situations based in part on the cultural norms they've learned.

The Dutch history of individual enterprise from merchants and traders has given the nation high scores for individualism—the Dutch are not afraid to break society's rules and feel empowered to explore new solutions. They also rate highly on egalitarianism—and this makes them perfect team players, comfortable broaching new ideas and eager to build long-term relationships.

Today, the Dutch are world leaders in creating land from the sea, in transportation, and in technology. They've even leapfrogged ahead on Edison's signature invention—the century-old lightbulb—at Philips.

Dr. Joerg Habetha, a tall man with an even temperament, is senior director at Philips Research. He heads the department that is developing innovations for Personal Health Solutions—things like body sensors and smart clothing. Much of the company's research is conducted at design centers in Europe, the United States, and Asia with 1,500 researchers from every country around the globe.

Dr. Habetha is an expert in getting all those different kinds of specialists from all those different cultures to work through their differences and invent together. This process begins with the company philosophy: "We have very smart people here at Philips, but we don't have all the smart people." It's an insight shared throughout the company culture: more than 30 years ago, the company's engineers were pioneers in Open Innovation. That is, they buy technology from other companies, they sell their own, and they create partnerships to develop new ideas.

One of these ventures is a 33-partner consortium underwritten by the European Union to fight cardiovascular disease through prevention and early detection. (Considering all the butter, cream, and fat, most European diets look like heart attacks waiting to happen.)

Among the diverse companies involved are large firms like Medtronic Iberia, Nokia, and Vodaphone Foundation, and Italian textile companies Nylstar and Smartex, major hospitals including university hospitals in Aachen, Heidelberg, and Madrid, and research universities in Italy, Spain, Portugal, and Germany.

How do people at Philips get all these people working together? They start by acting as third-party facilitators, in special creative headquarters about a 90-minute drive from Aachen and in eight branch studios in Europe, the United States, and Asia. Here they bring in anthropologists, cultural sociologists, psychologists, and trend researchers in addition to the design professionals and engineers you might expect.

Habetha's MyHeart project began at an Application Workshop in Madrid. Mili Docampo Rama, director of Strategic Futures Design, described the workshop to us:

> MyHeart started with 33 partners developing 16 totally different concept ideas, all shaped through a process that is people-insight driven. In the first phase, they had to understand the whole domain—from prevention to chronic disease management.
>
> The original ideas had to work for all future stakeholders, and the business plans had to be thought through. Through Philips' carefully developed selection process, they unanimously decided on which directions to pursue.

The second step was getting the 75 participants to form eight cross-company teams focused on "work packages," such as functional clothes or on-body electronics. Creative collaboration was only one benefit of the workshop. By making the workshop a two-day event, the participants also had a chance to begin building trust and long-term relationships. They had time to sleep on their thoughts and play games of volleyball to encourage cooperation and competition.

This trust building is vital, because the teams will encounter some very sticky issues. Not the least of these is intellectual property, the stumbling block to many proposed collaborations. According to Habetha, "The way companies in Europe handle patentable ideas differs across countries. Also, the national laws give different rights to the inventors. The MyHeart consortium agreement has been written so it doesn't block partner companies from exploiting the IP."

This attention to the legal structure ahead of time results in a surprising openness among the 33 companies. The workshops build on that to create long-term, trusting relationships. The sunny spaces, games, and meals together create a shared history of successful collaboration and reward those early successes. And Philips' role as trained, experienced facilitator helps ease the conflicts that arise. It's a perfect recipe for inventive negotiation, and it is already paying off in breakthrough technology.

At the heart of this success, as always, are the people involved. Open to new ideas, willing to embrace diversity, connecting as people—all the traits that are key to inventive negotiators.

Leveraging the New Diversity

Human progress through the millennia has been driven by international trade. Good ideas are borrowed, and even invented, in cross-cultural interactions. Think of the ancient Silk Road or the Silicon Valley of the twenty-first century.

Working with diverse groups is not always easy, but studies show that diverse groups put more ideas on the table and provide different perspectives on those ideas, thus multiplying creative output—*if* you can overcome the initial problems in communication. This is precisely what brought John and an associate to General Motors' offices in Warren, Michigan.

On a cold spring day in 2007, we met with Dr. Lawrence Burns, a polished but exuberant executive then vice president of Research and Development and Strategic Planning. His R & D facility spread over a square mile and had once been one of the world's most innovative places, but that day it looked surprisingly shabby.

Because Burns believed that the only way GM could catch up with its rival Toyota was to leverage the diversity of GM's global workforce, we'd been hired to develop cross-cultural training programs. One typical problem: in GM global work teams the Americans and Brazilians did all the talking, while the Chinese and Koreans couldn't or wouldn't get a word in edgewise.

Our proposal therefore was based on a pathbreaking study on the long-term impact on work team performance that was reported by three researchers[2] at Midwestern universities in the *Academy of Management Journal* in 1993. The details are interesting.

Thirty-six teams of 4–5 mostly undergraduate business majors were formed to work on a variety of cases over a four-month period: 17 teams were culturally homogeneous (all from the same nationality and ethnic background), and 19 were diverse groups ("a white American, a black American, a Hispanic American, and a foreign national from Asia, Latin America, Africa, or the Middle East.")

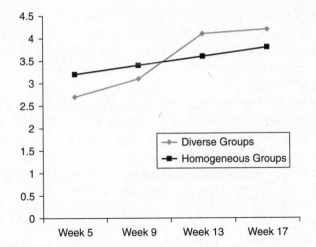

Exhibit 7.1 Average number of ideas put on the table.
Source: Watson et al. (1993)

In weeks 5, 9, 13, and 17, the groups were "required to (1) examine the case from a variety of perspectives, (2) identify the problems that had a bearing on the situation described in the case, (3) generate a list of alternatives that might be employed to deal with the problems they had identified, and (4) to select what they believed was the most effective of the alternatives and provide justification for their recommendation."

On average, both diverse and homogeneous groups increased their idea productivity over the 17-week period (see exhibit 7.1). Initially the diverse groups were at a disadvantage, but after working together they improved faster, and in week 13, they actually overtook their homogeneous counterparts.

The Mine Fields of Cultural Diversity

The opportunities of diversity are clear—more ideas, more perspectives on those ideas, and more innovative solutions. To avoid the pitfalls of diversity, the first step is to recognize some cultural differences in negotiation style.

For the past three decades, we've studied negotiation styles of more than 1,500 businesspeople in 17 countries (21 cultures).[3] We've interviewed experienced executives and observed actual negotiations in several of the countries. In a behavioral science laboratory, we've analyzed surveys and videotaped negotiations. We chose Japan, Korea, Taiwan, China (Tianjin, Guangzhou, and Hong Kong), Vietnam, the

Philippines, Russia, Israel, Norway, the Czech Republic, Germany, France, the United Kingdom, Spain, Brazil, Mexico, Canada (English-speaking and French-speaking), and the United States because they are America's most important present and future trading partners.

Looking broadly across the several cultures, there are two important lessons: (1) Regional generalizations very often are not correct. For example, Japanese and Korean negotiation styles are quite similar in some ways, but in other ways they could not be more different. (2) Japan is an exceptional place: On almost every dimension of negotiation style considered, the Japanese are on or near the end of the scale. For example, the Japanese used the least eye contact of any culture we studied, but they were also best at creating value in their negotiations.

Cultural differences cause four kinds of problems in international business negotiations:[4]

1. Language
2. Nonverbal behaviors
3. Values
4. Thinking and decision-making processes

The order is important; the problems lower on the list are more serious because they are more subtle. For example, two negotiators would notice immediately if one were speaking Japanese and the other German. Solving this problem may be as simple as hiring an interpreter or talking in a common third language, or it may be as difficult as learning a language. Regardless of the solution, the problem is obvious.

Cultural differences in nonverbal behaviors, on the other hand, are almost always hidden below our awareness. In a face-to-face negotiation, participants give off and take in a great deal of information nonverbally. Some experts argue that this information is more important than verbal information, and almost all this signaling goes on below our consciousness. When the nonverbal signals from foreign partners are different from their own, negotiators are most apt to misinterpret them without even being conscious of the mistake. When a French client consistently interrupts, Americans tend to feel uncomfortable without noticing exactly why. Thus interpersonal friction often colors business relationships, goes undetected, and consequently goes uncorrected.

Differences in values and thinking and decision-making processes are hidden even deeper and therefore are even harder to address and correct.

Language

Translation problems are often substantial, particularly when languages are linguistically different (see exhibit 7.2 on pages 103–4 for linguistic differences from English) in international negotiations. English speakers should expect more difficulties communicating with speakers of languages that are more distant—higher numbers in the table, such as Chinese or Arabic.

Global negotiation can be particularly daunting. Often English is a second language for most executives at the table. Even native speakers from England, India, and the United States often have trouble understanding one another, and translations are rarely exact.

Nonverbal Behaviors

According to anthropologist Ray L. Birdwhistell, words convey less than 35 percent of the message in conversations while a whopping 65 percent is communicated nonverbally.[5] Albert Mehrabian,[6] a UCLA psychologist, studied face-to-face interactions, and found:

7 percent of the meaning is derived from the words spoken
38 percent from paralinguistic channels—things like tone of voice and loudness
55 percent from facial expressions

While the exact percentages may vary, the truth is clear: *how things are said* is often more important than *what is said*.

In our research we have audio- and videotaped more than 400 business people from around the world in simulated negotiations. Our systematic analyses of these tapes has included the tallying what negotiators say (for example, the use of "no" and "you," and the percentages of threats, warnings, questions, self-disclosures). We also count nonverbal behaviors, such as silent periods, interruptions, eye contact, and touching used in one-half hour of negotiating. Here's a quick summary of the cultural differences we've observed:

Japan. Their style of interaction is among the least aggressive (or most polite). Threats, commands, and warnings are deemphasized in favor of more positive promises, recommendations, and commitments. Their polite conversational style means they use *no, you,* and facial gazing infrequently, and they are often silent.

Korea. Non-Asians often generalize about Asia. The findings demonstrate, however, that this is a mistake. In our studies, Korean negotiators used considerably more punishments and commands than did the Japanese. Koreans used the word *no* and interrupted more than three times as frequently as the Japanese, and there were no silent periods at all.

China (Northern). Negotiators from Northern China (i.e., in and around Tianjin) ask more questions (34 percent). Indeed, 70 percent of the statements made by the Chinese negotiators were classified as information-exchange tactics. Other aspects of Chinese negotiators' behavior were quite similar to that of the Japanese, particularly the use of *no* and *you* and silent periods.

Taiwan. Businesspeople in Taiwan behave quite differently from those in China and Japan, but similar to those in Korea. The Chinese on Taiwan looked at others more—on the average, almost 20 of 30 minutes. They asked fewer questions and provided more information (self-disclosures) than any of the other Asian groups.

Russia. The Russians' style was quite different from that of any other European group, and was quite similar in many respects to the Japanese group's style. They used *no* and *you* infrequently and used the most silent periods of any group. Only the Japanese did less facial gazing, and only the Chinese asked a greater percentage of questions.

Israel. Israeli negotiators were distinctive in three respects. They used the lowest percentage of self-disclosures, apparently holding their cards relatively close to their chests. They used the highest percentages of promises and recommendations by far. They were also at the end of the scale in making the most frequent references to competitors' offers. Perhaps most important, the Israeli negotiators interrupted one another much more frequently than negotiators from any other group, and this important nonverbal behavior is most likely to blame for the "pushy" stereotype Americans often use to describe their Israeli negotiation partners.

Germany. German behavior is difficult to characterize because the German negotiators fell near the center of almost every continuum. They were, however, exceptional in the high percentage of self-disclosures (47 percent) and the low percentage of questions (11 percent).

United Kingdom. British negotiators were remarkably similar to the Americans in all respects.

Spain. *Diga* is perhaps a good metaphor for the Spanish approach to negotiations. When you make a phone call in Madrid, the usual greeting on the other end is not *hola* ("hello") but is, instead, *diga* ("speak"). It is not surprising, then, that the Spaniards in the videotaped negotiations used the highest percentage of commands

(17 percent) of any of the groups and gave comparatively little information (only 34 percent self-disclosures). They also interrupted one another more frequently than any other group, and they used the terms *no* and *you* very frequently.

France. French negotiators were perhaps the most aggressive of all the groups. They used the highest percentage of threats and warnings (together, 8 percent). They also used interruptions, facial gazing, and *no* and *you* very frequently compared with the other groups, and one of the French negotiators touched his partner on the arm during the simulation.

Brazil. The Brazilian businesspeople, like the French and Spanish, were quite aggressive. They used the second-highest percentage of commands of all the groups. On average, the Brazilians said the word *no* 42 times, *you* 90 times, and touched one another on the arm about 5 times during 30 minutes of negotiation. Facial gazing was also high.

Mexico. Mexican behavior demonstrates the danger of regional or language-group generalizations. Both verbal and nonverbal behaviors were quite different from those of their Latin American (Brazilian) or continental (Spanish) cousins. Mexicans answer the telephone with the much less demanding *bueno* (short for "good day"). In many respects, the Mexican negotiators' behavior was very similar to that of the negotiators from the United States.

French-speaking Canada. The French-speaking Canadians behaved quite similarly to their continental cousins. Like the negotiators from France, they too used high percentages of threats and warnings and even more interruptions and eye contact. This aggressive interaction style doesn't mix well with some of the more low-key styles of some of the Asian groups or with English speakers, including English-speaking Canadians.

English-speaking Canada. The Canadian negotiators who speak English as their first language used the lowest number of aggressive persuasive tactics (threats, warnings, and punishments totaled only 1 percent) of all 15 groups. Perhaps, as communications researchers suggest, such stylistic differences are the seeds of interethnic discord in Canada over the years. In international negotiations, the English-speaking Canadians used noticeably more interruptions and *nos* than negotiators from either of Canada's major trading partners, the United States and Japan.

United States. Like the Germans and the British, the Americans fell in the middle of nearly every continuum. They did interrupt one another less frequently than all the others, but that was their sole distinction.

These differences across the cultures are quite complex, and this material by itself should not be used to predict the behaviors of foreign counterparts. It is important, however, to be aware of these differences so that the Japanese silence, the Brazilian "no, no, no," or the French threat are not misinterpreted.

Differences in Managerial Values

There are many ways to think about culture. The Dutch management professor Geert Hofstede refers to culture as the "software of the mind" and argues that it provides a guide for humans on how to think and behave; it is a problem-solving tool.[7] Anthropologist and business consultant Edward T. Hall provides a definition even more relevant to international negotiators: "The people we were advising kept bumping their heads against an invisible barrier. . . . We knew that what they were up against was a completely different way of organizing life, of thinking, and of conceiving the underlying assumptions about the family and the state, the economic system, and even Man himself."[8] Cultural differences are often invisible (as water is to fishes)—and ignoring them can hurt your company and your career.

Most traditional definitions of culture agree that it is the sum of the *values, rituals, symbols, beliefs, and thought processes* that are *learned, shared* by a group of people, and *transmitted* from generation to generation. Culture resides in the individual's mind. The expression "a culture," however, implies that large groups of people, including business executives, share those beliefs.

Underlying the cultural diversity among business systems are fundamental differences in cultural values. When Hofstede studied more than 100,000 IBM employees in 66 countries, he found that national cultures differed along four primary dimensions. Subsequently, he and hundreds of other researchers have determined that a wide variety of business behavior patterns are explained by two of those primary dimensions: the Individualism/Collective Index (IDV), which focuses on self-orientation; and the Power Distance Index (PDI), which focuses on authority orientation. Higher scores on IDV Index suggest valuing individual goals over group goals, and this index is the most useful dimension.[9] Higher scores on the PDI Index indicate greater acceptance of hierarchy over equality (see Hofstede's scores in exhibit 7.2.) Note that the correlation between Hofstede's scores and those for linguistic distance are quite high at $(r > 0.6)$.[10]

Exhibit 7.2 Individualism index scores and linguistic distance for selected countries and regions

Country	Individualism/ Collectivism	Power Distance	Primary Language	Distance from English
United States	91	40	English	0
Australia (total)	90	36	English	0
Great Britain	89	35	English	0
Hungary	80	46	Hungarian	4
Netherlands	80	38	Dutch	1
New Zealand	79	22	English	0
Belgium (Dutch speakers only)	78	61	Dutch	1
Italy	76	50	Italian	3
Denmark	74	18	Danish	1
Canada (French speakers only)	73	54	French	3
Belgium (French speakers only)	72	67	French	3
France	71	68	French	3
Sweden	71	31	Swedish	1
Ireland	70	28	English	0
Switzerland (German speakers only)	69	26	German	1
Germany	67	35	German	1
South Africa	65	49	Afrikaans	1
Switzerland (French speakers only)	64	70	French	3
Finland	63	33	Finnish	4
Poland	60	68	Polish	3
Czech Republic	58	57	Czech	3
Austria	55	11	German	1
Israel	54	13	Hebrew	5
Spain	51	57	Spanish	3
India	48	77	Dravidian	3
Argentina	46	49	Spanish	3
Japan	46	54	Japanese	4
Morocco	46	70	Arabic	5
Iran	41	58	Farsi	3
Russia	39	93	Russian	3
Brazil	38	69	Portuguese	3

continued

Exhibit 7.2 Continued

Country	Individualism/ Collectivism	Power Distance	Primary Language	Distance from English
Arab countries	38	80	Arabic	5
Turkey	37	66	Turkish	4
Greece	35	60	Greek	3
Philippines	32	94	Tagalog	7
Mexico	30	81	Spanish	3
Portugal	27	63	Portuguese	3
East Africa	27	64		8
Hong Kong	25	68	Cantonese	6
Chile	23	63	Spanish	3
China	20	80	Mandarin	6
Singapore	20	74	Mandarin	6
Thailand	20	64	Thai	7
Vietnam	20	70	Vietnamese	7
West Africa	20	77		8
Korea (South)	18	60	Korean	4
Peru	16	64	Spanish	3
Indonesia	14	78	Bahasa	7
Pakistan	14	55	Urdu	3
Colombia	13	67	Spanish	3
Venezuela	12	81	Spanish	3

Source: Geert Hofstede, *Culture's Consequences,* 2nd ed. (Thousand Oaks, CA: Sage, 2001).

Differences in Thinking and Decision Making

When faced with a complex negotiation task, most Westerners divide the large task into a series of smaller tasks. Issues such as prices, delivery, warranty, and service contracts may be settled one issue at a time: the final agreement will be the sum of the smaller agreements. In Asia, however, all the issues are discussed at once, in no apparent order, and concessions are made on all issues at the end of the discussion. The Western sequential approach and the Eastern holistic approach do not mix well.

Thus, American managers often report great difficulties in measuring progress in negotiations, particularly in Asian countries. After all, in America, you are half done when half the issues are settled. But in China, Japan, or Korea, nothing seems to get settled. Then, surprise, you are done. Often, Americans make unnecessary concessions right before agreements are announced by the other side.

An American department store chain executive traveling to Japan to buy six different consumer products lamented that negotiations for the first product took an entire week. In the United States, she'd be finished in an afternoon. By her calculations, she would have needed six weeks in Japan to complete her purchases. She considered raising her purchase prices to try to move things along faster. But before she was able to concede, the Japanese agreed on the other five products in just three days. This particular manager was, by her own admission, lucky.

Her near blunder reflects more than just a difference in decision-making style. To Americans, a business negotiation is a problem-solving activity, aimed at securing the best deal for both parties. To a Japanese businessperson, on the other hand, a business negotiation is a time to develop a business relationship for long-term mutual benefit. The economic issues are the context, not the content, of the talks. Thus, settling any one issue is really not that important—the details will take care of themselves once a viable, harmonious business relationship is established. And as our American buyer learned, once the relationship was established—signaled by the first agreement—the other "details" were settled quickly.

Other Sorts of Diversity

Diversity in negotiation styles can also be found across other kinds of groups: regions, industries, companies, expatriates, and genders. And while you may have a basic understanding of some other cultures, you don't negotiate with countries, cultures, or companies. You negotiate with people. What's more, any one person's behavior is determined by a number of factors aside from culture—personality, industry and/ or company culture, expatriate experiences, age, gender, regional differences, even brain chemistry. We can't help with the blood type that might interest a Japanese executive or the Asian calendar year in which you're born—pig, snake, or rat, for example. But we can show you the influences of some other factors.

Culture and Country Do Not Always Coincide

While you can generalize about national styles of negotiation, almost all natives of any country can quickly describe the nuances of culture across regions in their homelands. Mexicans say there are really five Mexicos. Vietnamese argue there are three very different cultures in their country: north, south, and middle. The toughest negotiators in Japan are from Yokohama, in Spain from Valencia, and in China from Shanghai.

Languages mark significant regional differences. Freeway signs near Barcelona mark exits in both Catalan and Spanish (Castellano) *sortida* and *salida*— and Catalan taggers often paint over the *salidas* in protest. Hofstede distinguished between French- and Flemish-speaking Belgians, and English- and French-speaking Canadians. If he studied in the United States today, he'd need to measure the work values of Spanish-speaking Americans separately. Even then, there would be an argument about lumping together immigrants from Mexico and Cuba.

The biggest cultural differences within countries are in the most populous regions. While tiny Switzerland includes four different official languages on its currency—French, German, Italian, and Romansch—a 20-rupee note in India lists 13 official languages. Indeed, there is more cultural diversity in religions and languages on the subcontinent of India than there is in Europe. Or consider China, these summaries of regional nuances in negotiation styles from our book, *China Now*:[11]

Northeastern negotiators. The stereotype is forthright. Negotiators from the three northeastern provinces above the Yangtze are industrious, competent businesspeople. They are generally honest and plain-spoken to the point of being uncouth. They are also not known for their risk taking or creativity.

Beijing area. Negotiators from Beijing are known for their unusual (within China) bureaucratic sloth and imperialist perspective, both yielding a relatively uncommon lack of creativity. Since they have often defined the box in the first place, they are not good at thinking outside it. Increasingly, cosmopolitan managers from the capital city may be outgrowing this generalization.

Shanghai area. In a word: shrewd. These negotiators are outgoing, big talkers and big spenders. They will try to impress you in ways and to an extent you won't see anywhere else in China. For them, anything is possible—they are very creative thinkers. Speakers of the Shanghai dialect are quite clannish and cunningly political. Some in China describe them as calculating, even devious. But more than anything, they are successful—really the dominant business group on the mainland.

The south. These Chinese have always been the closest to foreign influences, which has yielded a special strength in entrepreneurship and spontaneity. They are relatively honest and forthright. They are less calculating than folks in Shanghai, but they are excellent traders and particularly interested in making a quick buck.

Hong Kong. The business culture in Hong Kong is distinct from the general descriptions in important ways. Almost all the Chinese in Hong Kong are bilingual, at least speaking English fluently. Indeed, their English is probably better than yours. As Hong Kong executives have learned English, they've also deeply absorbed British culture. For most, their first language is Cantonese, and it's the roughest dialect. It almost always sounds like an argument is going on, and their swearing is legendary—incredibly vulgar at times. If you get mad at them, though, face is lost on both sides of the table, and usually the deal is dead. Oddly enough, humility and indirection are far more common in Hong Kong than in northern China.

Taiwan. Other Chinese consider Taiwanese the most conservative in behavior and language. Here the influence of Confucius and the Mandarin dialect won out, even though adjacent to Communist rule on the Mainland. Consequently, age, rank, and family play the most powerful roles on the island. Companies tend to be managed directly from the top and the decision-making style is autocratic. Managers can be down-to-earth practical, but on occasion they are also daring.

Singapore. Here the historical influence of the British is key. These islanders are known for their English-language skills and their underlying values: for following the rules and for their generally straightforward (not devious) business dealings. Chinese in Singapore are more individualistic; they move quickly, and decision making tends toward the autocratic.

Overseas Chinese. Overseas Chinese managers, often born and raised in Indonesia, Thailand, the Philippines, Canada, or the United States, are at least bicultural and therefore are capable of thinking and conversing as "natives" in their native countries. Yet they can also turn on the entrepreneurial spirit and skillful bargaining of their south coast Chinese ancestors quite quickly. They will continue to be tough customers and even tougher competitors, particularly on their home turf.

Overseas Chinese can be defined by their fluency in Chinese dialects, the recency of their immigration, and the location of their university experience. As you get to know the Chinese across the negotiation table, whether you're in Bangkok or Boston, it makes sense to take an interest in their personal histories.

Negotiation Styles Differ across Industries

There can be dramatic differences in negotiation styles across industries, even within any one country. Consider banking and retailing. Negotiations with bankers in all countries will almost always proceed in the most conservative and traditional ways—nobody wants a daring banker. The flamboyant Mario Conde, known ironically as *El Tiburon* (the Shark), was the owner of the fourth largest bank in Spain and was voted by his countrymen as their most admired businessman. He was frequently displayed handsomely on the cover of *El Tiempo* magazine, and he spent his last few years in jail for his daring "banking" practices. Ordinarily, however, you'll find more daring retailers than bankers across any negotiating table.

Company Culture

Anyone who has worked for two companies in the same industry and country knows that companies have cultures—unique ways of doing things and ways of thinking. Many a merger or acquisition strategy that made great sense on paper has failed because of differences in "management style." Consider Dieter Zetsche's DaimlerChrysler as a prominent example. Even forty years ago *Harvard Business Review* noted "When a company seeks to merge, it usually wants a partner whose operations will complement it in some manner, such as product line, marketing, or manufacturing capability. But a successful combination depends at least as much on compatibility of fundamental business "styles."[12]

More recently, regarding the AOL-Time Warner merger, commentators said: "AOLTW has already undergone a slew of personnel shakeups, which has seen top executives falling from the beleaguered company like rotted fruit from a tree: Former Time Warner CEO Gerald Levine in January, while company COO and interim head of AOL Robert Pittman followed in July. Pittman's departure came as part of an overall restructuring of the company that shifted power away from the renegade new media side and into Time Warner's old media court."[13]

Corporate goals and growth strategies drive corporate culture, everyday decision making *and* negotiation style. The stodgy "old media" versus creative "new media" is one kind of clash. Here's another: Neiman Marcus versus its sister brand/store Bergdorf Goodman. Both are high-end department stores, jointly owned, and they often even trade executives. But Bergdorf specifically aspires to serve only New York City, while Neiman Marcus is now expanding rapidly across the Unites States, and this affects the management cultures in many ways. For an extreme example, just imagine how a Microsoft/Apple merger might work.

Negotiators with Differing Expatriate Experiences

Foreign executives with experience living or working in the United States will usually adjust their bargaining styles and appear to understand Western approaches. We have noticed in our negotiation simulations that Japanese executives who've lived in the United States just six months begin unconsciously to reflect the communication style (eye contact, conversational rhythm) of American bargainers.

But the degree to which foreign executives will understand and respond to the American style of negotiations can differ depending on the length and quality of their stay in America. The answers to simple questions such as, "How long did you spend in the United States?" and "What were your responsibilities there?" will help gauge their level of understanding. Generally, higher level expatriate tours of duty (such as head of a subsidiary or middle manager) are shorter (three to five years) and involve primarily contact with their own headquarters personnel at their foreign corporate offices. You should also be aware that most foreign businesspeople with such bicultural competence are able to switch their American style on and off. We have seen, for example, Mexican associates who can play either role—indulging in business entertainment and nontask talk or in other circumstances getting down to business uncomfortably fast.

You are more likely to focus your attention on executives with long expatriate experiences because they speak English better, they appear to understand you better, and they appear to be smarter. This is a mistake. Often, the foreign executive with long expatriate experience is the least influential in the group. In either case, recent studies show that bicultural people are better able to think creatively—their experiences and languages deliver broader perspectives.

Age

"Youth today love luxury. The have bad manners, contempt for authority, no respect for older people, and talk nonsense when they should work. Young people do not stand up any longer when adults enter the room. They contradict their parents, talk too much in company, guzzle their food, lay their legs on the table, and tyrannize their elders." Sound familiar? It's from Socrates circa 500 BC. Today the generational divide is widening as younger people are better able to stay abreast of the almost daily changes in communication systems and other technologies. Some experts believe that these generational differences will become increasingly important as young people become more similar to their peers in other countries than they are to their own elders.

Gender

There are two things working against women in international negotiations. First is the perception that women are not effective negotiators. Second, the progress toward equality made by American women in management professions isn't shared by their foreign counterparts, so they feel that they will not be accepted as equals by their foreign counterparts. Both perceptions are false.

From our own studies of gender differences in negotiations among MBA students and a raft of similar studies, we know that women do not achieve the same levels of profits as men do in laboratory negotiations. We also know that in real life American women make less money than men, and one of the key reasons is that they do not ask for as much money as their male counterparts. But laboratory or salary negotiations don't tell the whole story.

In the most recent study of the pricing decisions made by American male and female veterinarians, women set lower prices.[14] Unlike men, however, the women take into consideration some traits of their customers and the number of their associates in their practices. The women charged higher prices when they had more associates, and the men did not.

As linguistics expert Deborah Tannen reports:

> In general, women are more comfortable talking one-on-one. The situation of speaking up in a meeting is a lot closer to boys' experience of using language to establish their position in a large group than it is the girls' experience using language to maintain intimacy. That's something that can be exploited. Don't wait for the meeting; try to make your point in advance, one-to-one. This is what the Japanese do, and in many ways American women's style is a lot closer to the Japanese style than to American men's.[15]

When the US Congress shut down the government in the fall of 2013, it was diversity that got it up and running again. According to *Time Magazine's* cover story, *Women Are the Only Adults Left in Washington*: "At one of the darkest moments of the government shutdown, with markets dipping and both ends of Pennsylvania Avenue hurling icy recriminations, Maine Republican Susan Collins went to the Senate floor to do two things that none of her colleagues had yet attempted. She refrained from partisan blame and proposed a plan to end the crisis."[16]

Other women Senators stood behind her. Indeed, most of the 20 women in the Senate had met informally the night before over pizza, salad, and wine in the Senate offices, and they had discussed several ways to compromise. None of the old cigars and poker chips there. No bluster or bluffing, just respectful positive discourse. Ultimately, Senate leaders Harry Reid and Mitch McConnell were shamed into better behavior, and that different sort of discourse among the women had led directly to more inventive options.[17]

None of this would come as a surprise to MIT psychologist Steven Pinker. In *The Better Angels of Our Nature,* he strongly supports four reasons for the ongoing decline in violence across the globe: rule of law, rule of information, trade, and women in politics. Pinker notes:

> From the time they are boys, males play more violently than females, fantasize more about violence, consume more violent entertainment, commit the lion's share of violent crimes, take more delight in punishment and revenge, take more foolish risks in aggressive tactics, vote for more warlike policies and leaders, and plan and carry out almost all the wars and genocides..... Historically, women have taken the leadership in pacifist and humanitarian movements out of proportion to their influence in other political institutions of the time, and recent decades, in which women and their interests have had an unprecedented influence in all walks of life, are the decades in which wars between developed states became increasingly unthinkable.[18]

American women are simply better at managing personal relationships than American men. They pay more attention to their coworkers. We also note from our laboratory observations of MBA negotiations that American men interrupt American women with surprising frequency.[19] American women are more relationship-oriented than their male counterparts. Moreover, the latest brain science shows that women literally have more brain power than men when it comes to managing interpersonal relationships.[20] And that trait serves them well (perhaps even better) in international negotiations.

The second misperception about gender equality is a bit more complicated. It is true that women in other countries do not hold the same level of equality that American women do—in some cases they're actually better off. In a survey on gender equality compiled by the World Economic Forum (www.weforum.org) America ranks #22 of the 115 nations included. Saudi Arabia (#114) and Yemen (#115) are at the bottom, and Sweden (#1) and Norway (#2) are at the top in real gender equity.

Things are improving for women around the world, albeit much too slowly in some places. In the United States, 57 percent of undergraduate students are women, and this trend is common in other countries, mostly in Europe, but it is found even in Iran (#108) and Saudi Arabia. This sea change in college enrollments has led to a changing landscape in professional programs. About half of law and medical students in America are women. And women make up about 30 percent (down from 40 percent in the 1990s) of MBA classes and account for about 20 percent of students in US engineering programs.

Implications for Managers and Negotiators

Considering the potential problems in cross-cultural negotiations, particularly when you mix managers from cultures with distant values and linguistics, it's a wonder that any international business gets done at all. Obviously, the economic imperatives of global trade make much of it happen despite the potential pitfalls. But an appreciation of cultural and other sorts of group differences can lead to even better international commercial transactions—not just business deals but inventive and highly profitable business relationships.

Thanksgiving Dinner and Inventive Negotiation

"There's a turkey there with the Persian spread. She'll make yams and stuff like that. The Persian food is there too. . . . There's one with lemons and one with potatoes, but they're all meat-based and with heavy sauce. She makes a lot of salmon and there's eggplant . . . and she'll make brown rice for me if I'm there. But there's always the white rice. Never rolls or bread on their table. It's always rice. She serves a salad usually. And the turkey. That's it. And mashed potatoes."

"Every year, in addition to the outrageous amount of Jamaican based food, we always have a turkey with stuffing, cranberry sauce, gravy. We decorate a table and place the turkey in the center. However, the turkey is NEVER eaten, except for one part. . . . The Turkey Neck. . . . The rest of the turkey stays on the table untouched. By the next day, it is wrapped and placed in the refrigerator in the garage. My brother-in-law may have cut a leg or maybe a slice of breast off, but 90 percent of it is left. By day 5, it reaches the garbage bin still basically untouched."

"Well, normally, for example, when we make the Thanksgiving we make the system here, but, for example, we cook the turkey in the Mexican way. . . . Oh, you put it with the banana leaves around and with some special stuff that I have here that is some Mexican flavor and spices, and you put it together. We put it in the oven and after 4 or 5 hours, and you take it away this stuff, and all the turkey is very juicy, very tasty, because if you do it the other way traditional, sometimes it is too dry.... Like I told you, we are going to take the good things from Mexico and put it in the American system and enjoy it. We don't need to break one regulation of the other system to feel better."

These three verbatim comments come from a study by two of our colleagues, and they show the positive aspects of cultural diversity in practice.[21] The comments are focused on bicultural families and Thanksgiving Day dinner, and the researchers' explanation can be summarized as follows.

The concept of creolization stems primarily from the field of linguistics and has been defined as "the coming together of diverse elements to create a vital, vibrant new entity." Stemming from the Spanish word "*criollo*," the Portuguese word "*crioulo*," and the French "*créole*," the noun "creole" has historically had several meanings, ranging from a person of French or Spanish ancestry born in the Americas to an individual of mixed parental heritage. As an adjective, the word "creole" has also been used to describe that which is mixed or blended, including people, food, and language. Edouard Glissant, the Martiniquan poet, novelist, and philosopher, sees creolization as an encounter that changes the parties involved to create something new. This view of creolization is also supported by other researchers who describe creolization as "any coming together of diverse cultural traits or elements to form new traits or elements."

Despite some immediate difficulties, cultural diversity always adds new and positive elements to your team. And that diversity makes for inventive negotiation at its best.

CHAPTER 8

Exploring Place/Space/Pace

Space is the breath of art.

—Frank Lloyd Wright

It's blazing hot. Sweat is pouring into your boots from under your body armor. Commands are coming through your headpiece from several different levels. Angry Somali villagers, wielding blood-drenched machetes and AK-47s, are banging on the gates. In the middle of the street, the mayor's brother lies dead.

Inside, US Marine Corps Civil Affairs Group (CAG) team is desperately trying to negotiate with the mayor. The shouts of the villagers nearly drown out the words of the players: a World Food representative trying to bring much-needed supplies to the village, a private contractor who wants to build a wind farm on the very beach the Marines have targeted for amphibious landings, leaders from two warring village tribes, all being recorded by an angry female journalist in her *hijab* and her aggressive cameraman. Captain D (as her troops call her) has her hands full.

The conflict seems very real. The Somali villagers are real. The forward operating base (FOB) is full of real Marines with a real mission. The cultural advisor, Claud Henri, is a 25-year veteran of the French army, posted for years in various parts of Africa. The weapons are definitely real, and so it seems is the anger of the villagers.

For William Hernández Requejo, however, some parts are optional. Helmet on, he's a participant in the engagement. Embedded with the team, he is subject to the same "life-threatening" circumstances as the others. Helmet off, he's just an observer.

Suddenly the villagers have crossed into the compound. You hear the safeties clicking off. "Who are you?" demands the Somali with the machete, inches away from William's face. "Who *are* you?" It seemed like a good time to switch to observer status. Helmet off.

Despite the authentic villagers, we are actually in Camp Pendleton near San Diego, California. Our mission during this innovative training exercise is to see if our team can use the negotiating skills learned last week in our classroom in this simulated environment that more closely resembles conditions in the field where the Marines' Civil Affairs Group will need to operate in a post-Afghanistan world.

It's been Henri's job to get the "atmospherics" right. He's brought in American immigrants from Somalia from tribes that are actually at war. The compound is an exact replica; the heat of the summer sun is identical. More important, Henri knows the culture because of his years in Africa. Unlike U.S. military teams, he's lived in the same villages, in the same housing, as the people he's protected. He can tell you that a machete is frightening, sure, but not too dangerous if you keep your distance and especially compared to the AK-47s. And that AK-47s held high are signs of jubilation, not threat.

Today's mission is to try to pacify the villagers, to convince them not to shoot at the main force of Marines when they arrive next week. Yet all the promises of food, energy, and safety may well be undercut by the feuding tribespeople who are unwilling to accept any leadership, especially after one of their own leaders has just been shot in the street. "Other places have democratic elections," observes one tribesman, referring to the butchered body of the mayor's brother. "This is how we hold elections here."

The first stage, as in any negotiation, is to observe everything closely. But if you get a surge of adrenaline walking into an ordinary business transaction, the effect is magnified in this kinetic (their adjective for bullets flying) situation. When emotions come into play, all those rational lessons head right out the door.

Since the contenders in the negotiation included women in their native garb, a police chief, the mayor, plus various tribal leaders and the press, all of whom had just walked by the pile of body parts that had been the mayor's brother, Captain D knew that selecting the people to be in the room was critical. If she made the selection, she could be legitimizing or negating important participants.

So she let the local experts decide. The mayor, the mayor's other brother, and the police chief agreed to allow one member each from the warring factions in the village.

Then there was the choice of venue. Ultimately, the villagers agreed on a fairly neutral location, the mayor's stifling hot two-story cement compound; it was unlit but surrounded by a fence where Marines secured the inner perimeter and locals hovered just outside. All except the mayor surrendered their weapons on entry, even the captain, as a sign of good faith.

The second major decision was again one that arises in every negotiation: the seating. The mayor occupied the only chair. When the captain asked for one, she was told that they were poor, and there were no other chairs. Perhaps the mayor could sit with the rest of them on the floor? No, he answered, he had a bad knee. In the hierarchy of nonverbal communication, she had lost major status points and would not be seen as an equal.

So she used her cultural knowledge to edge back up in status. Knowing that it was obligatory for a host to provide food and drink, she mentioned that she was thirsty. He had to provide something and, worse yet, serve a woman.

Her next challenge was to determine who had the final decision-making authority. Used to clear-cut military chains of command, at first she was bewildered. It seemed the villagers needed to reach a consensus somehow among all the factions, each with its own agenda. Each one wanted authority over jobs or just plain payment as a condition of allowing the main Marine force to land. She wasn't authorized to grant either request to anyone.

The situation deteriorated quickly. The group asked one member to leave. After a brief time outside the fence, during which the crowd got more agitated, he returned. The mayor abruptly halted the meeting. Slipping back into her body armor, the captain escorted her team back outside through an even more hostile crowd.

Even then, she attempted to engage, listening to the men and women surrounding her team and answering their questions, while the team quietly worked its way back to the secure forward operating base.

During the debriefing, Captain D was upset. As a negotiator, she had failed to reach her stated goal—assuring a safe welcome for the Marines arriving in the next week. Then trainers revealed the real nature of the mission: in a situation that they had deliberately rigged as a lose-lose, they wanted to see whether the team members could keep their heads about them, apply their newly learned skills, make some progress, and get out alive.

Chances are, your negotiations will not take place under threats from bullets and machetes. But as Captain D learned, culture matters. Status matters. Geography matters. An experienced team matters. Even your definition of meeting matters.

If you're an American, the word "meeting" stretches to include everything from a half-hour two-person chat in Starbucks to a formal presentation with a cast of dozens in a corporate boardroom. Any meeting can require hours of preparation or a few minutes glancing at notes. Not so in other cultures, and these differing expectations can torpedo both short- and long-term goals.

Yet, to a much larger extent than you may realize, inventive negotiations depend on the right combination of place, space, and pace.

Place

In 2013, President Obama met with Chinese President Xi at Sunnylands in Palm Springs—a place with a pleasant climate, an informal resort town, and roughly halfway between their two capitals. Back in 1986, President Reagan and Soviet Prime Minister Gorbachev held a summit at Reykjavik, Iceland, (probably a good place to get things done as there's not much else to do there in October) but also equidistant from their two countries. Despite their differing climates, those neutral locations created an implicit equality between the world leaders that helped reduce their tensions.

For both practical and psychological reasons, the location of the negotiations may have a substantial impact on the outcomes. On the practical side, there may be legal consequences to creating an agreement in one jurisdiction or another. Far more important, though, are the other reasons.

In a competitive negotiation, Americans often seek a "home court" advantage. The home team has all its information and resources readily available, and all the necessary team members close at hand. The traveling team, on the other hand, brings the minimum of necessary resources, information, and players, and that team has to stay in hotels.

But perhaps a greater advantage the home team enjoys is psychological—a perception of power. If the other side is coming to you, that means you have something they want. You are in control of the scarce resource, whether it's a product or service (you're the seller) or access to a key market (you're the buyer). Competitive negotiators will always try to hold negotiations in their own offices. Inventive negotiators will always opt for a neutral location that promotes an egalitarian sharing of information.

The location is even more important when dealing with clients or partners from relationship-oriented cultures, for it communicates power much more loudly to them. In Japan car salesmen will visit you in your home. Thus, in international business dealings, expect a strong emphasis on getting to a neutral location, such as a restaurant, karaoke bar, spa, golf course, or some other off-site location where diversity can best yield invention.

The US government's current restrictions on visas for some foreign executives deliver a big disadvantage to American firms. It will often be impractical to invite your Chinese or Middle Eastern counterparts to visit you, given the frequent delays and denials of the American immigration officials. You could, however, invite them to one of your offices in another country. For example, General Motors negotiators arranged a visit to their Brazilian plant for their Shanghai Auto counterparts during those crucial negotiations.

If you do travel to your partner's home turf, you can create a more neutral space to reduce your disadvantages. You can make arrangements for meeting facilities at your hotel (or your bank, or a subsidiary's office) and invite the other team to call on you. You might argue, "I've already made the arrangements and everything is all set," or "You can get away from the telephone," or perhaps you actually do need to wait for an important FedEx delivery yourself.

Or you can consider an unusual off-site location. When John worked as a market analyst for Solar Turbines International, now a San Diego division of Caterpillar, the company owned and operated a corporate boat. Before the days of cell phones and wireless communications, clients would be invited for a day of dolphin chasing and deep sea fishing off the tranquil coast of Coronado. Time to talk, debate, laugh, drink, and even catch a few fish. And the clients couldn't get away.

Getting to Paris, Finally

In 1973, the Paris Peace Accords ushered an end to the Vietnam War and earned Henry Kissinger and Le Duc Tho the Nobel Peace Prize. Yet just selecting the venue for those talks had taken weeks of negotiations.[1]

Back in April 1968, President Johnson began by suggesting Geneva, the location of the negotiations that had originally divided Vietnam in half. His people argued that Switzerland was a neutral country and its facilities would support the world press that was expected. Hanoi countered with Phnom Penh, Cambodia, which the Americans immediately rejected. Johnson then offered Asian sites—Vientiane (Laos), Rangoon, Djakarta, or New Delhi. The Vietnamese said no and suggested Warsaw. Then the United States offered Colombo (Sri Lanka), Tokyo, Kabul, Katmandu, Rawalpindi (Pakistan), Kuala Lumpar, Rome, Brussels, Helsinki, and Vienna.

Hanoi argued all were either not neutral or did not have diplomatic relations with North Vietnam. On May 2, Hanoi rejected a proposal for a secret meeting in the Gulf of Tonkin on an Indonesian ship. Finally, the United States reluctantly agreed to Paris; the Americans had been afraid of Charles de Gaulle's potential interference. Given that it took 34 days to agree on place, it's not surprising that space was also a tough subject.

SIDEBAR 8.1

Place and Space: Lessons from Science

According to scientific studies, the place where you meet can have unconscious but significant effects on the outcome of any discussions. If you want to focus on details, make sure you're in a room with a low ceiling and red walls. If, however, you're looking for inventive outcomes, try to maximize these proven game changers:

1. Go off-site to a neutral environment[2]
2. Paint the room blue[3]
3. Stretch the visual space with a high ceiling[4]
4. Stock the room with toys and tools[5]
5. Keep the room warm[6]
6. Make sure there are scenic views[7]
7. Add plants and flowers[8]
8. Hang some modern art[9]
9. Infuse a lavender scent[10]
10. Get people in close physical proximity[11]
11. Arrange soft chairs and sofas[12] and encourage people to relax and lounge around[13]
12. Make the room just about as noisy as a coffee shop[14]

Space

Fortunately there are fewer shapes of tables than there are countries in the world. The Vietnamese wanted a round table that would give equal recognition to the National Liberation Front (NLF) fighting for the North in South Vietnam, particularly because the United States invited the South Vietnamese government to sit with them. The South Vietnamese argued for a rectangular table representing the two distinct sides in the negotiations. Ultimately, they compromised by having both. The two Vietnamese governments, North and South, would sit at a round table, and the others—Americans and NLF—would sit at square tables surrounding the round one.

The talks started on May 13, 1968, at the International Conference Center in the old Majestic Hotel. President Johnson had given the US negotiators instructions that included as the first word "prompt." The North Vietnamese delegation's orders were the opposite: "stall." The Americans initially stayed in hotels; the North Vietnamese leased a convenient chateau. The negotiations took another four years to bear fruit, and millions died during those four years. It's a perfect example of the effects of place, space, and pace.

Pool versus Conference Room

Underneath a canopy of bright orange umbrellas, adjacent to the pool cabanas, a group of Miami attorneys are conducting a business negotiation. According to the story in the *New York Times*,[15] "the contract negotiations were progressing well until the woman in the tiny bikini interrupted to ask Mitchell Stevenson and his client if they wanted drinks."

And while distractions like this can be a downside, more and more companies are choosing poolside venues for serious negotiations. For decades, blockbuster movies were green-lighted in the cabanas at the Beverly Hills Hotel. The Cosa Nostra managed its mob empires from oceanside lounge chairs in South Beach or over a mojito at the iconic Hotel Nacional in pre-Castro Havana.

Today, however, "I'm increasingly seeing small groups of people wanting to get together in unusual or nontraditional spaces," says Betty Wilson, the vice president of divisional sales at Starwood Hotels. The demand for "sun and fun" settings has sold out the 20 thatch-roofed beachfront huts at the Marriott Beach Resort, and the two-story air-conditioned cabanas at Loews Miami Beach. In cooler cities, meetings take place on outdoor terraces in summer and in spas all winter.

According to the *Times*, part of the appeal is simply that people actually like to go to meetings in such pleasant places. Part is the perpetual drive for the new and the novel. But more important is that professionals are now having smaller meetings, and they seek more collaboration.

As Stevenson puts it, "Your mind can kind of run free when you're not in a white office building that has the same table in it as the office next door."

He's right, and there's lots of science to prove his point. But to really understand why choosing the right space in the right place is so important to inventive negotiators, just look at the typical setting for most businesses and organizations.

Two companies, A and B, have agreed to negotiate a joint venture. The meeting has been scheduled in the conference room in a high-rise building. At the massive table, surrounded by twenty high-backed leather swivel chairs, each place is carefully set. There is a new yellow pad, a corporate pen, and a small stack of financial documents neatly corralled in a small ring binder. A heavy crystal glass stands next to a plastic water bottle. At one end of the room, there is a flat screen monitor mounted above a credenza, and a silver-plated thermos warms coffee next to a matching set of mugs with the corporate logo.

Even though there are no place cards, everyone knows exactly where to sit—there are only two possibilities. If the heads of the two firms are sitting at the head and foot of the table, each will be surrounded by his associates, ranked in order from his right, then lined up neatly left and right to the exact center of the table. The final two places will be held by the attorneys, who arrive with their own (large) stacks of documents in thick black binders. In the alternative scenario, all of team A's people will line up opposite those of team B. There is to be no deviation from this order, and little small talk is tolerated as everyone files in and waits for the leader to take his seat. It is precisely seven minutes after the appointed time, and the meeting will adjourn promptly as scheduled, in exactly two hours.

Before a single word is spoken, we can guarantee that this meeting will not result in an inventive negotiation. In fact, the chances are very good that both teams will emerge frustrated, less likely to want this project, and set on an adversarial path that will doom this venture and the prospect of any more to follow.

Let's examine why.

1. Assume both teams have decided that working together is a good idea—they will be sharing technology or marketing or distribution or ganging up against a competitor. They've already agreed to the idea in principle, but those pesky details need to be ironed out. It is, however, an important decision and thus not left to underlings.

   Each company has had a hard time selecting the lucky ten who will constitute its team, and some of the team members may be secretly against this venture because it will threaten their personal domains. Except for the leader (and possibly not even him, if he has a strong board of directors looking over his shoulder), there are no risk takers in the room. And just to make sure, there's a lawyer or two for extra precaution.

Of the twenty people in navy blue power suits, one is from another country, one has different-colored skin, and only three are women. Not only are the wrong people in the room, there are way too many of them. And way too few of the right people.

2. As in all business ventures, there is an assumption that the decisions will be made rationally. This is dead wrong. Much recent neurological research shows us that people make decisions emotionally and then wrap those decisions in rational trappings to justify them. The notebooks on the table will just provide the props they need for that justification.

3. The team members have given themselves both too little and too much time. Two hours is certainly time to raise and discuss objections, but far less than what they'd need to form a team or agree on mutual objectives that would preclude a lot of quibbling. There's not even enough time to step outside for a break.

4. Since all the place settings are virtually the same, the hierarchy has not been established physically, and this means that all the players will need to establish it themselves. The easiest way to do that is to say no to any suggestion made by someone else.

5. The large table reinforces the adversarial nature of the proceedings. In fact, research shows that the smaller the barriers between people, the softer and rounder the surfaces on which they sit, the more they need to lean forward or touch, the more they work from the same sheet of paper, the more they will collaborate. Here we have a huge, hard hunk of wood separating the decision makers by about 30 feet. Between them stand armies of defenders, not sharing so much as a single piece of paper or pitcher of water. And these warriors are each ensconced in their personal armor—a hard leather chair with a high back and arms that will allow them to lean far away from every idea on the table.

6. The view is designed for sterility. A blank TV screen. A wall of windows high above any possibility of greenery. Possibly an abstract painting on one wall. Matching navy-blue coffee cups and yellow pads. Near silence. No people, nothing interesting, no life. Yet, decades of research prove that people are creative when they can look at live trees moving in the wind. When they hear the sounds of people in a coffee shop. Or have odd things to see. Random intrusions. Every single rule of creative space is killed in a corporate boardroom.

7. There's no food. This 10 a.m. meeting will allow for no sharing of cookies, no swapping of unwanted potato chips, no funny

stories about Dad's World-Famous Chili. This group will not be breaking bread together, violating the ancient rule of hospitality that was in place long before traders traveled the Silk Road through hostile territory. And nearing that noon break, everyone in the room—especially those who skipped breakfast—will be thinking of nothing but the next meal.

It's little wonder that there's no trust, no sharing of ideas, no relationship building in this setting. Everything is stacked against these outcomes.

Now for contrast, take a peek inside the Design School at Stanford or IDEO, the creative shop that's had a hand in everything from your computer mouse to your mop, from the way you bank or shop for lingerie to how you're admitted to a hospital. And that has built dozens of joint ventures and long-term relationships along the way.

Conference spaces seat three or six or ten. There's an Airstream trailer and a round triple-chair-like thing with a roof and a tear-off pad where a coffee table would be. Open spaces can seat a hundred and outdoor plazas even more. Floors are concrete, so chairs and red sofas, tables, and wall dividers can roll around. There is not a conference table in sight, though workbenches host half-built mystery designs. People are perched atop tables, in beanbags on the floor, lying on sofas, standing at whiteboards drawing, knee-to-knee over low tables. There's a pleasant hum of laughter and conversation in the background, smatterings of other languages. Outside the windows, there are trees and cars and people walking about. Everywhere you look, there's something interesting to see. Bins of spare parts. Bikes. Piles of crayons and colored paper. Whiteboards covered in neon sticky notes. Rolls of brightly colored duct tape. Toys. Hats. Feathers. Game boards and Nerf guns.

Meetings may take 10 minutes or seven hours if you're on a creative roll and you send out for Chinese food. Apparel ranges from the casual to the bizarre, and while the staff trends to be a little young, there's plenty of gray hair and a few hairless pates shining in the sunlight. When a team has an idea, they can enlist an instant focus group to poke holes in it or add to it. There's a kitchen stocked with snacks and casual tables inside and out. The smell of popcorn or brownies fills the room, and late afternoons feature wine and beer.

Clients usually book a night or two in Palo Alto, share dinner or breakfast with their collaborators, and have time to sleep on their ideas and improve them before they leave with something brilliant in hand.

Honestly, where would you rather negotiate your next deal?

SIDEBAR 8.2

The Actual "Walk in the Woods."

Perhaps the most famous creative sidebar negotiation was that between Paul Nitze and Yuli Kvitsinsky. It was 1982 in Geneva when they took their proverbial "walk in the woods" and came up with an inventive solution to the American/Soviet impasse about nuclear arms reductions. The discussions were informal, involving physical movement among trees. Ultimately, their concoction was dismissed by both sides—but all agree it set a new tone for the ongoing talks and paved the way for significant progress between Reagan and Gorbachev in their October 1986 summit in Reykjavik. Sometimes the best space is the wide-open type.

International Negotiations

When you're negotiating outside the United States, the space you choose can be even more important (see anthropologist Edward Hall's classic description of the language of space excerpted in Sidebar 8.3). Americans value and feel comfortable with informality. Executives from most other countries value and feel comfortable with formality. If you travel to Thailand, for example, the Thais will manage the physical arrangements of the negotiations including time, place, refreshments, and breaks (that is, unless you make the arrangements). The only advice we have for Americans in these situations is to ask the Thais where to sit. They will have a specific arrangement in mind, and if you ignore their arrangement, they will feel uncomfortable.

If your foreign partners are calling at your offices, then we recommend setting up the space to make them feel comfortable and more cooperative. To show that you are interested in the prospective business deal, meet in a comfortable living room setting without desks or conference tables. Many chief executives have these areas in their offices, and for more reasons than one, a brief nontask encounter with the American CEO may be the appropriate first step. For companies that have frequent visits by foreign clients, a specific room could be furnished just for this purpose and it will maximize information flows and creativity.

Some competitively oriented firms take steps to create an auction atmosphere in their negotiations by arranging competing bidders to sit in adjacent rooms. PetroBras, the Brazilian national oil company, is famous for using this tactic with its suppliers. Then the company's

SIDEBAR 8.3

The Language of Space

Like time, the language of space is different wherever one goes. The American businessman, familiar with the pattern of American corporate life, has no difficulty appraising the relative importance of someone else simply by noting the size of that person's office in relation to other offices around it.

One pattern calls for the president or the chairman of the board to have the biggest office. The executive vice president will have the next largest and so on down the line until you end up in the "bull pen." More important offices are usually located at the corners and on the upper floors. Executive suites will be on the top floor. The relative rank of vice presidents will be reflected in where they are placed along "executive row." The French, on the other hand, are much more likely to lay out space as a network of connecting points of influence, activity, or interest. The French supervisor will ordinarily be found in the middle of his subordinates where he can control them.

Americans who are crowded will often feel that their status in the organization is suffering. As one would expect in the Arab world, the location of an office and its size constitute a poor index of the importance of the man who occupies it. What we would experience as crowded, the Arab will often regard as spacious. The same is true in Spanish cultures. A Latin American official illustrated the Spanish view of this point while showing me [Edward Hall] around a plant. Opening the door to an 18-by-20-foot office in which 17 clerks and their desks were placed, he said, "See, we have nice, spacious offices. Lots of space for everyone."

In the Middle East and Latin America, the businessman is likely to feel left out in time and overcrowded in space. People get too close to him, lay their hands on him, and generally crowd his physical being. In Scandinavia and Germany, he feels more at home, but at the same time the people are a little cold and distant. It is space itself that conveys this feeling.[16]

purchasing agent can easily go from room to room to grind down both suppliers. Walmart is also famous for having its vendors sit down in the same room while the purchasing agent simply runs an auction—the lowest price gets the business. All this is at the opposite end of the high-pressure scale from tipping back a few Coronas aboard the Solar Turbines boat off the Coronado coast. These pressure tactics may make money in the short run but will destroy any creativity or long-term business relationship.

Pace

Tokyo. The *aisatsu* (formal greeting) was scheduled weeks in advance, in the Japanese company's corporate boardroom in Tokyo. John Graham, working with an American capital equipment manufacturer, had arrived a week early to prepare for this critical step in negotiating a distribution agreement for the Japanese market.

There he and his associate attended several meetings with lower-level executives at the Japanese firm, making sure every detail was in place for the Thursday meeting.

Then things began to go south. The forty-something American VP had never been to Japan and was scheduled to arrive Wednesday evening for a briefing and a good night's sleep. The flight was delayed, then delayed again. The frazzled, sleep-deprived VP and his Far East sales manager didn't get to the hotel until nine the next morning.

The second hiccup also happened Thursday morning. The American legal agreement, which was supposed to precede this meeting, did not arrive. Approval, if it came at all, would not occur until after the scheduled meetings, and this meant that the American had to act positive but not say yes.

In a hastily arranged briefing, the Tokyo rep for the company and John met the VP and the sales manager. Without the legal agreement, they agreed to "dance" during the meetings, avoiding any commitments. Given that it was customary to avoid any talk of business in an *aisatsu* meeting, that part should have been easy.

Then he asked about protocol and behavior. The rep, assuming the VP understood something about the culture, just told him to "be natural," and the travelers ran upstairs to get a shower.

Graham and the three American executives arrived at the Tokyo offices promptly at 2 p.m.

They were politely escorted by a uniformed receptionist to a formal meeting room, where they discovered 16 expensive easy chairs set in a square, with coffee tables placed nearby. They were not asked to sit.

Shortly afterward, three Japanese executives, with whom John and the rep had been meeting all week, arrived. There was a surprisingly formal exchange of business cards, and the seven of them made polite small talk in English about travel from Singapore.

By the time three more senior executives joined them, the meeting had already taken on a more respectful, formal air than the Americans had anticipated. And status distinctions, which made them uncomfortable, had already emerged. Since the Americans had been on an equal social footing with the junior executives, they scrambled to adjust from their now-inferior status to the older executive staff members. Before they could establish parity, the Japanese company president entered. With all six Japanese being even more deferential to their boss, the Americans were effectively two levels down.

Another formal exchange of business cards. When finally asked to sit, everyone sat in the *exact* order of their status rankings. The Japanese president and the American VP sat next to each other at a choreographed corner (at a right angle) with a junior executive perched on a stool a bit behind them to interpret (even though the Japanese president spoke English very well). Tea was served.

Now the Japanese president had total control. He asked questions of each American in turn, using the interpreter. Then the dialogue began between the two top officers. Only it wasn't exactly a dialogue. First, the president would ask a question in Japanese while looking at the American. While the interpreter spoke, the American had to shift his gaze, while his counterpart had more time to study his face and reactions. When the American spoke, the president understood immediately but had the same lag time while the interpreter translated—giving him twice the time to respond and twice the time to study the American. And he never had to shift his gaze, establishing another kind of nonverbal dominance.

Everyone in the room was focused on the American VP, so when there were any conversational gaps, he rushed to fill them. So far, all the participants had been careful to avoid any business discussion, and they wandered to the topic of golf. Since it was the American's favorite sport, he brightened considerably, describing courses and tournaments near his headquarters.

His next sentence would have left everyone with a dropped jaw if they had not been too polite. He invited the Japanese president to play in a golf tournament when he next traveled to the United States—*to sign the distribution agreement*! This led him to even more business comments and to predicting a long and prosperous relationship for the two companies.

The Japanese president hid his surprise and responded courteously. And then promptly excused himself, suggesting the Americans go into another room for a presentation by the executive staff. For the remainder of their relationship—if it even happened—the Japanese could dictate the terms of future negotiations.

What had happened?

The American was young, inexperienced, and totally ignorant of Japanese business culture. He was eager to close a deal and too sleep-deprived and jet-lagged to notice the nuances or even to remember his explicit instructions not to discuss business. Thanks to the interpreter, he didn't have time to calculate his next responses, and he felt the pressure of ten sets of eyes on his every word.

Most important, however, was the instruction to "act naturally." Coming from a culture that puts a premium on quick action and individual decision making and that pretends to ignore status differences, he simply didn't have the cultural tools to participate in a much more formal transaction. And his natural sense of timing, which worked well at home, backfired here.[17]

Americans and Time

"Just make them wait." Everyone else in the world knows that no negotiation tactic is more useful with Americans, because no one places more value on time, no one has less patience when things slow down, and no one looks at wristwatches more than Americans do.

But Americans can also learn to manipulate time to their advantage. Solar Turbines Incorporated (a division of Caterpillar) wanted to sell $34 million worth of industrial gas turbines and compressors for a Russian natural gas pipeline project. Both parties agreed that final negotiations would be held in a neutral location in the south of France. In previous negotiations, the Russians had been tough but reasonable. But in Nice, the Russians were not nice. They became tougher and, in fact, completely unreasonable.

It took a couple of discouraging days before the Americans diagnosed the problem, but once they did, a crucial call was made back to headquarters in San Diego. Why had the Russians turned so cold? They were enjoying the warm weather in Nice and weren't interested in making a quick deal and heading back to Moscow. The call to California was the turning point. Solar's headquarters people in San Diego were sophisticated enough to allow their negotiators to take their time. From that point on, the routine of the negotiations changed to brief, 45-minute meetings in the mornings, with afternoons at the golf course, beach, or hotel, making calls and doing paperwork. Finally, during the fourth week, the Russians began to make concessions and to ask for longer meetings. Why? They couldn't go back to Moscow after four weeks on the Mediterranean without a signed contract. This strategic reversal of the time pressure yielded a lucrative contract for Solar.

National holidays can also play a role. PetroBras invited a team of American negotiators to bid on a $5 million contract for equipment for an offshore oil platform *right before the Christmas holidays*. Summers are nice in Rio, but the Americans were at an awful disadvantage in their negotiations because of the unspoken demands of their own families waiting for Santa back home.

Finally, one last point about time limits. While creative processes and brainstorming can be enhanced by time pressure, the best international commercial relationships take time so viable personal relationships and innovative business structures and processes can be developed.

Taking It Slowly

His timing is flawless. He knows when to speak, when to shut up, when to wait. Let Father Gregory Boyle tell you two more stories from his book, *Tattoos on the Heart*.[18]

> I met Anthony through legendary Eastside probation officer Mary Ridgeway. "Help this kid," she pleads over the phone.
>
> Mary told me where I might bump into him, since his last known address was his car, left for dead on Michigan Street.
>
> At nineteen years old, Anthony had been on his own for a while. His parents had disappeared long ago in a maelstrom of heroin and prison time, and he was fending for himself, selling the occasional vial of PCP to buy Big Macs and the occasional Pastrami Madness at Jim's. He was a tiny fella, and when he spoke, his voice was puny, reed-thin, and high-pitched. If you closed your eyes, you'd think you were "conversating" (as the homies say) with a twelve-year-old.
>
> One day we were both leaning up against his "tore up" *ranfla*, and our conversation is drifting toward the "what do you want to do you want to be when you grow up" theme.
>
> "I want to be a mechanic. Don't know nothing 'bout cars, really. But I'd like to learn it."
>
> My mechanic, Dennis, on Brooklyn Avenue, was something of a legend in the barrio.
>
> Dennis could fix any car. A tall, pole-thin Japanese-American in his near sixties, Dennis was a chain-smoker. He was not a man of a few words—he was a man of no damn words at all. He just smoked. You'd bring your car in, complaining of some noise under the hood and hand the keys to Dennis, who would stand there with a cigarette dangling from his lips.
>
> He'd take the keys, and when you returned the next day, he'd give you your car, purring as it should. No words were exchanged during this entire transaction.

So I go to Dennis to plead my case.

"Look, Dennis," I say, sitting in his cramped office, truly a smoke-filled room. "Hire this kid Anthony. True enough he doesn't know anything about cars, but he sure is eager, and I think he could learn stuff."

Dennis just stares at me, nodding slightly, a long ash hovering at the end of his *frajo*, deciding whether to jump off the cliff or not. I redouble my efforts. I tell Dennis that this won't just be one job for one homie but will create a ripple effect of peace in the entire neighborhood. Long drags of silence and a stony stare. I get out my shovel and my top hat and cane. Nobel Peace Prize, will alter the course of history, will change the world as we know it. Nothing. Dennis just fills his lungs with smoke, as I fill the air with earnest pleas. Finally, I just give up and shut up. I've done the best I can and I'm ready to call it a day. Then Dennis takes one last long sucking drag on his cigarette and releases it into the air, smoke wafting in front of his face, clouding my view. Once every trace of smoke is let out, he looks at me, and this the only thing he says that day:

"I will teach him everything I know."

Another demonstration of Boyle's exquisite sense of timing:

"Mass is about to begin at Camp Munz, and I've been shaking hands with the gathering homies filing into the gym. They are all dressed in their military fatigues, smiling and courteous. There is one kid covered in tattoos, face and arms, which is not usual with this young age group. I pull him out of line, and he says his name is Grumpy. He only offers his gang moniker and seems tougher on the first bounce than most kids are.

"Look," I say, fishing one of my cards from my pocket, "call me when you get out, and we'll remove your tattoos for free."

Now, usually when I say this, the response is nearly always the same. They grab the card and stare at it and say something like, "Really?...Wow...For free?...*Firme*." But not Grumpy. He doesn't take my card. He looks at me, as the homies would say, "all crazy," and on the total LOUD status says, "Yeah, well, why'd I get 'em if I'm just gonna take 'em off?" He's huffy and belligerent. This almost never happens. In the face of this rare occurrence, I become quite placid and find my preternatural calm voice.

"Well," I say, "I don't even know you—but I KNOW why you got all these tattoos."

"Yeah," louder still, he says, "Then why'd I get 'em?"

"Well, simple," I say, my voice as quiet as his is loud. "One day, when you weren't looking, your head...got stuck...up your butt. That's right, dog, you straight-out keistered your *cabeza*. So," and I force my card into his hand, "you call me...the minute...you locate your head."

Not my proudest moment, but as the homies might say, "I don't let myself," which is to say, you get crazy with me, I tend to get crazy back. I'm working on it.

Some five months later, someone gives me a slew of Lakers tickets, enough to fill the parish van with the *pandilla mugrosa* (a group of trouble-making little ones from Pico Gardens, who all seemed to have a common allegiance to bad hygiene, an allergy to bathing). It was when the Lakers still played in the Forum, and we had been blessed with seats not in the nosebleed section, but in the cerebral hemorrhage section. The gaggle of project kids was running up ahead of me, but I took my time climbing the stairs. Suddenly, in about fifteen aisle seats, a group of Camp Munz youth all stand to salute me. "Hey G," one says, "It's us from Camp Munz." They come into focus for me. They are all in their camouflage garb—given free tickets as well. I shake the hands of each one, seated all behind one another on the aisle. The hollering, "DOWN IN FRONT," does not make us speed up our greeting. We're all mutually excited to have bumped into one another.

I'm nearing the end, and the third to the last *vato* is Grumpy. We fix eyes on each other, and I extend my hand to his. He refuses to shake it. I think, *Not good*. There is a beat before, quite unexpectedly, Grumpy throws his arms around me and squeezes tight. He leans into my ear and whispers, "I get out Tuesday...I'll call you Wednesday...I want-cha ta...take my tattoos off."

That's it, the essence of Boyle's success. He understands that boy and all the others in this place. He's deeply embedded in their culture. It's no surprise that his homies call him G-Dog and that they would do absolutely anything for him. Not only has he built those long-term relationships—he's created a space where people are happy to come and interact and the community structure that will sustain it. And, of course, he started with a pie factory.

Notice that Father Greg Boyle's stories demonstrated uncommon patience twice: waiting for Dennis to collect his thoughts and waiting for Grumpy to change his mind. No matter how carefully you select the space where you'll meet and the way you furnish it, the amount of time you allow for negotiation is critical. Remember the days that Ford spent in Vietnam with the retreats in a luxury resort? The years that the geothermal teams met over dinner in Oregon? The more you can create bonding in informal settings, the better the outcomes you can expect. The more you know about the people you're negotiating with, the more you can determine just how long each phase of your talks should take.

CHAPTER 9

Preparing for
Emotions/Power/Corruption

The human species thinks in metaphors and learns through stories.
—Mary Catherine Bateson

He must have practiced it. The chair cartwheeled through the air and—*thunk*—embedded itself in the wall. On both sides of the table, the Koreans and Americans just stared in awe as it rested, stuck in the wall, suspended above the floor. After a long moment of silence, the American stood, stuffed his papers into his briefcase, and announced, "We're done."

Not exactly an ordinary negotiating tactic, but one that was extremely effective. And it led to a disastrous outcome for one or perhaps both the teams.

First the background. Cellular phone purchases in the United States were declining. Everyone who wanted a cell phone already had one, and the demand for the semiconductor chips inside the phones was falling too. Making things worse, an ongoing recession dimmed long term prospects as well.

The Korean manufacturers demanded lower prices from the American chip makers, and at this point profit margins were already minimal. Throughout this tough negotiation, the Koreans kept pushing, even though both sides knew their long-term futures depended on the innovation only the Americans could provide.

The four members of the Korean team had done their homework. Led by an "old-school" executive in his sixties, the team included two financial and technical experts in their forties and a hotshot young manager who had earned an MBA at a top American university and spoke fluent English. (He was the chair launcher.)

The American team had been hastily thrown together and included a business manager, a project technician, and the Korean-American project manager. None of them had much international experience, and being tech experts, they lacked the social skills of most business negotiators.

As the Americans walked into the room, the tension was palpable. The Koreans were worried about escalating threats from their northern neighbors. The Americans were jet-lagged from 18 hours of flight and a layover. At the first point of contention, the Korean stood up and the chair went flying.

The Americans were nonplussed: this was not the behavior they expected from their brief cross-cultural training about the reserved, quiet Asians. So instead of just walking out, they hesitated as they tried to understand what had just happened.

What they didn't know was that the whole chair-tossing incident had been carefully planned. The young Korean manager knew the Americans believed the stereotypes and that they were familiar with hotheaded bar fights in their own country—knowledge he'd gathered during an internship with their company. His team had worked together for years and had traveled many times to the United States, specifically to study US negotiation techniques. They'd honed their skills in increasingly difficult negotiations. And then they'd rehearsed. And rehearsed. By the time they pulled this stunt, every gesture was perfect, the timing impeccable.

Then the Korean leader took advantage of the Americans' confusion. He sent his young manager out of the room and apologized profusely for his "inexcusable anger." He explained that the project was vital to their continuing success. But he left the chair in the wall.

The Americans, still rattled, sat back down and gave away the farm.

Those tiny profit margins disappeared altogether. They had come to the table believing that they would simply reason with the Koreans, and the Koreans had outsmarted them by using the power of emotion—dramatic irrationality.

The Koreans won this skirmish using unconventional methods. But that is the exact opposite of inventive negotiation. Instead of finding common ground, trying to innovate together to create new phones and increase their joint sales, both sides lost.

It's just one example of how emotion can drive any negotiation and how important it is to harness the power of those emotions—not to win a conflict, but to build relationships.

Neuroscience tells us that people respond to emotional triggers almost instantaneously. They feel, then filter information through those feelings any time they interact in similar circumstances. When strong negative emotions enter the room, creativity exits—and it stays gone. University of Southern California neuroscientist Antonio Damasio explains that our cognitive processes—reasoning, recognition, and memory—operate in hundredths of a second. We can change our minds about a fact when we learn a better one. But the emotional parts of our brains are much slower to change. Empathy, imagination, love, fidelity—all of them repair "in their own sweet time."[1]

Emotions: Watch for the Wrinkled Brow

Corporate trainers and neuroscientists have known for a couple of decades that sharing emotions can create unbreakable bonds and loyalties. Hence the team-building activities at many corporate retreats: Ziplining, leaping off mountains, whitewater rafting, making embarrassing videos, singing badly. Any activity that evokes a strong emotion will make the moment memorable and important and increase the amplitude of your feelings for the people with whom you share it.

For an even stronger emotional bond, you can't beat the army. You may have hated your drill sergeant, but by the end of boot camp, you would be willing to literally die for your buddies. Having a common goal, having a common enemy, sharing wretched physical conditions—all this is designed to promote group solidarity.

So how do emotions figure into inventive negotiation?

Paul Ekman, Professor Emeritus of Psychology at the University of California, San Francisco, is the leading authority on facial expression and emotions. In his seminar back in the late 1970s, John Graham learned much about the fundamentals of emotions. The coolest part of Ekman's presentation was his illustrations of the muscle map of his own face through his unbelievable control over them all. The raised eyebrow of Paul Newman or Steven Colbert could not compare to the facial movements dancing across Professor Ekman's face as he demonstrated his Facial Action Coding System (FACS).[2] Ekman argued that there are six fundamental emotions: happiness, sadness, anger, fear, disgust, and surprise. All these feelings can be directly observed by measuring movements of particular facial muscles.

While at Berkeley and the University of Southern California, John pioneered the use of Ekman's FACS in the study of face-to-face business negotiations.[3] In that work, he and his colleagues demonstrated that frowns (indicated by Action Unit 4 movements), interruptions, and facial gazing hurt negotiation outcomes, while smiles (Action Unit 12 movements) and facial expression synchrony helped. These findings have led us to focus on two aspects of emotion here. First, we will consider the effects of anger on inventive negotiation. Later, in chapter 12, we will consider the effects of humor on negotiations. Generally, and as you might guess, anger is a bad thing, and happiness is a good thing.

Anger's Negative Impact

The Korean chair story aptly demonstrates the potential damage that can be done to inventive negotiation processes. When that chair hit the wall and the Americans just sat there, all opportunities for creativity were gone.

When anger is threatening or intimidating, it is likely to end inventiveness not only at that meeting but in the personal relationships as well. If you're feeling angry, you need to take a break and sort out why. If your partners are displaying anger, you need to take a break and sort out why. Anger and invention rarely coincide.

And things often get worse fast. It is natural for humans to reflect the behaviors they witness on the other side of the table. Interactional synchrony means that smiling begets smiling, threats beget threats, raised voices beget raised voices. The anger only escalates from there. Consider Father Boyle's response to Grumpy on pages 131–2.

The Opportunities of Anger

In four specific circumstances, however, anger can work in your favor. But use it with extreme caution.

First, while you may never have seen a chair thrown during a negotiation, if you're an American, you've seen folks get mad. Chester Karrass, who teaches a mix of competitive and integrative bargaining in his popular courses and books, advises that anger can be good when it's used to emphasize the importance of particular issues—that is, when you use it as a communication tool.

Second, anger can be used to shake someone out of routine thinking. It's a cliché (for good reason) of the science of creativity that thinking outside the box is key. For example: Jim and Andrea were watching TV one night when their teenage daughter crawled into the room, doubled over in pain. She'd been suffering from stomach pains for months without a diagnosis, but this time the pain was acute.

Andrea called the doctor immediately, sobbing and screaming. Either her anger or her fear caused him to rethink his diagnosis, consulting some other physicians. Within two days, he discovered that the girl had a tropical infection, one he'd never thought to test for. Within a few more days, she was finally cured with a simple round of antibiotics.

SIDEBAR 9.1

Driveway dispute

On a cliff top high above the Pacific in Laguna Beach, California, two multimillion-dollar houses shared 180-degree views, the sound of the waves—and a long driveway.

While the original owners of the properties had no problem with this arrangement, the new owners were quickly at loggerheads. One had parties that annoyed the other. One had cars that were routinely parked in the shared stretch of the driveway.

Neighbor A installed concrete bumpers that made parking difficult or impossible. Neighbor B sued over the right of access. A countersued. The litigation escalated for years with no end in sight. Numerous financial settlements were offered and refused. The emotions had taken over, and nothing could move either neighbor to give in.

Finally, the parties agreed to try a mediator. Since both neighbors were quite wealthy, the monetary issue seemed as if it would be easy to solve—but it wasn't. When the judge probed further, he found the real issue:

"I don't care about the money. I'd be glad to pay to take the bumpers out. It's just that I don't want to give that jerk a penny."

So the mediator came back with an inventive suggestion. What if A didn't pay his neighbor a penny—but gave half the settlement money to a charity selected by B, and half to a charity selected by the judge?

To neighbor B, he made the other half of the suggestion: what if he didn't receive any money, but the settlement went half to a charity of his choice, and half to the judge's selected charity.

Before the day was out, the neighbors and their lawyers had agreed to a settlement offer.

By harnessing the litigants' positive, charitable emotions, the judge was able to bypass their mutual hostility and genuine anger. And the charities were able to really use the money that these wealthy neighbors had been throwing into their ongoing driveway dispute.

In Andrea's case we aren't sure what worked, the anger or the crying. Both affect others emotionally. Indeed, Ekman's Action Unit #4, the brow wrinkle, can indicate anger but also sadness or fear.

Third, everyone who takes a marketing class these days learns that complaints are important information. Entire companies have been built around the notion of "complaint handling." And complaints become louder when folks accompany them with emotions like anger and sadness. Thus, when your negotiation partner blows up, take a break, calm down, and then learn why this discussion caused so much pain. The more you know about your partners, the more creatively you can work with them—perhaps.

Fourth, frustration is the first step in any creative process designed to solve problems. After all, if you weren't frustrated by a situation, you would never want to fix it. Lynda Lawrence, who worked on different creative teams for many years, soon learned that a team's working relationships always began in the same way:

A bitch session (she claims that's the technical name for it). After the account people would come in with a new assignment, the art directors and copywriters would start their complaints. "That's the stupidest assignment we've ever been given. The competition is doing it better. There's no way we can do this by Friday." New account people were always taken aback. It's their job to bring in business, and they expected the people on the creative team to leap at the chance to show off their skills.

The curious thing about this response, however, is that it always led to very creative solutions. When the account people asked the creative team to stop complaining, the creative team just held their tongues until the account people left the room and then kept bitching. After years of participating in these sessions—and the resulting solutions—Lynda learned that there was something magical about that joint bitching. It allowed the team to discover the real problems to be solved, and it allowed team members to develop some solidarity around a perceived enemy—whether that was the time limit or the difficulty of the assignment. Thus when scheduling for any project, she always allowed for some complaint time, told the account people to expect it, and advised them to leave the room as quickly as possible so the team could work through the issues and go on to be brilliant.

Back in chapter 3 we discussed our thought experiment about having the Olympics in Jerusalem in the *Harvard Business Review* blog; the reactions to that blog entry were often very negative, in some cases even nasty. In sorting through them, though, we learned three quick lessons:

1. Venting emotions about the impossibility of the task can be a useful prelude to creative thinking;
2. Ad hominem attacks almost always damage the process of invention; and
3. It is essential to focus on the future, not the past, for the sake of invention.

SIDEBAR 9.2

The Japanese Poker Face

A common American complaint about negotiating with Japanese is their apparent lack of facial expressions: "We can't tell what they're thinking, whether they're happy, sad, angry, or what?"

Paul Ekman[4] and his colleagues wondered about the universality of facial expressions and went to their lab to find out. There they showed Japanese and American male subjects the same videos, one about a puppy and one documenting a circumcision rite in New Guinea where a stone was used as the "surgical instrument." Ouch! The Americans expressed a combination of surprise, fear, and disgust on their faces. By comparison, the Japanese showed nothing.

The immediate conclusion would be that facial expressions are not universal, but that would be wrong. Ekman wondered what would happen if the subjects viewed the videos alone, with no researchers in the room. The hidden cameras showed no differences—the universal response was surprise, fear, and disgust. The Japanese are socialized to control their expressions of emotion in social settings, and the Americans less so.

In our own laboratory we videotaped Japanese and American businesspeople's facial movements during simulated negotiations, and then we counted the expressions. We found no differences. Our interpretation is that the Japanese move their faces just as much as the Americans, but the Americans cannot read their Japanese counterparts' facial expressions because of timing differences and other social factors. Thus the Americans report they see nothing except the Japanese poker face.

The implications for negotiators are clear: Body language (or in poker parlance, "tells") can provide useful information, but the chances of misinterpreting them, particularly in cross-cultural circumstances, are great.

(See the comments for yourself at http://blogs.hbr.org/2011/07/bring-the-olympics-to-jerusalem/; they are not much fun to read. You can still add your own comments if you wish.)

Venting those emotions in a negotiation can lead to disclosure of more information and reveal real problems, and this in turn can lead to more constructive ideas. Even the worst comments can be the source of inventive negotiation outcomes. The trick is to distinguish complaints from anger. Once that line is crossed, immediately take a break. Cool off. Anger escalates and can ruin your current negotiation and your personal relationships. Use it rarely and very, very carefully.

Power: A Second Enemy of Invention

The most important idea about the role of power in negotiation is presented by Fisher and Ury in their book *Getting to Yes*. They define the concept of "best alternative to a negotiated agreement" or BATNA, and they describe how it lets you measure your power in any negotiation: if you have lots of good alternatives to reaching an agreement with your current negotiation partners, then you have the power. That is, if you have the patent on a unique product, even if you're negotiating with Walmart, Microsoft, or Donald Trump, you have the power. This is a market-based definition of power.

In physics, power is defined as the time rate at which work is done. Defining social power is a bit more difficult, but here's one popular list of all the different kinds of power people use:

Power of:
perception
competition
legitimacy
risk taking
commitment
expertise
knowledge of needs
investment
reward and punishment
precedent
persistence
attitude

Psychologists John French and Bertram Raven have come up with a simpler list: [5]

Coercive Power—Forcing someone to do something that he or she does not want to do. "If you don't give me a lower price, we're done here."

Reward Power—Granting someone things that he or she desires or decreasing things the person does not desire. "If you give me a lower price, we will be able to do business for a long time."

Legitimate power—Making someone feel obliged or responsible. "You cannot charge such high prices in a government contract."

Referent power—The ability to grant someone a sense of personal acceptance (rejection) or personal approval (disapproval). "Your low prices will help your reputation in the market place."

Expert power—Dispensing knowledge or expertise. "Based on my long experience in the business, your prices are completely unreasonable."

Informational power—Informing someone. "Based on the most recent marketing data, your prices are much too high."

We believe in a different concept of power: in social relations there's no such thing. Power is a concept that is useful only in retrospect if you are an academic or a journalist. In particular, political scientists are fond of "power" explanations: "They won the negotiation by using their _____ power." (You fill in the adjective.)

The 19 terrorists on September 11th, made nonsense of the idea of America as the most powerful nation in world history. The fans of power would explain that the terrorists had developed "countervailing power." But this is a post hoc explanation.

We think there are only negotiations and human exchange. Thus, as an inventive negotiator, you will need to stay vigilant against attempts at coercion, that is, power plays; if you spot them, work to turn things back immediately to invention. Maintaining a focus on opportunities in partnership makes that old notion of best alternatives inefficient and unproductive. Instead of worrying about alternative partners, consider how to build a better partnership.

Corruption: The Third Enemy of Invention

It was a hot day in August when William and John met Miguel Alfonso Martinez at the Hotel Nacional to discuss setting up joint programs between UC Irvine and the University of Havana. Martinez had held a number of big jobs: President of the new Advisory Committee of the UN Human Rights Council, spokesman for the Cuban Foreign Ministry, and president of the Cuban Society of International Law. He spoke three languages fluently—English, French, and Spanish—and he taught international negotiations at the University of Havana Law School, much like our courses at UCI.

Martinez was a big man with a graying ponytail, and he was huffing and puffing as we first sat down. He appeared tired from his recent travels and long meetings at the UN in New York.

In a typical non-task sounding session before discussing potential joint venture programs, Martinez suddenly asked if we ever played poker or chess. We wanted to talk about inventive negotiations, and he wanted to talk about games? Of course, he was really sounding us out about our own metaphors and therefore about our values and about our concept of negotiation. A chess metaphor signals a Machiavellian view because chess requires players to plot several moves in advance. Poker implies that lying is ok, even expected. Both games lend themselves to metaphors of competition.

Four years later, we took thirty UCI MBA students to Cuba for a nine-day residential course on real estate and healthcare systems on the rapidly changing island. The success of that innovative program grew from Martinez's instrumental role in our mutual inventive negotiations though, unfortunately, he did not live to see it. He died early last year.

His question about chess and poker, though, highlights the two key corruption and ethics issues for inventive negotiation: lying (misinformation) and withholding information. Inventive negotiation depends completely on the unfettered flow of accurate information, and misrepresentations and withholding information can do great damage to creativity.

Paul Ekman, our expert on facial expressions, is perhaps best known for his discovery of microexpressions, which show up on our faces for fractions of a second as indicators of emotion.[6] In his studies he found that a small fraction of people, approximately 50 of the 20,000 he and his colleagues tested, could spot deception without formal training. In his current professional work he also uses sociolinguistic clues to spot liars (he says he could tell former President Clinton was lying during the Monica Lewinsky scandal because he used "distancing language.")

Unless you're in the tiny fraction, the .25 percent of people who can naturally detect lying or you've been trained in Ekman's system (see www.PaulEkman.com), you're stuck with judging the veracity of your partners' information based on your feelings. If you feel like they're misinforming you, there is a good chance they are. This is where poker fits in—looking for "tells" is a crucial skill in that competitive game, where it is perfectly acceptable to bluff and withhold information. If your cultural or ethnic backgrounds are different, however, then your chances of making mistakes using your "lie-dar" are very high.

Which Truth?

The definition of truth varies across cultures. Consider the problem of wa (maintaining harmony) in Japan.

Western negotiators universally complain about the difficulties of getting feedback from Japanese negotiators. There are three explanations for this complaint. First, the Japanese value interpersonal harmony, or wa, over frankness. Second, the Japanese may not have come to a consensus themselves on the offer. Third, Westerners tend to miss the subtle but clear signals given by the Japanese.[7]

Wa is one of the central values of the Japanese culture. Negative responses to negotiation proposals are almost nonexistent, and when they are given, they are given very subtly.

We've all heard the classic story about the Japanese response to an American's request: "We'll think it over." Usually, this means "no" in American terms; if the Japanese really wanted to think it over, he would explain the details of the decision-making process and the reason for the delay. As we mentioned on page 99, a Japanese negotiator would be loath, however, to use the word "no."

One Japanese scholar, Keiko Ueda, has described sixteen ways to avoid saying no in Japan. In fact, we have found that Japanese negotiators tend to use the word "no" less than two times per half-hour in bargaining simulations, while Americans use "no" five times per half-hour, Koreans seven times, and Brazilian executives forty-two times!

In more ambiguous responses, Japanese negotiators follow the cultural double standard of tatemae and honne. Tatemae can be translated as "truthful" (or "official stance") and honne as "true mind" (or "real intentions"). It is important for Japanese to be polite and to communicate the tatemae while reserving the possibly offending, but also informative, honne. This difference in the Japanese value system shows up in statements by Japanese negotiators in retrospective interviews: The Japanese often describe Americans as honest and frank, to the point of discomfort for the Japanese.

Finally, eye contact is much less frequent during Japanese negotiations (13 percent of the time in negotiations between Japanese, 33 percent for both Americans and Koreans, and 52 percent in negotiations between Brazilian executives).

Thus, in Japan leakage of potentially offending feelings is limited, and the honne is kept intact. To Americans, this distinction between *tatemae* and *honne* seems hypocritical, even deceptive. Yet, this distinction is made by the Japanese in good conscience and in the interest of the all-important *wa*.

Given these cultural differences, many Americans accuse Japanese of lying. In turn, Americans can be seen as "beating around the bush" when they soften the truth to German or Israeli negotiators—both nations are noted for their brutal frankness. (The word in Hebrew is "*doogri*" and our word "frank" comes from an old German tribe called the Franks.)

Don't Be a Sucker

In the United States we usually trust people to tell the truth unless we're given evidence to the contrary. In most places around the world the opposite is true—trust must be built up over time. Nowhere is this more the case than in Israel. A central theme of negotiations there is, "Don't be a *freier*." You might translate the Hebrew into English as "sucker," but that word doesn't capture the importance of the concept in Israeli thinking.[8] Thus, we often hear Israeli leaders warning their American counterparts about being too trusting. Of course, distrust kills invention—and this is perhaps another explanation for the endless discord in the region.

More Ethical Issues

Back to Seoul and the thrown chair. As an unplanned, visceral reaction of anger to the Americans' obstinacy, the action would have damaged the possible process of invention. If the histrionics were planned, however, that action was a lie—perhaps a combination of chess and poker in Miguel Alfonso's view. This multiplies the damage.

Fraud is a form of lie and is punishable by law. Fraud is not an ethical matter; it's a legal matter that can come up in the course of negotiations. Just ask the big banks about their misrepresentations in the latest financial crisis.

Another kind of corruption that occurs in negotiations is bribery. The international legal establishment is tightening its standards and the laws are becoming clear, particularly the US Foreign Corrupt Practices Act, which prohibits American firms and individuals from bribing officials of foreign governments. While we don't condone bribery, to many people around the world (and it often seems so in Washington, DC), paying tribute can be seen as a form of creative negotiation. Moreover, almost all American politicians will lie about this—just ask them in public if donations influence their votes.

For example, recall from chapter 5 that Americans used money as a better weapon than bullets in Afghanistan, and that this approach was seen as pragmatic. No matter who is handing out the cash, the lack of transparency is most often bad for society and therefore damages the "grand inventive negotiation."

Information leaks can be another form of lying, particularly when information is leaked selectively. Yet, more people having more information is always good. Openness and transparency should always help inventive negotiations.

Inventive Negotiation as an Ethic

Given the better alternative of inventive negotiation, we believe it's actually unethical to take either a competitive approach or an integrative approach to negotiations. Both focus on interests, not the opportunities of collaboration. And both approaches limit what humans can accomplish when they work together.

CHAPTER 10

Changing Roles

When written in Chinese, the word "crisis" is composed of two characters.
One represents danger and the other represents opportunity.
—John F. Kennedy

As any parent can tell you, it's hard to get kids to eat their vegetables. It's even harder when getting those vegetables to the table involves two bus rides after a long day standing on your feet, plus spending a big chunk of your paycheck.

For decades, the California Department of Health Services had tried everything in their arsenal to encourage families to eat better to avoid diabetes, cancer, and heart disease. Yet even in health-conscious California, most people were getting just two servings of vegetables a day—and one of those was probably French fries.

The barriers were substantial. Inner-city neighborhoods where obesity runs highest are jammed with fast-food outlets, and markets with fresh produce are rare. Fast food is cheap, tasty, and convenient. Ads for junk food run nonstop on TV, while the department's ad budget was miniscule.

Long before Michelle Obama began her nationwide campaign, nutritionists in California decided to do something different.

They started with research, learning why busy, low-income moms were choosing high-calorie fried or processed food. Some of the answers were expected: fruits and vegetables are expensive, heavy to carry, time-consuming to prepare, and they go bad quickly. Some answers were cultural: among African-Americans, a meal without meat is simply not a meal. Among Hispanics, using family recipes (often frying with lard) is a sign of love. In fact, for all audiences, taking the family out for fast food was seen as a treat, a reward, a way to demonstrate your love.

In focus groups throughout the state, mothers routinely believed that they were doing their best for their kids. When confronted with evidence that those treats were hurting their families, almost every mother asked for advice about how to change the family's diets.

Even with information, however, there's a gap between what people intend to do and what they actually do. And that's where inventive negotiations came in.

When the department worked with us to try to bridge that gap, we started with another piece of the research: within the past 48 hours, half of all American households have eaten at a fast-food outlet.

Until that point, the department's strategy was to fight the proliferation of fast-food outlets, city by city, block by block. They encouraged grocers to consider building inner-city stores. They worked within the schools to ban fast-food contracts and soda machines. But their resources were limited, and their long-term efforts were not getting short-term results.

We began with one of the principles of inventive negotiation: creating a story of a perfect world. Obviously, this was one where within the past 48 hours everyone has been eating 10 servings of fruits and vegetables.

We encouraged everyone to consider even the craziest ideas and work in short bursts to get as many ideas on the table as fast as possible.

It was some of those crazy ideas that led to the breakthrough. Since research showed that kids believe food in branded fast-food packages tastes better than the same food without the packaging, someone suggested that we could just wrap carrots in a French fry bag. Someone else suggested we just switch ad budgets with the industry. Another thought we should include toys with broccoli. And suddenly there was a big idea: instead of treating the industry as the enemy, we should treat it as a partner—using the companies' ad budgets, their cachet, and their convenient outlets as an efficient distribution channel. Perhaps kids could have carrots or apples as a choice in their Happy Meals.

Of course, it's a long way from having that thought to achieving that goal, and that's where we used another principle of inventive negotiation. If we asked McDonald's to carry our products, what would they get out of the deal? What would help us build a relationship with them?

We began a role-playing session to see what we might have to offer. One nutritionist, playing a fast-food operator, stuck a beach ball under her sweater, crossed her arms, and growled, "Show me the money."

Just by physically mimicking her sworn enemy, she had changed roles. Instead of being the dedicated health professional, she became a franchise owner, understanding his primary concerns—not anonymous waistlines, but his own bottom line.

Before we went to see the franchisee organization, we needed to know how this idea could help franchisees make more money.

Again the research helped: if half of all Americans were eating fast food, half were not. Many of those were moms who wanted to give their kids healthier choices, and by offering those choices, the fast feeders might regain the families they had lost to health concerns.

It took two years, working with regional associations and test markets, but soon kids all over the country could have milk or juice instead of soda and apples instead of fries.

The biggest barrier, it turned out, was simply an attitude: that fast-food operators were the enemy. Once the nutritionists changed roles, embracing their former antagonists to create a mutual story, their new partners helped them reach more kids with healthier choices.

Changing Roles

Whether you realize it or not, everyone enters every encounter, every day, in a certain role. Some of the roles are stereotypes: The stern father. The nurturing mother. The class clown. Some are dictated by the circumstances: The innocent victim in a car crash. The quarterback who scored the winning touchdown. Some are defined by family dynamics: Every family has the smart one, the pretty one, the rebellious one, the stubborn one, the religious one, the reliable one—the list goes on.

In life, we change roles all the time. In the course of a day, the dutiful daughter can also be the creative writer, the loving spouse, the watchful mother, the adoring sister, and the outrageous jokester at Girls' Night Out.

Sometimes people are forced to change roles. In Woody Allen's *Blue Jasmine*, the plot revolves around a woman married to a very successful man. She quickly goes from college girl to snob, taking her designer shopping sprees, country houses, racehorses, and fleet of luxury cars for granted. She can't be bothered entertaining her downscale little sister and is willing to ignore her husband's infidelity to keep up her illusions and her lifestyle.

Once her husband is revealed as a Bernie-Madoff-type con man and she's stripped of her wealth, she can't adjust to her new role. She keeps flying first class when she's deeply in debt, and taking a job is far beneath her imagined station in life.

Like Jasmine, too often in business or political negotiations, we assume a role in the beginning and then forget to use our innate flexibility to change roles when that could really help. Worse yet, we see the other people in the room in the roles we assign them and forget to imagine them as anything other than adversaries.

Even people who work together for months and years in formal settings get stuck in their initial impressions. So when we facilitate workshops on collaborative thinking, we open with a very simple exercise. We ask people to pair up with the person they know least in the room. They have two minutes to learn their partner's name and title, why that person is involved in the project and what his or her secret talents are. Then the partners introduce each other to the room.

In every case, coworkers or board members discover that the person they had neatly filed in one role has a totally different role in other settings. There's always astonishment when the quiet finance officer is a kung fu master, or the chairwoman of the board is a competent belly dancer. In larger groups, you might uncover an entire band of musicians or a team of volleyball players.

Once people have revealed another aspect of their personalities, they are much more open to changing roles and to discarding the stereotypes they hold about others.

During the course of a negotiation, roles can, and often should, change. The naysayer on the other side of the table can see the long-term prospects of a successful negotiation and suddenly become a champion. Someone may get promoted into working with you or get transferred away to another country, and the new player will have different views. Someone seen as a taskmaster may shift to a more relaxed role in gathering information. An introvert may suddenly take a leading and outspoken role when talks center on his area of expertise. By being able to assume other roles, an inventive negotiator can trigger unexpected and extremely positive outcomes.

Here's a good example.

War and Peace and Prisoners

For Dr. Bernard LaFayette, one of the most important negotiations of his life featured lunch and the element of surprise. Plus a change in the role he was expected to play.

Dr. LaFayette worked with Martin Luther King Jr. and was with him on the day of his assassination. For the past fifty years, he has taken King's philosophy of nonviolence and taught it to people around the globe. One of the least understood principles of this theory is this:

violent people may want to take your life. But if you have already given your life to the cause of peace, there's nothing left for them to take.

In Colombia, since 1964, up to 30 percent of the country had been controlled by an armed revolutionary group known as FARC (Fuerzas Armadas Revolucionarias de Colombia). Yet, like ordinary people all over the world, people within these areas want to live in peace, so Dr. Lafayette had traveled there to teach his nonviolent methods.

He was visiting a small village, accompanied by the High Commissioner for Peace, a priest, and the governor of that state, when FARC guerrillas decided to seize the coffee produced in the village. Since the dignitaries objected, the guerrillas kidnapped them and took them on a long trek through the jungle. Two of the four would be killed, but by that point the groups had been separated, and Lafayette was traveling with his own band of guards. Their commander, who controlled 400 troops, was known among them for his violence and his need for absolute control. In fact, one of Lafayette's guards was without a hand—it had been chopped off when he killed and ate a wild chicken without the leader's permission.

Lafayette had been a model prisoner, walking for five days up steep mountain paths, and he was limping and about to collapse when he sat down to rest. He was ordered back to his feet by the guards. No resting. So LaFayette stood, but as he did so he glanced at his watch. It was 2:30, and the marchers had not stopped for lunch.

Summoning his limited Spanish, he said "Quiero comer" (I want to eat). In response, the guard stuck his AK-47 into LaFayette's side.

So LaFayette grew more insistent. He walked over to a flat rock, sat down, and said again, "Quiero comer!" For emphasis he added, "Pronto! Aqui!" (Right now, right here).

The guards were astonished and summoned their leader to deal with this prisoner. When he arrived, Lafayette repeated his demands, pointing to his watch, and repeating them a third time.

Now the leader had a decision to make. Clearly, this prisoner has a problem. He doesn't know how to be a prisoner. No training at all. Doesn't he know we're going to kill him?

But LaFayette had decided that if he was going to live, he needed to eat. And if they were going to kill him, well, then he wouldn't need that lunch after all. And he used one of the principles he taught: Unusual but genuine behavior, in extreme circumstances, has the potential to arrest the conscience of your assailant. So he simply changed roles from compliant prisoner to a demanding one.

Perhaps it wasn't his conscience that persuaded the leader, but the leader's own pragmatism. He, too, had a decision to make. He could continue marching with this difficult prisoner, knowing that he'd only become more difficult. He could kill him. Or he could free him.

So lunch arrived. The guards smiled as they ate their tamales—if LaFayette couldn't eat, neither could they. And shortly thereafter, a horse arrived, and the leader ordered LaFayette to mount. As LaFayette had never ridden before, he was a bit reluctant, but faced with the choice between his potential freedom and more marching, he complied.

Of course, he made a beginner's mistake. Grabbing on for dear life, he hooked his feet tightly under the horse's belly. The horse, naturally, reared up. Lafayette's Spanish had run out. He knew enough to get food, but "Whoa" and "Settle down" were beyond his scope.

The guards were laughing after they got the horse calmed down. They taught LaFayette a few basics and sent him on his way down the mountain.

If you'd like to see LaFayette telling this story (and he does it much better than we do), you can watch him on YouTube at http://www.youtube.com/watch?v=pZ57_prZ9e4.

Thus, whether you're promoting peace or stuck on a deal point in negotiations, you can draw a lesson from these professionals: Go eat lunch and think of something unusual to break the impasse—like changing roles.

Role Changes in Grand Negotiations

Sometimes you need to change roles because your partners or your adversaries change. And that can open up a path for more inventive negotiations or close them off entirely.

The front page of the *New York Times* on September 20, 2013, featured three stories—all perfect examples of how role changes can help inventive negotiations. Obviously, we have no idea how these three negotiations will turn out, but each was a positive step in an otherwise stalemated situation.

It's hard to imagine having a worse negotiation partner than former Iranian President Mahmoud Ahmadinejad. The daffy logic of his speeches was matched only by their inflammatory delivery. No Holocaust—really? The *Times* headline, "Iran Said to Seek a Nuclear Accord to End Sanctions," was not even remotely possible while he was in office. Now, however, the new Iranian president, the more moderate Hassan Rouhani, is exchanging olive-branch correspondence with President Obama. Apparently, Rouhani also has the (perhaps weak) assent of the Iranian Supreme Leader, Ayatollah Ali Khamenei. This is a remarkable turn of events given the last decade's war of words and the embargo of Iran.

The change in the person filling the role of Iranian president is just one factor. According to Thomas Erdbrink and Mark Landler of the *Times*, "The [Iranian] leaders considered the tone of Mr. Obama's letter a very promising sign, and paradoxically, they view what they see as America's declining regional influence as a positive. Mr. Rouhani has publically applauded Mr. Obama's decision to refrain from striking Syria for its poison gas attack on its own civilians."

And there's no paradox at all in the Iranians' new reasoning. America's role in the Middle East has changed with our failures in Iraq and Afghanistan and our growing energy independence. Both circumstances provide new perspectives for American leadership and Middle East policy.

The second surprising headline was "A Shift to Diplomacy for Syria and Iran." Reporter David E. Sanger explained that in the rhetorical prelude to violence between the United States and Syria, Russia has taken on a new role, that of mediator. While the chess-playing Russians always seem to have a complex set of motives in diplomacy, perhaps they see an opportunity for a peaceful resolution of the bloody mess that Syria is at this writing. It's a role they've sought before— there's growing evidence that the Soviets were actually involved in attempts to mediate in the conflict between the United States and Vietnam in the 1960s.

Today's diplomatic sea change apparently also benefitted from Secretary of State John Kerry's "offhand" suggestion that further violence could be avoided if the Syrians immediately turned in all their chemical weapons. Perhaps if Vice President Joe Biden had made that suggestion, it would have been easier to sell it as "offhand." Diplomacy is an interesting game, seldom involving creativity, though maybe the Russians can push things in an inventive direction.

The third remarkable headline in the *Times* that day was "Pope Says Church Is 'Obsessed' with Gays, Abortion, Birth Control." Laurie Goodstein reports that very clearly the change in leadership at the Vatican is affecting thinking and potentially policy making in the church. We apologize to those who might object to characterizing this as a kind of negotiation, but literally God only knows how things will work out in this arena.

A Man of Many Roles

First lieutenant, gubernatorial nominee, federal district judge, senator from Maine, US Senate majority leader, champion of NAFTA and

SIDEBAR 10.1

Iraq

Even when tensions are high and the situation is life-threatening, it is possible to shift roles to produce an inventive negotiation.

It was in the early weeks of the war in Iraq, and Iraqis of every faction were hostile to the American troops. Without any government of their own, the Iraqis' sectarian rivalries were surfacing after decades of resentment. Religious leaders were being killed, mosques were blown up, civilians were at risk every time they left their homes, and often even when they didn't.

Without much knowledge of the culture, the American military was trying to slow down the violence and sent troops to guard religious leaders. The presence of heavily armed troops, however, served only to enflame the locals, who took to the streets with their own weapons. Every encounter was a firefight waiting to happen.

A small contingent of American soldiers stepped out of armored vehicles at the opening of a cul-de-sac where a major religious leader was inside his mosque. Sent to protect him, the soldiers had only a single translator.

As they mustered at the street corner, a few passersby quickly gathered and swelled to a crowd. The translator tried to explain that the soldiers were there to protect their leader, but the crowd couldn't hear him or didn't believe him. The people formed a solid, shouting, armed blockade, their weapons trained on the soldiers. One wrong move and hundreds would die.

The young colonel could not perform his mission, and the situation was rapidly deteriorating. Then he did something creative—a move that went against every bit of training he'd ever had and that astonished his troops.

He ordered them to lower their weapons, kneel in the street, and smile.

Thoroughly trained in field combat but also trained to implicitly follow their leader, they complied. The fear still showed on the nineteen-year-old soldiers' faces, but as they knelt, one by one, with their weapons lowered, pointing to the ground, the crowd grew silent. Why would hostile foreign soldiers be kneeling? The colonel then held his rifle high in the air, holding it by the barrel. Another sign of friendship.

As the Iraqis grew quiet, the voice of the translator could be heard. Now the people in the crowd listened and noticeably calmed down. This gave the colonel an opportunity to withdraw his men with no blood shed on either side.

By changing roles, from armed invaders to humble fellow humans, the soldiers transformed a potentially deadly encounter into one of peace.

the WTO, in 1994 he turned down President Clinton's nomination to the Supreme Court. A director of companies such as Disney, Federal Express, Xerox, and the Boston Red Sox, law partner and chairman, and peacebuilder. Twice he's taken a run at the Israel/Palestine conflict, in 2001 and 2009.

But one of George Mitchell's greatest successes came in 1998 when he was mediator of the Northern Ireland peace process. The interesting thing is that this peace was not his first assignment related to The Troubles. At least not directly.

Bill Clinton doesn't like to hear the word no. After Mitchell resigned his Senate seat in 1994 without Clinton's blessing, he turned down Clinton's Supreme Court nomination. The president then asked him to chair a White House Conference on Trade and Investment in Northern Ireland. Mitchell was told at the time it would just take a few days of his time—though it actually took three years.

In this new role Mitchell met with business leaders in Belfast on both sides, unionist and nationalists. Both made arguments he had heard before: "they told me there is a high correlation between unemployment and violence." He had heard this same "nothing stops a bullet like a job" argument from Robert Zoellick (another role changer, most recently president of the World Bank) during the hearings on both NAFTA and the WTO.

Mitchell's work with the trade groups displayed many of his fine traits, particularly his sense of fairness. And those perceptions led to perhaps the most satisfying (and perhaps most emotional) aspects of his career. He was asked to lead a three-person mediation team and chair the all-party peace talks that culminated in the Good Friday Agreement in 1998.

The story of those three years is like a Six Flags rollercoaster. In his book, *Making Peace*,[1] Mitchell still regrets sacrificing family time over what often seemed a hopeless task: disarmament or decommissioning weapons on both sides. Yet, he persisted, thinking outside the box, to stress the suffering from economic deprivation in addition to the violence.

Meanwhile, Mary Robinson was connecting allies from royalty to street fighters. Anne Gallagher, a former nurse, changed roles to found Seeds of Hope, creating dialogue between prisoners and those they'd hurt.

These grassroots peace efforts were bolstered by the economic development Mitchell had come there to promote. Primarily supported by the European Union and American investments in the Republic of Ireland, the great economic divide between the two parts of Ireland began to decrease (see this dramatic change in exhibit 10.1). Income parity in the two countries arrived at about the same time as the peace accords—and all because Mitchell had delivered the message as a business promoter and a peacebuilder.

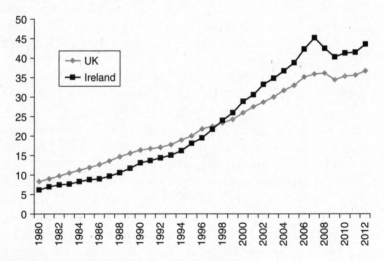

Exhibit 10.1 GDP per capita, UK and Ireland (PPP).
Source: World Bank, WDI online.

We Are in the Midst of the Greatest Crisis of Our Age[2]

The single biggest problem facing Americans in the next twenty years is lurking right in our homes. It's not foreign wars or even terrorism. It's not economic, although many have defined it that way. It's not drugs or diets. No, it's the changing roles of 75 million Americans. The biggest problem facing Americans circa 2014 is the evolving decrepitude of the baby-boom generation. But as Kennedy suggested, this problem can also be seen as an opportunity—for inventive negotiation. Indeed, as Franklin D. Roosevelt once said, "Like charity, peace begins at home."

Happiness is having a large, loving, caring, close-knit family. In another city.

George Burns

The advantage of growing up with siblings is that you become very good at fractions.

Robert Brault

On this topic, humor is important for a couple of reasons. First, a little levity will help us all get through the rather serious adjustments we'll be making to our family lives during the next decades. Second, we know that humor is an important tool for stimulating creative thinking. So, while we very much appreciate the quips by Burns and Brault, the people we've interviewed hold very different views. Today, millions of American families are inventing ways to live together with the rapidly changing needs and constraints of our twenty-first-century society. Their stories are about living *close by* one another to work together creatively and cooperatively *rather than just dividing things up.*

The burgeoning population of older people with their inevitable infirmities, their failing finances[3] and pension systems, the expense of childcare when parents work full time, and the volatility of employment and housing markets are the most obvious challenges facing Americans today. Baby boomers are changing from breadwinner to retiree, parent to grandparent, head of household to negotiator. Increasingly, multigenerational families need creativity to design new structures and interactions as more people live in extended families.

American culture is changing:

1. The retirement and infirmities of American baby boomers are causing a complete restructuring of government and corporate support for elderly in the United States (Social Security and other pension funds, Medicare, and medical care in general). This will be a ten-year process of adjustment that will be difficult for individuals and institutions.
2. Our fifty-year national experiment with nuclear families (the ideal of two parents, two-and-a-half kids, and the white picket fence) is ending. The old and faithful interdependence of extended family relationships is reemerging as a cultural norm.
3. New housing will be built that is appropriate for mixed-age neighborhoods and multigenerational family proximity.

One-third of today's single-family houses can and will accommodate an accessory apartment or some variation of one.

4. The current growth of "boomerang kids," adult children living with their parents in the midst of the present economic travails, is a kind of spring training for the long, hard season of the babyboom retirement years. Millions of Americans are now *re*learning the tricks of balancing proximity and privacy that will be crucial in the next decades.

5. Our unusual American cultural fetish with interpersonal independence will fade away in the next decade, partially in response to economics. And that will lead to different building codes and more creative versions of "home."

In 1940, more than 60 percent of elderly widows lived with their children.[4] By 1990, that number had dropped to less than 20 percent, thanks in large part to Social Security. By 2010, this trend was reversing, for both economic and social reasons (see exhibit 10.2).

Consider the phenomenon known as "boomerang kids." Estimates vary, but according to the US Census Bureau, almost one-third of all Americans between the ages of 18 and 34 are now living with their parents. That's more than 21 million young adults (see exhibit 10.3). A decade ago, newspaper headlines, books, and movies called this phenomenon *Failure to Launch*, and a minority of American parents of twentysomethings were complaining. Now it's clear that boomerang kids are just another symptom of the greater cultural change affecting American society: the reunification of the extended family.

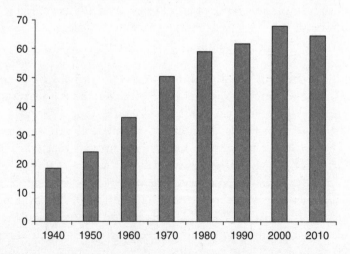

Exhibit 10.2 Percentage of widows over 65 living alone.

Sources: McGarry & Schoeni (1998) and U.S. Census.

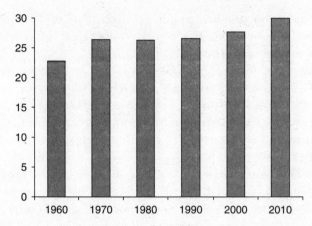

Exhibit 10.3 Percentage of 18–34 year-olds living in parents' home.
Source: U.S. Census.

Grandparents are also moving back in with their children. Three-generation households are on the rise in America, according to the Census Bureau. The Pew Research Center estimates that more than 17 percent of the population—54 million Americans—lived in multigenerational housing in 2011, up from 28 million in 1980. That's 6 percent of all American households (see exhibit 10.4). Moreover, the census understates the trend—folks living next door, across the street, in duplexes, and apartments are not counted. People are moving back

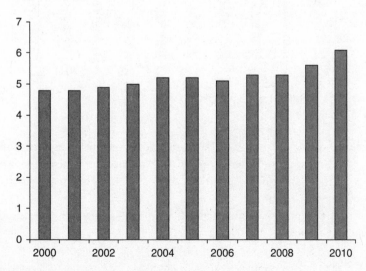

Exhibit 10.4 Percentage of multigenerational households.
Source: AARP analysis of US Census data.

together again because the grand experiment of the World War II generation hasn't worked. Three generations belong together and not just for financial reasons.

Humans have evolved, psychologically and physiologically, to live in extended families. We are happiest in our tribes. And we are quickly learning that other institutions (companies, unions, governments, or religious organizations) ultimately cannot take care of us. Only our families can and will, as they did in those primordial times on the West African savannah.

America's elderly population is now growing at a moderate rate. But not long into this century, the rate will accelerate. According to census projections, the elderly population will double between now and the year 2040 to more than 80 million (see exhibit 10.5). By then, as many as 1 in 5 Americans will be elderly (65 or older). And more than half of them will have at least one disability.

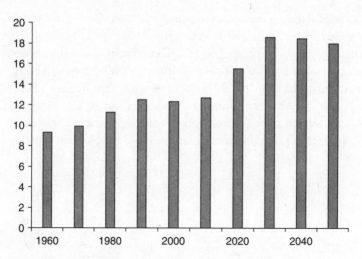

Exhibit 10.5 Percentage of US population over 65
Source: US Census.

These families must negotiate to design communities and homes that will accommodate a fast-graying America in innovative ways. And within those homes, people must keep changing roles to thrive in these new situations.

Like the family in northern California described in the *San Francisco Chronicle*.

It's 5:55 on a Sunday afternoon at the house in Fairfield. Five-year-old Grace Curry walks around ringing a small bell to summon everyone to dinner.

By 6 p.m., they're all seated around the dinner table: Grace's parents, Bernadette, 37, and George Curry, 42; her brother, Jack, 3; her aunt and uncle, Teresa, 41, and Steve Lavell, 42; their children, Jennifer, 15, Michael, 13, and Danny, 11; and her grandparents, Gretchen, 70, and Joe Shilts, 72. The family dog, Roxie, also shows up. They all live in a 6,800-square-foot house on 4.8 acres along the Putah South Canal. The Shiltses live downstairs, and each of the other two families has an upstairs wing.

The idea for the family compound started after Joe was diagnosed with Parkinson's disease in 1999. The five Shilts daughters had all moved out and married, so the Fairfield house where they had grown up was too big and too much work. In the meantime, the Currys and Lavells were outgrowing their Fairfield homes.

Teresa Lavell came up with the idea of everyone living together. She and Steve had moved all over the world while he was an Air Force pilot. After he had completed his service, "She said, 'We're moving back to Fairfield, and then we're going to live together,'" Gretchen Shilts said.

Three of the Shilts daughters and their families had moved away, but the three Fairfield families were already spending time together, "so there was a natural integration of our lifestyles," Bernadette Curry said.

The search for a site began in 2000 and ended with the purchase in November 2000. Next the family settled on an architect, Jacobson, Silverstein & Winslow in Berkeley. "We spent hours not only talking with them but also poring over books" to get ideas, Gretchen Shilts said.

Finding financing for construction was difficult. The family invited loan officers to lunch to explain the dream, but possible default was a worry. Finally a loan officer from First Northern Bank agreed to lend the money. "He caught the vision," she said.

The project cost $1.4 million—the equivalent of $466,666 per family—for the land, design, and construction except for the pool, landscaping, and solar panels.

The Shiltses used some of Joe's retirement money to buy the land, and all three family groups pitched in for the down payment after selling their houses. They own the house as joint tenants, and each family contributes to a joint account that pays for the 15-year mortgage and other shared costs. Although the new house is unique, Joe Shilts estimates that buying three new Fairfield houses suited to each family's needs would have cost "at least twice what we paid." New single-family detached houses in Fairfield can cost anywhere from about $600,000 to more than $1 million.

If the families had built three separate houses, they would have had to buy three lots because city zoning allows only one house on the lot they have. Shilts estimated that three lots would cost a total of $100,000 more than they paid for their land. Construction costs would have totaled nearly $500,000 more.

The entryway is flanked by a hall spanning the center section. The hall is lined with book shelves beneath large windows on the outer wall and openings into the great room with its two-story-high ceiling. On the left end of the great room is a conversation area with a fireplace, TV, piano, a window seat, and another wall of windows overlooking the backyard, which has decks, pool, lawn, and a dry, grassy hillside sloping down to the canal.

The center of the great room is dominated by a long dining table that can seat up to 20. It was the first joint purchase because of "the communal value of sharing a meal," said Bernadette Curry.

This table also has allowed the family to have Thursday night soup suppers during the winter. They started with friends and neighbors who sometimes brought others along, making for lively discussions. "It was a way to have a wider community," George Curry said.

Each family chose the colors for its living area. Colors and other details for the communal areas were collaboratively chosen. "It was work," Gretchen Shilts said. Everyone would meet around the Shiltses' dining room table to make decisions during construction.

Collaboration is a huge key to the success of this living arrangement. Families take turns cooking dinner for a week at a time. Everyone is on his own for breakfast, lunch, and Friday dinner, which often winds up to be leftovers or pizza. The family that cooks also plans the menus and does the grocery shopping.

Housekeeping tasks for the communal areas are divided eight ways and rotate weekly, excusing Joe and the Curry kids. Each family takes care of its own area.

Eating dinner together at 6 p.m. is "quite an experience for the young people," Gretchen Shilts said. It gives everyone a chance to talk about the day.

It's also a chance to head off conflicts, she said, noting that the family spent a lot of time talking about that issue before moving in. The family also tries to have regular meetings for everyone, but the kids are excused when finances are involved. "The chemistry is here to make it work. We have the commitment to one another," said Gretchen, a nurse who works on call as a lay Catholic chaplain with North Bay Hospice.

In planning the house, "we saw it as a marriage of families" and a way "to be there for Mom and Dad," Steve Lavell said. "This isn't an experiment. We're going to make it work."

George Curry agreed. "No matter what happens, we can work it out. It's a more impressive family than it is an impressive house."[5]

SIDEBAR 10.2

Inventing a Grandparent

The attending physician asked, "Who's his next of kin?" Anne Gallagher blurted out, "I guess I am." And ultimately the words made it so.

Seventy-year-old Dick Madden lay in bed in a Dublin hospital ward for indigents dying of pneumonia. The doctors kept him alive, but Anne saved his life. Trained as a nurse, Anne had already changed roles to become Ireland's greatest connector (*tertius iungens,* to use David Obstfeld's more comprehensive term). As founder of a peace-building organization named Seeds of Hope, she seemed to know everybody on the island, North and South, Protestant and Catholic, ex-prisoners and policemen, rich and powerful, and folks in the direst of straights, like Dick. She found common interests and made introductions and thus strengthened the peace that's held in Northern Ireland during the past few decades.

She also rescued people like Dick, a stranger she met on a cold and rainy street and brought to the hospital. She visited him during his recovery, and when he was well, she and her husband, Jerry, moved him into a small flat near their home in a Dublin suburb. Every Sunday, her suppers sustained both his body and soul, and soon they'd given him a key to their front door. In turn, he helped them care for their 14-year-old son, Jared, while they worked full time.

Jared's a youth champion at both hurling and Gaelic football, and his biggest supporter was Dick. He never missed a game and was the community's most ardent fan for five years. During the past year, when Dick's health failed him again, he moved into Anne's house to die, and the three of them kept him comfortable as he faded away.

Dick died at home, surrounded by his adopted family. Jared was holding his hand when he passed, and he kissed Dick's forehead at the services attended by scores in his adopted community. Jared misses his best friend.[6]

With eight siblings to care for her own mother, Anne created new roles for her family, and for Dick that led to a rich and rewarding relationship.

We tell this story with some recent sadness. This past year Anne herself passed. We miss her.

This extended family had changed roles to make their life together work. A decade later, when John interviewed them again, all are still living together in their Fairfield home. The toddlers have become teens, the teens are adults, and parents have become grandparents. The families have discontinued the regular biweekly family meetings but still address problems on an ad hoc basis. Like 50 million other Americans, the family members reinvent their agreements continually. And they've converted a host of dangers into opportunities.

Yes, ten people in three generations and a family dog! Meanwhile, in China, the next decade will reap the harvest of the government's one-child policy—each middle-aged couple will need to care for four parents, and with little social structure in place to care for them, the government is considering passing laws to compel those children to do it. In Ireland, there's an opposite problem. With large families the norm in the 1950s, often there are eight adult children for every grandparent. So some adults have created their own alternatives.

CHAPTER 11

Creating Surprises

The half hour between waking and rising has all my life proved propitious to any task which was exercising invention.

—Sir Walter Scott

Paula Garb has spent her entire life building peace and teaching others to do the same, from gang prevention workers in Los Angeles to international postwar reconciliation councils. She has probably spent more time negotiating than most people do in several lifetimes. And her favorite stories are about the element of surprise.

As an American student in the Cold War years, she took a rare opportunity to study in Moscow. There she met a handsome young Russian, and over the next 20 years she married and raised two children before returning to the United States as a professor at the University of California, Irvine. Her deep knowledge of the language and culture of both countries helped immensely as she studied and then participated in peace negotiations between the former Soviet Georgia and the region of Abkhazia that is seeking recognition as a separate country.

For many years, it was nearly impossible to get the two sides of the conflict to even meet for discussions. After working with grassroots activists, building trust for more than a decade, the two sides had agreed to have a joint meeting where each participant would present a paper on his or her differing point of view.

Before the conference could begin, however, there was the little matter of publishing their recommendations. Generally, conference papers are all published together, either by topic or by alternating points of view. Given the inequity in their relationships (the Georgians have the money, the arms, and the power of the status quo), one Abkhaz participant was adamant that the papers be published as separate books. He believed that publishing together would send an implicit signal that the Abkhazi people had agreed to remaining minions of Georgia.

Rational arguments simply did not work. It's always done that way. It's too expensive to publish two books. The more the Georgians insisted, the more he resisted. After a long morning, the participants took a break for lunch. Paula tested different arguments with the remainder of the Abkhazi contingent, but nothing they could invent would satisfy him.

After lunch, talks resumed, with both teams now having no expectation of agreement. Then the Georgian negotiator did something unexpected. He gave in. "You know," he said, "I'm OK with two publications." And at that point the stubborn Abkhazi let go of his resistance. Once the atmosphere in the room felt equal, he agreed that it made more sense to publish together.

One final hurdle: Which side would get the opening paper? Being the first paper, or even taking the first half of the book, might suggest that one side had prevailed. Taking a clue from academic negotiations about publishing she'd experienced, Paula jumped in with a simple suggestion: Alphabetical?

Both sides considered, nodded, and the conference planning was allowed to proceed. One small step toward lasting peace between two regions long hostile to each other.

Even if you're not guiding an international peace conference or matching wits with a band of guerrilla fighters in a tropical jungle, there are ways to bring elements of invention to every negotiation. The techniques come from innovation workshops, theater, sociology and psychology experiments, plus decades of trial and error in the field. You may already have used some of them without realizing that they are sophisticated and proven. They can be used in inventive sidebar negotiations (that is, "parallel informal negotiations," using Lawrence Susskind's terms, or "prenegotiating," using Howard Raiffa's terms as described in chapter 1) or to help break impasses. Consider how you—or your facilitator—might use these to stimulate imagination.[1]

Make a Small Offer

You've done your homework. Selected the right team members. Set up a friendly atmosphere. Arranged to meet in a congenial space. Perhaps even identified shared goals. Yet once you enter the room, everything changes. The old script automatically kicks in: You are on one side of the table championing the forces of good. Your enemy is on the other side, representing the forces of evil. You need to win.

So your first surprising move is to lose something. Of course, it is something you have planned in advance that is of little consequence to you or the future outcome of your collaboration. It may be something that was thrown into earlier failed negotiations, or it may be something you invent. In your research, perhaps you've discovered that it's really a minor issue for the other side. But it should still be a worthy negotiating point.

This may well be what the Georgian negotiator did in the story that began this chapter. He probably knew that there was no money to publish two reports, so he surprised the other side by giving up something that really made little difference to him or the outcome. His surprise might have been planned.

The earlier you spring this offer, the better. First, it breaks that old stereotype: you are not an evil enemy, prepared to fight to the death over every detail. It changes your role dramatically. Oddly enough, by giving up something, you put yourself in the role of the gracious host, and the others may begin to follow that leadership.

You see this dynamic in many indigenous cultures around the world, where gift-giving is both the start of negotiation and the expression of power: The one who gives the most lavish gifts is perceived as the most powerful.

Celebrate Small Wins

Once that offer has been accepted (and you should have done enough research to make sure it will be), the whole team can chalk it up as a win.

This establishes a new pattern—one of cooperation, so that everyone begins to feel like the whole group is one team working together. More important, it is an early success, establishing that this team can accomplish things quickly. If somebody has to call back to the head office to report at the first break, that person can honestly say that the group is already making progress. Some boxes on that long list are being checked off.

It also changes the self-perception of everyone in the room. Instead of feeling cautious and distrustful, they feel confident and successful.

And people who are negotiating from strength are always more generous than those who feel they're hanging on by their fingernails and have much to lose.

To reinforce that feeling, celebrate the win with a toast. Obviously, if this offer and acceptance is early in the morning, you may be "toasting" with coffee and a bagel, but make it a small ceremony.

At this point, the break gives you an opportunity to introduce another surprise element.

Change Chairs

Whether you're in a traditional setting around a big table or you've managed to start your negotiation in a more informal setting, chances are very good that you're sitting in adversarial positions: one team lined up on one side, the other team on the other.

Sometimes it's even worse, as in the Japanese *aisatsu* cited in chapter 8: you've been silently manipulated into taking seats by power ranking, and you're not the one in power.

So change it up. Whatever you suggest for the celebration, it should include getting out of your chairs—walking to the buffet for coffee or standing to list something on a whiteboard. While people are up, suggest an informal discussion about something relating to that win or the next steps and form cross-teams for a few minutes of discussion.

This is actually harder than it seems. Humans are by nature territorial, and that instinct governs behavior from the first moment they enter a room. In a classroom, you can guess at future behavior by where people sit: the eager learners are at the front, the reluctant ones in the back. Extroverts sit casually next to strangers; introverts skip a chair or two. But everyone creates a personal space—much like dogs lifting their legs at the corners of the street, people set out their markers: water bottle here, briefcase just here, coat draped, chair at a particular angle, pen and paper lined up just so. If you don't create a different seating plan, people will automatically head for the same space and configuration for the duration. And they'll be annoyed if a visitor or newcomer accidently sits in that space.

When people arrive at creative workshops, faced with sofas and beanbag chairs, they often ask where they are supposed to sit. When we tell them it doesn't matter, they'll be moving soon, they are always disoriented.

You expect that possessive behavior in a workplace, even for creative people who seem to thrive in chaos. Famously, when Apple's advertising agency, Chiat Day, moved into a revolutionary new space designed by a prominent architect, people weren't assigned a work space in order to foster more group interaction and creativity. They instead had little rolling carts to keep their work papers, and they were to check out computers each day and hang out wherever they wanted in the bright, tree-filled space.

People were miserable. They wanted their own spaces, places for photos of their kids and dogs, spots they could retreat to or simply where other people could find them the next day. The television producer created a space for herself by building a wall using big audition tapes as individual bricks. Needless to say, in the company's next building, along with lots of creative collaboration spaces, there were dedicated spaces where people could establish their nests.

Asking people to change seats will make them uncomfortable. Someone else will be in their recently established territory, next to their briefcases and water bottles. And they will feel like trespassers in someone else's space. The first time you ask, you will get resistance.

Here's where your facilitator comes in handy.[2] As a participant, you can't suggest how the negotiations are to be conducted while you're in the room. But you can suggest ahead of time how you'd like the day to proceed and what the ground rules could be.

So your facilitator can overcome that resistance by establishing the possibility of movement early in the day. He or she can tell people they'll be forming small work groups all day, and so briefcases should be stashed against an outer wall to make it easier to shift from one team to another. This is a neutral move, and people tend to follow that kind of logistics instruction from a facilitator.

If your facilitator didn't establish that rule before you began, she can make the first move seem temporary by asking people to find a space for a five-minute discussion. Once they've moved for those five minutes, those temporary teams report out from their new spaces, and then the facilitator just moves on to the rest of the agenda—leaving people slightly uncomfortable, but in their new chairs.

Given the difficulty of operating against instinct, it may not seem worthwhile to change chairs, but the change has two important benefits. First, it changes the adversarial environment. Unconsciously, people will feel that they are operating in a new team. Because they are without the briefcase and water bottle walls they've built to establish their territories, they will be more open to offers and suggestions.

If seating has been established by power ranking, this change is even more important. If those rankings aren't physically reinforced every minute by the seating chart, people may feel a bit more powerful and able to contribute their own suggestions.

All of this leads to the second reason for changing seats. Recent studies show that when you change the composition of the temporary teams, you vastly increase the flow of new ideas.[3] If you want to foster inventive thinking from everyone in the room, keep finding excuses to get people working in different temporary teams.

Now that you've established a winning and creative atmosphere, you can begin applying some new techniques to keep that spirit alive through the interactions to come. You are starting a journey together, but for most people the end goal is just splitting that first pie. You need to get partway through the journey before you can share a bigger vision and head for the pie factory. This means that you should start using some different techniques in the very next stage.

Random Juxtaposition

The first one is sharing startling information.[4] Because people come into the room with their own points of view and information, find five to eight things that everyone is not likely to know and have your facilitator pass out one page descriptions of those findings.

The findings can be your industry statistics with their implications. For example, imagine that you want to negotiate a distributorship in a new country. You might present something like: In our country, 40 percent of consumers use our product in a certain way. In the prospective target country, only 10 percent of people do. By informing the new consumers of additional ways to use our product, we could quadruple our sales.

Or you could be borrowing ideas from other industries. The best examples may be from industries far from your own—one hospital chain used lessons from Nascar pit crews to inform discussions with their staff about hospital admitting procedures.

At first glance, this may not seem like the most efficient way to start a negotiation. But it is a proven way to get even the most moribund thinkers to begin imagining more possibilities. It's a technique called random juxtaposition, which just means putting two random things together. Thomas Edison is probably the most famous inventor who relied on the technique—when he wanted a filament that would burn for a long time inside his new lightbulb, he tested thousands of random materials: spare parts from machines, bits of cotton and wire, even weeds from the parking lot.

Of course you can't just hand out a piece of paper and expect a new light bulb. You have to get the teams engaged. So your facilitator should invite people with similar skills—say, engineers or lawyers from each side—to pair up and make a list of all the ways that new information could change their approach to the issue that's currently on the table.

For example, suppose the topic is as mundane as the term of a proposed contract. One side wants it short; the other wants more time to build its new client base. The startling news you bring could include items about companies that work with month-to-month contracts and companies that immediately forge twenty-year deals. It could showcase unique triggering methods, such as flexible contracting approaches, a topic that will be covered in some detail in chapter 14.

When your facilitator asks your teams to think about how they could work together under those different scenarios, they'll discover a wide range of possibilities and put more options on the table. You won't end up with a frustrating fight over three-year versus five-year contracts, and more important, everyone will have the experience of creating new possibilities themselves.

There are four rules of engagement that make random juxtaposition discussions most productive.

Maximize Ideas

First, the facilitator must emphasize that you're looking for more options, not necessarily good options. The vast majority of good ideas are stillborn because people self-censor and never even say them out loud. Even silly options can lead to inventive outcomes, but they can't spark discussion if they're never offered.

Speed

The second condition that encourages creative thought is speed. Research shows that more ideas are generated in five-minute brainstorming sessions than in thirty-minute ones.[5] When people think they must perform quickly, they do. And the short time limits keep people from overthinking, and thus criticizing, the ideas that emerge. In our executive workshops, we've actually found that two minutes is the optimal time for generating ideas from random juxtaposition.

And because some people are introverts and some extroverts, here's the best way to structure these brainstorming minisessions:

- Two minutes for people to silently write down their ideas (brightly colored Post-it notes are ideal for capturing ideas without too much detail)
- Two minutes to share the ideas with each other
- Three minutes to add to their shared list and improve on the ideas together[6]

Sharing Ideas

The third rule is to have all the teams share their ideas, briefly, with the group, even if they are working on different parts of the same issue.[7] We usually give teams one or two minutes to share all their ideas. So if you have eight people in the room, you're likely to get 20 different ways to approach the issue in less than 15 minutes, with no hard feelings and little room for hidden agendas or power plays. Now you see why the method is pretty efficient after all.

Reject Nothing

The final condition is that you cannot rank or prioritize these ideas immediately. The human brain likes novelty, but not too much. People also like safety, and new ideas may seem strange and dangerous when they are first presented—especially if they aren't your own ideas.

So, just leave all those fledgling ideas lying on the table. At this point, everyone feels productive and invigorated. Solving a problem quickly actually releases oxytocin in the brain, the same rewarding chemical boost you get from good sex or laughing with friends.

While everyone is walking around in this fine chemical glow, consider what you've accomplished so far:

1. You've proved that your entire team can agree on the issue you offered first.
2. You've acknowledged and celebrated that victory.
3. You've created cross-functional teams from each side that have successfully worked together.
4. You've established that everyone in the room is creative and has good ideas.
5. You're well on your way to solving the first difficult issue in novel ways.
6. You've eliminated the automatic adversarial mindset.

And you've accomplished all that in less than an hour. You definitely deserve a break.

Breaks

A break at this point is not just a chance to relax. It's a scientifically proven way to get consistently better outcomes.[8] Here's why: human beings were not made for sitting still and concentrating. Our ancestors on the plains of Africa were not likely to survive long, whether they were hunters or gatherers, unless they kept moving. You know this subjectively if you've ever suffered through an hour-long PowerPoint presentation after lunch. Or even fidgeted through a two-hour movie that your spouse selected. In executive workshops, we've found that 20 minutes is about the longest you can keep people focused in the same chairs, even if they are actively participating.

What you do with that break is important too. With today's technology, a totally unstructured break will usually result in people checking their e-mail, and that successful feeling will dissolve in worries about the plumbing problem at home or the package that did not get delivered at the office. Obviously, busy executives will need to stay in communication, but your facilitator can limit those check-ins to longer breaks when the discussions will have more time to recover afterwards.

Your facilitator should suggest that the five- to seven-minute break is to accommodate both bathroom breaks and a few minutes to glance at all the ideas literally lying on the table. If you've used sticky notes for capturing raw ideas, the facilitator can stick them up on a nearby window or wall to encourage people to mill around in front of them. Lists generated by the subgroups can also be taped to a window.

You've now created a situation that most negotiators never face. Let's assume you're still working on that term of contract issue. In a standard negotiation, each side would by now be offering slight compromises—four years instead of five on one side, three years instead of two on the other. But you have 20 options now, and somebody has to choose the ones to work on.

Sidebars

There are several ways to tackle this dilemma. The facilitator can appoint a small subgroup to discuss those alternatives later in the day. Or participants can volunteer. Either way, that issue seems solvable since there are so many possibilities, and the good mood is maintained to move on to another topic.

The downside of this method is that for people who are used to working in a linear fashion, this approach leaves them hanging. They want closure; they want a decision, right here, right now. A good facilitator will make an educated guess about whether this approach might work or not.

Idea Selection

Another approach is to decide on perhaps five of the twenty options that could be debated later in a subgroup. One way to do this is to give every participant three colored sticky dots (the same color) and ask each one to affix them next to the three ideas they think would be the most productive possibilities. In our executive workshops, this provides some measure of control, promotes egalitarian values since everyone has the same number of votes, and results in surprising consensus around the best ideas. Instantly, without debate, the less promising ideas are off the table, without any wasted time or hurt feelings.

For some people with an outstanding need for control, however, this very egalitarian voting is frustrating precisely because it is egalitarian. In hierarchical companies or cultures, the idea that the leader will not make the decision is heresy.

In this case, the facilitator can make the rules clear: the ideas will be discussed later in a subgroup (for which the leader can volunteer if this is a big issue). That group will cull the list of options down to three, make suggestions, and the decision makers can ultimately decide from those three selections.

One successful step in negotiation accomplished, it's time to try some new techniques.

Thinking Backward and Flying Monkeys

After you've dealt successfully with a couple of items on your list of issues, you have a whole different team from the one you started with in the early morning. They are working together, maybe even laughing at times, and they know they can deal even with difficult issues. Yet at this stage, all of them are still working from the vision they entered the room with: we are going to get through this negotiation intact, and we won't lose our share of that pie.

Here's where you can change that vision to a vision of the pie factory, and all the participants will believe they envisioned it themselves. First, you have to create that vision and then you simply work backward to figure out how to achieve it.

It's best to start when people are relaxed, fed, and have had a change of scenery. Depending on your schedule, that means after a lunch with time for a walk among the trees.[9] If you're not at a resort or near a park, even a window with a view of treetops will help.[10]

Thinking Big

Getting a group to dream big is not an easy process, particularly when the group members have come to the meeting believing that they are on separate teams. Again, here's where a skilled facilitator can make all the difference. It's time for your facilitator to suggest a short break in the substantial progress you've already made.

In an ideal world, you'd call this a blue-sky exercise. In reality, those words will immediately produce resistance, especially from technical or financial people who are likely to be in your meeting. They came here to get something done and don't want to be distracted talking about things that will never happen.

Most engineers, scientists, and financiers, however, are very comfortable with creating what-if scenarios. Often those scenarios are for disaster control, though, so you need to shift the focus. The best way to get people to think big is to demonstrate how other people have done it, so here's where the facilitator can add information.

The first step is to collect stories of other collaborators who have achieved things they had never imagined—from your industry, other fields, maybe from this book. Find five stories, tell them in a couple of sentences each, and have the facilitator pass out that information to three-person cross-functional teams.

The facilitator sets up the rules: You have three minutes to imagine the world 10 years from now if this collaboration led to a hugely successful partnership. What would it look like? What would you be building? What share of market would you have? In which countries? How would you maximize the talents of each participant? (And while you're at it, solve world hunger and create peace.)[11] Some groups call this a Big Hairy Audacious Goal. Everyone silently jots down thoughts on brightly colored Post-it notes.

In the next step there's one more rule: since this is an imaginary scenario, there's no room for "yeah, but." When people share their thoughts, the only comment should be "yes, and." The facilitator gives teams five minutes to share their ideas and create a unified scenario that includes their best ideas and ones they create together during the discussion. Then they briefly share their vision with the whole group. So far, in total 10–12 minutes have elapsed.

Here's where the process often fails because reality sets in, and people have been trained to be linear thinkers. When they create next year's plan, they start from where they are. The barriers arise. Expectations dim. Version 2.0 is rarely much of an improvement over this year's version because people don't want to be held accountable for failure.

The cure for this limited thinking is to think backward. The facilitator gives each team two minutes to answer this question: What would the world have to look like in eight years in order to achieve what you see in ten years? What would need to be in place at that stage? Then each team gets six minutes to answer the same questions for year six, year four, and year two. Finally, two minutes for what they'd need to do next year to reach year two. During the whole thought experiment (Einstein's terminology), they are to assume that any barriers they imagine can be overcome. Ten minutes for this whole experiment; a total of 20 minutes has elapsed.

In executive workshops, we call it "If Monkeys Could Fly." The term comes from a conversation Lynda Lawrence had on a long flight from Geneva to California. Her seatmate was a director of innovation for Johnson and Johnson and she asked what he did when his research teams hit an insoluble problem.

He explained that his division made stents (tiny metal scaffolding designed to hold open clogged arteries). The problems his people dealt with were most often with the metal—it was hard to make something durable that would stand up in the long term and not cause blood clots. And metals are metals—they have certain properties that no amount of wishing can change.

When his engineers encountered a problem that would otherwise stymie them, they simply set it aside and proceeded with the phrase, "Oh, yeah, and if monkeys could fly." As he explained it, rather than get bogged down in reality, they just thought about how it could work if that particular monkey weren't in the way. And by imagining a positive outcome, they could often work backward and see a different way around or under or over that barrier. "Right. Let's put jetpacks on that monkey." And more often than not, they created new ways to combine metals or try coatings that would make their creations work in the real world.

To incorporate this technique into negotiation, your facilitator can borrow this story and this term, or simply talk about barriers and explain the process: Five minutes to identify barriers. (We find that resources, staff, money, and time almost always appear.) Then five minutes to pick their five most troubling monkeys and figure out who could adopt them. In other words, should they encounter these difficulties along the way, which person in their organization or among the people they know or have access to could help eliminate this barrier?

Often the person who could adopt the monkey is already in the room.

As one executive at a technology firm once told us, "It's amazing how we have no money in the budget for anything. But when our CEO falls in love with a new project, the money appears."

It's magic—or the power of a vision.

The break is over. You've spent half an hour, and everyone in the room is thinking in a larger way. The possibilities are lurking in their imaginations. Step five is to integrate that bigger vision into your discussions, and this is very simple. The facilitator asks if there are any new items that should be added to the agenda for further discussion today or later.

No one had to agree to those visions. They haven't spent a year making those plans. But the door to the future is open wide.

Sleeping on It

If you have the luxury of keeping the negotiating teams together for parts of two days, you have a unique opportunity. Because the single most productive thing you can do on your journey to the pie factory is to let people sleep on it.

Humans evolved to exploit opportunities. They're very good at it, even if they don't realize it. In fact, the subconscious brain is at work when we think we've pulled something from our rational brains during the day and always when we're sleeping.

Numerous studies prove that people learn more, produce more new solutions, and cooperate more with new teams when they've had a chance to sleep between sessions.[12] Even if they have only taken a nap.[13]

Often, at the end of a long negotiating day, participants are left with an issue that is not resolved. Or two or five. And here's where the facilitator can play another important role—by asking them specifically *not* to think about the problem. Instructions for the evening include: eat, drink, have fun, sing, dance, laugh. But do not, under pain of death, think about these unresolved issues.

Of course, in addition to being problem solvers, most humans also get a kick out of breaking the rules. Or at least their subconscious brains do. Just ask a group of people *not* to think about white tigers, and they'll have trouble thinking about anything else but those tigers.

In our experience in two-day workshops, for about two-thirds of day one's insoluble problems a solution occurs to someone while he or she is drifting off to sleep, showering, or taking a morning run. The stories of famous inventors are full of those inspirations: Einstein's theory of relativity. The structure of DNA. The helium balloon. After thoroughly immersing themselves in the problem, these creative people made the decisive leap when they weren't thinking at all.

If you have a two-day session, you might want to anticipate a half hour first thing in the morning to hear those unrequested, unexpected, truly inventive solutions.

There's also lots of science about eating, drinking, and playing that can improve your outcomes. Depending on the participants and their personalities, you may want to try some of the techniques that have been proven to work.

The simplest is eating. Remember that the word for working together is collaboration, from *co-* and *laboring*. But forming even stronger bonds—say, a companion or a company—comes from the Latin *con pane*, "with bread."

In our executive workshops and MBA classes, we have long known that a little candy goes a long way toward boosting creativity. We hand out miniature candy bars to teams who have the most ideas in two minutes or to those with the most creative solutions, or to groups that laugh the most. When people are working hard on a project together, we hand out bowls of M&Ms, which we call thinking pills. Now there's even a study proving that candy makes people happier and thus more creative.[14]

Of course, nutritious food works too. We supply generous fruit and bagel trays, nuts, and veggies along with cookies, crackers, cheese, and wine. Unexpected offerings like these seem to have even more effect than when they're on the agenda, so you might add these to your surprising techniques on negotiation days.

If food in the negotiating room is wise policy, lunch and dinner can really improve teamwork and outcomes. Just eating together can help form the bonds that lead to long-term relationships, as people find interests and friends in common. A little wine can help the process too (though we don't think we need to spell out the perils of a little too much wine).

Finally, the activities planned for the evening hours can demonstrably improve innovation. Five minutes of predinner play—say, a trivia game—using pairs and assigning them colors for competition can mix up the teams again and boost creativity.[15] Singing and dancing are a plus.[16] In fact, any kind of synchronized physical activity builds bonds.[17] For a complete list of ways to boost your team's performance, check "82 Ways to Generate More Ideas" in the appendix. And don't embarrass yourself too much while you're line dancing.

Beg, Borrow, or Steal

Consider a typical US citizen, who begins breakfast with an orange originally cultivated in the eastern Mediterranean, a cantaloupe that first came from Persia, or perhaps a cup of coffee that still comes from the hills of eastern Africa. After her fruit and first coffee, she goes on to waffles, cakes made by a Scandinavian technique from wheat domesticated in Asia Minor. Over these she pours maple syrup, invented by the Native Americans of the northeastern woodlands. As a side dish, she may have the eggs of a species of bird domesticated in Indochina or thin strips of the flesh of an animal domesticated in eastern Asia that have been salted and smoked by a process developed in northern Europe. While eating, she reads the news of the day, imprinted in characters invented by the ancient Semites on a material invented in China by a process also invented in China, or more recently, she may read the news on a computer with parts from all over the world, but most likely assembled in China.[18]

Like this breakfast scenario, many of our basic ideas about inventive negotiation are borrowed from others. Some are from the great international negotiators of the world, the Dutch and the Japanese, and much of what we recommend will sound quite familiar to them.

For example, it's easy to get Japanese negotiators in close physical proximity—they've been living that way for millennia. And it's easy for them to work in small groups with others—since executives may have worked in several functional areas, they understand their peers, eliminating the "silo effect" that can occur in American firms.

As for physical movement, picture the start of the day at a typical Japanese factory—with group chanting and physical exercise. Singing? The Japanese invented *karaoke*—even when you can't do it well. Taking breaks is the norm too.

Not criticizing solutions too early? The Japanese already have difficulty criticizing others, especially foreigners. And scientific studies prove that Japanese are even more likely than Westerners to use visuals and holistic thinking, two of the shifts that are imperative in inventive negotiation.

Of course, culture also explains why some of these techniques will *not* be comfortable for Japanese negotiators. Diversity is not their strong suit—purposefully adding women and other ethnic groups would seem odd to them. And they are not known for their inherent creativity, despite their new focus on it: in Japanese elementary schools, columns of third graders bow and chant their school motto in unison. Ironically, that motto might include "we will be independent thinkers."

Chinese negotiators may also be uncomfortable with many creative techniques, even as they address a creativity gap vis-à-vis the United States. Ann Hulbert in the *New York Times Magazine* recently asked the uncomfortable questions: Can China create schools that foster openness, flexibility, and innovations? And what happens to China if it does? She adds, "Even as Americans seek to emulate China's test-centered and math-focused pedagogy, Chinese educators are trying to promote a Western emphasis on critical thinking at home.... Throughout China, middle school exams have been abolished and vacation review classes are widely discouraged.... The Chinese government worries that too many students have become the sort of stressed-out, test-acing drone who lacks the skills necessary in the global marketplace."[19]

In addition to the skills inventive negotiators have already borrowed from the Japanese, there are two that Americans should also embrace.

First, the Japanese are the absolute champion information vacuums on the planet. They keep their mouths shut and let everyone else do the talking, and thus, they use the diversity of their international colleagues (customers, suppliers, competitors, scientists, etc.) to a greater extent than any other society. We often disparage this approach as copying and borrowing, but being open to everyone's ideas has always been the key to creativity and human progress. The Japanese, like everyone else around the world, are ethnocentric. But at the same time they very much respect foreign ideas.

Second, the Japanese prefer to work with dolphins, individuals who can swim together and rely on one another for protection. Trust and creativity go hand in hand. And the Japanese even train their partners to behave more like a dolphin for their own good: witness the 25-year joint venture between Toyota and General Motors, the successful NUMMI plant in Fremont, CA, or the decades-long collaboration between Mitsubishi and Boeing.

What's more, while Lawrence Susskind and his colleagues should be credited with introducing "consensus building" to Americans in 1987,[20] that's an approach the Japanese were using in negotiations decades earlier. And decades before Henry Chesbrough published *Open Innovation*,[21] the Dutch were perfecting it. Of course, both the Japanese and Dutch have also been wise enough to borrow from the United States. The folks at Philips Research, for example, learned all about innovation techniques from the Silicon Valley gurus such as David Kelley at IDEO.

One reason Americans have trouble borrowing is our cultural ethnocentricity. Like people everywhere, we think our country and our ideas are the best, even when they are demonstratively not.

For example, who has the best health care system? The United States has the best health care technology, but it doesn't deliver the longest lifespans. The Japanese rank best in that category. The World Health Organization says the French deliver the best health care—and on their list, the Japanese are 10th and we're down at number 37. We do have the most expensive health care system in the world, spending more than $8,000 per person annually; the Japanese spend about $4,000. Or consider our southern neighbor—Cuba spends $400 annually per patient and achieves pretty much the same longevity as the United States with WHO rankings just two places below ours. While the Cubans don't have the best technology, their delivery system is very efficient and effective. Perhaps we should be borrowing good health care ideas from both these island nations.

CHAPTER 12

Improvising

"Yes, and..." When each person in an improvisation agrees that this imaginary item is indeed a large beach ball, the interaction spirals upward.

—Eli Simon

I n the history of mankind, there are a fair number of stories about people negotiating their way out of prison, but very few about people negotiating their way into one.

Luke Boughen and Gwendolyn Oxenham were soccer fanatics. He was a leading player at Notre Dame, and she was the youngest NCAA player and goal scorer at Duke, who went on to play for the women's professional soccer league. When the league folded and he graduated, they found themselves suddenly without an outlet for their love of the game.

So they set out to play soccer in pickup games around the world. They scraped together a tiny budget, enlisted a pair of film-school friends from Duke, and headed for Brazil, where Gwendolyn had played in a summer league. In Brazil and Argentina, they simply asked people on the street until they were directed to the best pickup games in the city: they each joined a team and their crew of two filmed the game.

Then the group arrived in Bolivia, where the best pickup soccer is played in the San Pedro prison. As Gwendolyn describes it in her book, *Finding the Game*:[1]

> A game in a prison sounds extraordinarily far-fetched. Would we wander up to the gate, our backpacks stuffed with cameras, put our hands on the bars, and say, "Can we come in?"

Pickup games are spontaneous . . . that's not how prisons work. There's bureaucracy. We probably needed to obtain permission months in advance. Even if we had that kind of time, where would we start? Do we send an email?

Working from an internet café across the street from the prison, they eventually found a phone number and talked to a prisoner inside, who couldn't help them. Going through official channels wouldn't help much because in San Pedro "the inmates are in charge. The guards patrol the outside; they do not enter the inside."

The intrepid young filmmakers tried anyway. They showed a post-card with the name of the film they were attempting to make. They were shown a side door with a sign above it that read "Director." Someone shooed them away and told them to go to the embassy. After a long taxi ride, the filmmakers discovered the embassy was closed.

The next day they asked the owner of an Internet café, who promptly whistled to some guards walking by, and the guards, in turn, took them to the same office where they'd been kicked out the day before.

A bald man with eyeglasses sits down at the desk without speaking to us. He writes out directions on a pink sheet of paper. "Go to the Bolivian Ministry of Prisons," he says. "You must speak to Alejandro. If he gives you permission, you may talk to the prisoners." He stands up and shakes our hands. "It is difficult, but not impossible."

At eight the next morning we sit at a conference table. Alejandro has a scar running the length of his face. Everything's in Spanish.

There's nodding, shaking hands, and when they reached the elevator, Gwendolyn asked Luke "Did we get it? Permission?"

"The prisoners are the ones who ultimately decide," Luke says, pulling up the hood on his sweatshirt as though preparing for covert operations.

Since only two of the team spoke or understood any Spanish, those two went to negotiate. On their return, the four sat on the bed.

"We explained the film . . . "Luke says.

"They listened with, like, rapt attention," Ferg says.

"They were enthusiastic—got it right away. Made all these insightful comments about the connectivity of the world's game. And then they said, "Now for the painful part . . . what it's going to cost you."

"You must bring fruitcakes for one-fourth the prison."

At first the filmmakers thought they hadn't heard right. Then they did the math and asked, "How will we carry three hundred fruitcakes?"

The prisoners assured them that all they needed to do was bring the money, and the prisoners would buy the fruitcakes. The sum was about five hundred dollars, but there was one more glitch: "'They say you can't play. No women. They seemed pretty adamant.'"

Since they had gotten this far, the crew showed up at the gate, and the guards let Luke enter. "I use my pointer finger to signal I'd like to go in too. Eyebrows raised, he says something, and even though I don't speak Spanish, I know he's saying 'You too?' I nod as though I know for sure that I want to go in there." The group used the same process to get Ryan and Ferg through the gate.

Inside they found a city with prisoners and their women and children, food cooking, everyone dressed as they please. The filmmakers went up a flight of stairs into a room where the prisoners who ran the place were waiting.

> Luke hands them an envelope of cash and says in Spanish, "Here's the first part."
>
> Here is the first part: we have this idea, formed from watching action movies, that we'd split up the cash, give them half of it up front, half once we're out safe.
>
> I watch the thick gold rings on Teofilo's fingers as he thumbs through the money. We wait for him to realize it is only half of what we said we'd bring. He finishes counting and looks up at Luke.
>
> Luke clears his throat and tries to explain. His voice trails off. I sink back into the couch. Had we really thought we were going to go into a prison and call the shots?
>
> "No," Teofilo says. "Give us all of it now."
>
> Luke doesn't hesitate. He hands over the second envelope.

Here's the next problem. The prisoners had asked for enough money for 375 fruitcakes, about $500. The crew had brought only $400, thinking they could just act innocent, as if they couldn't do the math.

> Teofilo licks his thumb as he fans through bills. "*Tres mil bolivianos*," he calls out. The man across the room nods approval, and Teofilo reaches under the desk and pulls out a yellow fruitcake carton. Maybe they really do buy fruitcakes.

One more hurdle: Gwen is not supposed to play. The crew walked into the courtyard, past the popcorn vendor, the man with the fresh six-inch gash bleeding from his side, the signs advertising cell phones for sale, the laundry drying in the sun. After a short conversation with the players, Luke turned to her. "Gwenny, you can play."

Both of them played their hardest. Gwen stole the ball from a strong, graceful player. He fell, she stayed up. Later she learned that he was a famous criminal, in prison for murder. At the end of the game "a prisoner with tattoos of a heart and barbed wire on his forearm crouches down and pours warm Fanta into a pink plastic cup that looks straight out of a little girl's tea set."

The footage of the money coming out of the ATM, the tense scene at the transfer, and the game on that courtyard, painted with a mural of a giant tiger in a soccer uniform, are some of the most compelling in their film, *Pelada*.

In the end, everybody got what they wanted—and a little more. The lesson for inventive negotiation, however, is pretty simple: You have to get the right people to the negotiating table. And you have to stay pretty flexible.

Like everything else in life, in negotiation, Murphy's law applies: Anything that can go wrong, will go wrong.

In fact, even the extreme version is often in play: If anything just cannot go wrong, it will go wrong anyway.

Another Pitch in the Dark

Skilled negotiators have developed strategies for dealing with sudden emergencies, but even novices can learn them. It all starts with the attitude that anything can change at any time. For example, the key negotiator on the other team, the one you've studied and with whom you've cultivated a long-term relationship, breaks a leg and can't travel to your meeting. Or on the morning of the big meeting, you wake to the news that the company you're negotiating with has been sold. Or in a cross-cultural setting, someone may commit an unforgivable offense, and the other side walks out. The list of negative possibilities is endless.

Some situations just require a little tap-dancing at the moment, such as the time Lynda Lawrence's advertising agency was pitching a huge client. One of three agencies invited to the final meeting, her agency had assembled an elaborate demonstration of its services. Lynda and her team had negotiated rights to the music they proposed to use and recorded two versions for different markets. They'd enlisted subcontractors with stellar credentials and met all the government contracting requirements in advance. They'd created three alternative campaigns with multiple ads in print, TV, outdoor, radio, and collateral, complete with illustrated storyboards and recordings. They developed a media buying partnership to save millions of dollars and had partnered with a public relations agency to reach impossible-to-reach communities. They'd manufactured prototypes of premiums and outlined all costs and plans for the next five years in six-inch binders that had been distributed two weeks in advance to the 14 decision makers who had to agree on selecting the ad agency. Finally, they'd rented thousands of dollars of sound systems, lights, computers, projection and display equipment, including the necessary union contracts, in Sacramento, California.

After a week of rehearsal, the agency team felt ready for prime time. The 12 key executives and major subcontractors flew in from around the state. It was a high-stakes game because the client could provide solid revenue through a recession when other agencies were going under. Months of work would culminate in this two-hour meeting. The team had already negotiated the prime spot on the agenda—last—and they were ready to dazzle the prospective clients and end on a high note, with a rousing chorus of their catchy theme music and stunning visuals on a big screen while they asked for the business.

For the first hour and a half, things went very well. The team was ready for the final fifteen minutes, prepared to end a few minutes before six and send the decision makers home early. And promptly at 5:30, the power went out.

The meeting was being held in an interior conference room—and it was pitch black. The person from the client team closest to the exit groped her way toward the door and let in a sliver of light from the windows in the hallway, but the sun was setting. The agency team was offered an option: finish the pitch in the dark or reconvene and go through the whole pitch the next time all 14 people on the client side could coordinate their schedules.

Thousands of dollars in equipment rental, airfare, and hotels. Coordinating 26 schedules. Some unknown amount of time when the client could remember the finished pitches of the other two contenders while Lynda's agency lost momentum and any element of surprise.

There really wasn't a choice. Within five minutes, the team had sent someone to retrieve a battery-powered radio from deep within the adjacent cubicles. The two agency principals found tiny flashlights, meant for reading menus, in their purses. And they soldiered on, delivering their final plea for the business to the tinny sound of the music on the radio, holding the flashlights under their chins like kids at camp as they sincerely asked the prospective clients to choose them.

A week later, the verdict arrived. The agency had been selected, and the client explained why: "Your flexibility in a difficult situation—we figured that you guys could handle just about any crisis that came up in the next five years."

Pretty Darn Funny

Looking back, it's a pretty funny story. And that leads us to the huge role of humor in creating a flexible, successful negotiation. You've seen it in stand-up comedians: when a joke dies, as it often does, a great comedian will make that failure part of the next joke, and that one will kill, leaving the audience in hysterics. What the audience may not know is that the comedian has practiced that recovery, rehearsing the lines he'll need, just in case.

It's always astonishing to watch a good improv troupe. The political ones are constantly watching the news, preparing a few good bits about the topic of the day in advance. But it's their skill in taking unpredictable questions from the audience—and routinely cracking them up—that really impresses.

It all comes from that first rule of improvisation: *Yes, and?* . . . .

Improv actors accept whatever comes at them and turn it into something better. (See the "Clowning Lessons" on the next page).

Obviously, no one expects you to be a great comedian or a skilled improv actor. But you can take that attitude into every meeting—no matter what surprises come from the other side of the table, your first response should be positive. Try to frame every interaction as a *yes, and*, and soon everyone in the room will be enlisted in the same attitude.

Humor can also serve to mask awkwardness. If you've made a verbal offer the other side clearly thinks is too much, you can add a ridiculous element to make people laugh while you regroup:

You: "Let's agree we can get this accomplished in six months."
Them: Stony silence and glares that could pierce glass.
You: "O.K," with a chuckle, "how about six weeks? No, seriously, what kind of deadlines did you guys have in mind?"

We're not suggesting you make every offer or counteroffer a joke. But sometimes a little humor can be all you need to keep an offer in play and the other team in the room, especially if you've been building a relationship all along.

There's even some science to support this strategy. When people laugh together, they end up liking each other more. Specifically, if

SIDEBAR 12.1

Clowning Lessons

Eli Simon teaches clowning around the globe—to actors and business executives. And oddly enough, these lessons in emotion, improvisation, self-expression, and empathy are the same tools used by inventive negotiators.

Here are the insights we had from his book, *The Art of Clowning*.[4]

1. **Be authentic.** Every person has an inner child who reacts with complete honesty. Once you've explored that real self, your emotions will guide your actions—and won't pop out to surprise you with anger or hurt during a critical negotiation.
2. **Understand the other players.** When you know yourself, you can concentrate on getting to know the others. You can see when they are frightened, unsure, uncomfortable.
3. **You never know what will happen.** No matter how well you think you've anticipated events, the only guarantee is that there will be surprises. In fact, you should prepare to fail, because that attitude will rescue you when you ultimately hit setbacks.
4. **Accept every offer.** People in theatre call it "Yes, and...." When each person in an improvisation agrees that this imaginary item is indeed a large beach ball, the interaction spirals upward.

Try it yourself over your next business lunch: Start with a random statement, say, "I like chocolate ice cream." The next person has to accept and add: "I like chocolate ice cream and I love it with strawberries." It should take about two turns before everyone is smiling or laughing. Now try a conversation with everyone turning down the offer. "Yeah but ice cream makes you fat." By one turn around the table, you will be talking to a mighty cranky group of people—who will never agree on anything.

5. **Stay curious.** Actively engage in exploring options: How did other people solve this? Could we try a pilot program? What if we never had to worry about money? I wonder...

you can make someone laugh at something you've said, you get a shot of oxytocin, that same wonderful brain chemical that kicks in during good sex and produces bonding—while it improves creativity.[2] And, as we mentioned in chapter 9, in our laboratory studies of negotiation we found laughter was the key linguistic variable that influenced liking.[3]

Expect the Unexpected

Good negotiators plan for a certain amount of upheaval: planes are delayed, people get sick, computer systems fail, lawyers don't approve the documents, the power goes out. If they've rehearsed, they are prepared with contingency plans in case the other side gets stubborn about a deal point.

Yet, there will always be totally unpredictable events. You could get kidnapped. Or caught in an earthquake.[5] Or get grounded for a week by flying volcanic ash. Obviously, you can't prepare for every possible setback. But you can remember one technique that nearly always helps: when catastrophe strikes, begin converting it to a funny story. By reframing, sometimes you can see new perspectives that lead to solving the problem. Studies show that people who are in a good mood are often more creative. And even if you can't immediately solve the problem, you'll demonstrate your good will and eagerness to continue building the relationship. At the very least, you'll have a great story to tell your friends next time you're out drinking.

The Other Side

The other side of flexibility is your preparation to make positive changes. Situations can change: (See how Pixar and Disney modified their contracts when *Toy Story* was a surprise hit in chapter 14.)

Roles can, and often should, change. The naysayer on the other side of the table can see the long-term prospects of a successful negotiation and suddenly become a champion. Someone may get promoted into working with you or be transferred away to another country, and the new player will have different views.

If you have gone through the primary stages of negotiation, then expanded the scope of the work or partnership, you'll often realize you need more partners to get your goals accomplished. A whole new team could make the project succeed, as it did in the chemosensitivity venture in Sao Paulo. Those new minds and new resources can take you further than you ever imagined when you were in those first stages. The more flexible you are, the better your chances at building that pie factory.

SIDEBAR 12.2

Inventive Negotiation, In the Dark

In any negotiation, to get the outcomes you want, you need to sell your vision—to persuade the other participants that working together will be better than they imagined. That can be tough when you don't know the people you need to persuade.

And this is precisely what you have to do in advertising—only in that field, the adage is to sell the sizzle, not the steak. Sometimes you can persuade people that buying your product will make life better for them, and usually you have some reason to back it up-it's easier, cheaper, faster, better-looking.

Imagine, then, what fun it would be to sell this product: It's exactly like its competitors. The technology is about 500 years old. You buy it maybe once or twice a year. It costs thousands or tens of thousands of dollars. You have no guarantee that it will improve anything, but you're still out the money. And by the way, you have exactly 30 seconds to sell it. Without personal contact or even any visuals. Over a tinny speaker while your audience is busy doing something else.

Yes, your assignment is to sell printing services in radio spots.

When Lynda's agency tackled this task, she and her creative team did what anyone else would do—they headed for Hollywood. Over the years, they'd often worked with a production company to record radio spots, but this group offered something else: some of the funniest people ever assembled. Their floating team came from famous improv troupes, stand-up comedy clubs, and writers from sitcoms. The way one agency writer described their sessions? "As much fun as you can have with your clothes on."

This time, everyone agreed on one thing: the assignment was impossible. It could not be done. So the team started talking about stuff: what they'd done on the weekend, how dogs feel about fetching balls (complete with imagined dog dialogue and panting tongues). Comparing dogs and men in their attitudes toward playing with balls. What we would order for lunch. The unfairness of life in general. The unfairness of life in particular.

Ahah! A theme. People who buy our printing go on to be enormously successful. People who don't turn out to be losers. There were twin brothers who owned yard decoration companies featuring flamingos. One drove a luxury car and ate caviar, the other a battered off-brand vehicle that could barely make it into the fast-food drive-through. There were a pair of business competitors—one who summoned high-end services to his penthouse, the other . . . well, you get the idea.

The discussion led to talking about high-end services, the more absurd the better. Massages? Lynda shared her story about a German masseuse on a remote Italian island who definitely did not understand the English for "Gentler, please." Now *that* was funny.

In the recording session, the voice-over artists, inspired to improvise, named this imaginary masseuse Helga and began demonstrating her work by pounding on their own chests while attempting to talk. The results were hysterical, as each actor added a little something in each succeeding take. By the end of the session, their chests were aflame from the repeated self-pounding. And the resulting radio spot increased sales all over the country so much that the printers could barely keep up with the orders. It was inventive negotiation at its finest: a trusted team with a long-term relationship. A creative venue. A shared vision. Permission to improvise and improve. And a wildly successful outcome no one could have imagined. Feel free to try it yourself any time. Maybe without the chest pounding.

CHAPTER 13

Playing Together Nicely

Director Ingmar Bergman was once famous for his tantrums. When he switched from "throwing chairs to cheerleading," his productions became international icons.

—Robert Cohen

Your job as a leader is to be right at the end of the meeting, not at the beginning of the meeting.

—David Cole

Back in 1987, there was a tiny line item in Reagan's budget submission to Congress about a scientific project that most people had never heard of. Since the budget passed both houses, by 1990 the Department of Energy and the National Institutes of Health had a memorandum of understanding and had begun the project to map the human genome. It was research on a massive scale and to date the largest collaborative biological project in the world. Even with several government departments involved, plus universities around the world, everyone assumed it would take 15 years. Within a decade, the researchers had a working draft of the genome, and three years later they had a pretty decent map. By 2006, they had sequenced the last chromosome (though 8 percent of the genome is still unsequenced at this writing).

Meanwhile, another group of scientists, led by former NIH geneticist Dr. Craig Venter, thought they could tackle the task more efficiently, so they launched the Celera Corporation in 1998. With just $300 million, these researchers had less than a tenth of the funding of the public project. They used a "shotgun" approach to speed up the process, and since they were privately funded, they intended to patent their findings.

The race was on. The public project collected samples from a large number of donors; a few of them became DNA resources, but more than 70 percent of the final work actually came from a single male donor from Buffalo, New York. Celera collected 21 samples and used five—and one of those came from Venter himself. The cross-country rivalry seemed to spur innovation, the public group also adopted some shortcuts, and by 2000 both teams were close to the goal.

In April, Celera made a surprise announcement to the House of Representatives. Its researchers had completed the sequencing. Yet, because of an agreement they'd signed in 1996, they couldn't publish their findings until after the public group published theirs. Three months later, the NIH released the first working draft of the public group on the web, and within 24 hours scientists downloaded a half trillion bytes of that free and accessible information. By February, *Nature* had published the public paper and *Science* had published Celera's.

In theory, the two projects were rivals. Yet, each built on the other's work, and the net result was a more thorough understanding of the genome and the process of decoding it. Their competition cut nearly five years off the anticipated completion date (a rare outcome from public *or* private ventures). Their joint insights launched a half dozen more specialized projects, with enormous possibilities for more effective medical treatments for people around the world.

In the real world, these competitive collaborations are more frequent than you'd anticipate, though they're usually not quite so public. Which is why the definition of working together is much broader than most negotiators understand.

Remember the health department people who ended up working with McDonald's instead of fighting them? The angry Iraqi civilians who later cheered the armed American soldiers? So whether you start out on the same team (say, labor and management negotiators who both want their company to succeed) or as deadly rivals who could eventually work together (like the terrorist and his interrogator), there are certain principles that apply.

First, remember that humans are hardwired to trust their own tribes and instinctively eschew everybody else. Recent scientific studies have proved that cooperation is a basic survival skill, and even babies and our chimp relatives are happy to share.

To put it simply, in an ideal world, we like working together. It's intrinsically rewarding—even in a world that's less than ideal. Just imagine:

Inside a bottle factory on hot summer day in Monterrey, Mexico, is probably as close as most people get to hell. An average day is likely to be 99 degrees Fahrenheit. A good night might cool down to

80 degrees. Then there's the furnace: to make glass from sand, you have to heat it to 4,172 degrees. Even the best-insulated furnace is going to add a little ambient heat.

Lynda Lawrence and her colleagues, melting in their business suits, trooped through this vast complex to try to understand why the average employee had been working there for more than a decade. It is grueling, repetitive, ill-paid work, with a roaring furnace, clanking assembly lines, and forklifts dropping wooden pallets. Yet there appeared to be no big labor issues, and certainly no strikes.

The consultants met with small, randomly selected groups of employees to find out why. Lawrence met with the quality control group—men and women who spent eight hours a day, five days (or nights) a week, watching finished bottles coming down an assembly line. The vast majority of the time, the bottles are perfect, but every once in a while something goes a little bit off, and they have to stop the line and fix it. Ninety-nine percent monotony, one percent catastrophe. To a white-collar American, this does not seem like an ideal job.

Rather than interview the workers through an interpreter, Lynda paired them off to interview each other, a process more likely to reveal issues they wouldn't share with a stranger. These pairs then sat with two other pairs, so that each group of six could report out to the employees and consultants. After some basic biography (how long have you worked here? Why?), the workers had to answer two questions: Tell me about your best day. And how could you have more like that?

The first answers were not surprising. They worked at their plant because it was a steady job. They lived nearby. It felt like a family—in fact, many of them *were* family, with half a dozen members of their extended families recruiting the next generation. They cited the workers' holidays with picnics and gifts for the kids.

The other two questions, however, revealed the secret to the lack of labor disputes. When asked about their best days, some workers started by listing petty grievances—things that definitely did not make for a good day at work. Soon they began describing the good days, and even though they cited different examples, all of those days had one thing in common: they'd worked as a team to solve a challenge.

The response to the second question was even more surprising. Within minutes the workers were throwing out suggestions, filling easel pad after easel pad with ideas about better teamwork, better response time, better accident prevention, money-saving techniques that wouldn't require a peso of capital expenditure—more than you'd expect from a months-long report by highly paid consultants. Half an hour later, these teams and their supervisors were presenting the ideas to top management.

SIDEBAR 13.1

Lessons from the Theatre

Whether you're staging a Shakespeare festival or a blockbuster movie, arranging a corporate merger or reviewing a union contract, striking a peace treaty or discussing which family member gets the remote control, the same principles apply.

In his book, *Working Together in Theatre*, Robert Cohen[1] shares a lifetime of observations about how you get a cast and crew of hundreds to create a production, on time, every night.

1. **A dictator dictates. A leader collaborates.** Unless you have a standing army at your disposal, you will need to persuade people to join you to get anything done at all. Leadership is simply organizing collaboration. It's a quality, not a title. It is vision, integration, and organization—throughout the whole team.

   According to award-winning choreographer Twyla Tharp, "Collaborators aren't born...they're made. A day at a time, through practice, through discipline, through attention, through passion and commitment—and most of all, through habit."

2. **Get to know everyone before you begin.** Do some research, ask around. Arranging a meeting, even by e-mail, should show your eagerness to meet and work with everyone.

3. **Trust and respect are the foundations of any team,** including a team of rivals. If people don't feel safe, they retreat into untenable positions or stubborn opposition. If the situation is bad enough, they'll just walk out.

4. **Conflict is necessary, but tone is everything.** Any creative enterprise improves when it's built on ideas from everyone involved, so disagreements are vital to success. Instead of yelling "No!" good directors acknowledge and add. "I like that move, maybe you could use it more effectively in the next scene."

5. **Have fun. Break bread.** The word "company" comes from the roots for "with bread." The Moscow Art Theatre, the oldest collaborative enterprise in the world, began in 1897 with a dinner that lasted until breakfast.

When you contrast this with labor and management disputes throughout the world, you can see what makes a difference. First, workers, supervisors, and managers at the plant believe that they are part of a family. Just like a real family, there will be some members who drive you crazy, but ultimately you need to get along for the long haul. Second, they all have a stake in their success. If the plant suffers, they all lose their livelihoods. And third, like every human being since the beginning of time, they love conquering challenges together.

With those three elements, international business people, peacemakers, rival gangs, or political parties could stop worrying about splitting pies and create pie factories. Or in this case, a bottle factory.

Lessons from Kindergarten

So how do you ensure that your own team—on both sides of the table—can learn to profit by cooperating? This is, after all, the exact opposite of what most people believe they know about negotiation.

When Lynda Lawrence went back to school in mid-career to study organizational development, her friends often asked what the heck that meant. Her answer? "It's a way to get grown-ups to play nicely with others. And stop running with scissors."

The first step is to get everyone on your team indisputably on your team. It's astonishing how many negotiations are derailed because team members unconsciously sabotage their own efforts. In a large team, some people may be on board because they've been told to be there, while they have personal stakes in just the opposite. If the planned merger goes through, it may be good for the company, but the second vice president may well lose his own job in the inevitable consolidation and executive downsizing that will follow. If our firm buys that upstart with the new technology, what happens to the product I created a decade ago? No matter how many team-building retreats you fund, if individuals stand to lose from the proceedings, they are hardly going to be open to the team's efforts.

Some of these conflicts will be obvious—others may stem from sources you would never expect. Several years ago, we worked with a nonprofit that was trying to take on new partners for expansion. The problem was that the partners couldn't get along internally. The two women who ran the nonprofit's major departments were constantly feuding, and nobody could figure out why. After all, they had been friends and neighbors before they worked together, and one had actually recruited the other. But now, for every step forward the organization achieved, they managed to pull it back.

After a series of candid interviews, we finally learned the story from the women's coworkers. Yes, the two had been friends, until one night when the department head had called the police about a noisy neighborhood party. This unfortunately resulted in the arrest of the other woman's son. Since that kind of bad blood could not be dissipated by a few words from the executive director, the nonprofit changed its organizational structure and never again sent the two out together to talk with potential partners. No running with scissors.

Sometimes the people with opposing agendas are at the top. In recently released tapes from the Nixon administration, famously anticommunist Nixon was heard telling his archenemy Russian premier Leonid Brezhnev, "If we decide to work together, we can change the world." Brezhnev responded that both of them should forget "the bad past" and start sketching out plans for mutual visits. Their aides would have been dumbstruck since each man was publicly proclaiming the other to be pure evil.

Obviously, no team will share consistent views on every item, but you can minimize discord if you select your team members carefully and then make sure you share a vision. (Remember Eli Simon showing off his imaginary Shakespearean theater to the chancellor on page 22) The more often you meet, and the more informal the setting, the more likely your team will not stray from the fold.

If playing well with others is a strain for your team, the degree of difficulty increases exponentially when you consider all those on the other side of the table. Rarely will you know the players intimately or have the opportunity for enough contact to get to know them. Then there are the twin obstacles of culture and language—if you can misinterpret a colleague's intentions, it's that much easier to misunderstand your counterpart's motives when you don't share common expectations and ways of doing business.

In most Middle Eastern cultures, for example, reaching an agreement is a starting point. Americans expect that this stage is a done deal. When the other side wants to continue negotiating, Americans feel betrayed and angry. A normal part of life for one side is grounds for blowing up the relationship for the other.

Chinese and Japanese executives usually look to long-term relationships. Americans are surprised at the slow trust-building process and reliance on referrals, and their counterparts don't understand why the Americans are rushing things at the risk of undermining the relationship in the long haul.

As we've discussed throughout the book, it pays to understand the culture and the individual personalities and backgrounds of everyone on every negotiating team. And if that sounds like a tall order, consider that as soon as you've got that down pat, things will change.

The company you're negotiating with will be sold. The people you've come to know will be transferred to another division. The economics of the firm—or even the country—can and will change throughout any relationship that's longer than a single deal.

All this, of course, could happen before you reach your first agreement. And playing nicely with others is even more important in the long run.

Another good strategy is also drawn from kindergarten wisdom: Learn to share your toys. If your negotiation results in a partnership with unexpectedly good results, consider rethinking your compensation agreements. (In the next chapter, you can see how Disney reacted in this situation.) Consider working on additional projects together. Rethink your formulas for every part of your agreement.

The key is to walk into any situation with a degree of flexibility, whether early in a relationship or well into a decades-old partnership. It's this attitude that always distinguishes inventive negotiators from less-successful ones.

Getting the Marine Corps to Play Nice

Coercion is so last century. The big wars are over. The twenty-first century is a time where words dominate weapons. Of course, there will be necessary police actions around the globe, but nobody, not even the United States, can afford big military expenditures anymore. Thus, MIT professor Steven Pinker in *The Better Angels of Our Nature*[2] argues convincingly that the average human being is safer from violence now than at any time in history.

Sure, headlines suggest that the Middle East may explode at any moment in major war—but no governments in that region can afford that conflict. What about China, Taiwan, and the United States? The interdependence of trade among the three is tremendous, and a conflict across the Taiwan Strait is unthinkable. The so-called Pivot East of American military planning makes no sense when the Chinese and American navies are collaborating to keep trade routes open around the Horn of Africa.

So how does our military respond in this new world? Consider this story from our post in the *Harvard Business Review* of June 2011(See http://blogs.hbr.org/2011/06/negotiating-over-a-limited-res/ for the blog and comments):

> For more than two decades, leaders of San Diego and Orange counties in Southern California have struggled to manage the burgeoning needs of air travelers in the area. One potential solution is prominent—a new international airport at the south end of Camp Pendleton.

Dick Murphy, a former mayor of San Diego, laid out a plan some ten years ago that is still viable today: "The Camp Pendleton idea is to operate what I would call Southern California International Airport on a piece of Camp Pendleton. Now, we're not talking about shutting down Camp Pendleton ... But the new airport could be a joint venture with Orange County.... I would envision that airport being primarily an international-transcontinental airport like Dulles. So, basically, anybody out of San Diego County or Orange County or Riverside County who wanted to fly overseas or to Washington DC could fly out of that airport." The project would help create jobs in the region and further open the nation's most populous state to international trade. Plus, there's already a rail line to the area that would help flyers get to and from "Pendleton International."

Now for the other side. The U.S. Marines and the Department of the Navy want to retain all of the 15 miles of California coastline they now control for training purposes. As the assistant secretary of the navy told us in a letter,

Amphibious landings continue to be an integral part of Marine Corps operations and MCB is the premier amphibious landing training installation on the west coast of the United States ... The 1st Marine Expeditionary Force ... conduct daily training activities aboard MCB Camp Pendleton, including live-fire operations involving amphibious landings, ground movement, artillery, mortars, tanks, tactical aircraft, and laser systems. The presence of a commercial airport on the base would divide training areas, restrict access to airspace, and adversely reduce opportunities for Marine units to conduct realistic training.

Can civilian leaders in San Diego and Orange counties and their military counterparts reach an agreement that satisfies both sides?

The historical reality is that the branches of the military and the federal government have almost always taken a "dividing the orange" sort of competitive approach to the distribution of funding. But in the current federal budget-cutting environment, inventive negotiations are crucial to make the most of every dollar spent.

In this case, the best argument against a joint-use airport on Camp Pendleton is that the marines need the coastline to practice beach landings. But that tactic hasn't been used since the Korean War, as Secretary of Defense Gates himself pointed out last summer. However, America's military power now rests heavily on control of the skies. It could be that building additional air facilities on Camp Pendleton—some of which would be a commercial airport for civilians—could provide additional training opportunities for the military. Perhaps Pendleton International might be closed to civilian use on certain days and made available exclusively for military training exercises.

Negotiation could reveal other ways that a new airport could benefit the military as well as civilians. Perhaps high-paying service jobs could be made available at the new airport for both military spouses and reservists. Moreover, as America's wars wind down, and as efforts to rein in spending ramp up, soldiers, sailors, airmen, and marines will all be entering the civilian workforce in great numbers. The jobs created by this new international airport could help the substantial population of veterans already living in the Southern California region find employment. There's already some basis for collaboration between airlines and the military, as a large proportion of civilian airline pilots started as military pilots.

The decision about dedicating a part of Camp Pendleton as an international commercial airport need not be just a zero-sum choice between defense infrastructure and trade infrastructure. An inventive negotiation approach that considers the interests of the surrounding communities and the future needs of the Department of the Navy, the Marine Corps, and the marines themselves can result in a unique joint-use facility that accommodates the air travel needs of the seven million residents of the local communities and the ever-changing training requirements of a vital military.

How would you resolve this dispute in a way that leaves both sides better off than they are now? See how you could apply all that you've learned from *Inventive Negotiation* to create a plan, one that might include something like this:

A Brief Inventive Negotiation Plan

Find or create partners. Perhaps the most obvious partners in this enterprise would be local political leaders whose constituencies could benefit from an international airport at Camp Pendleton. That would mean Orange and San Diego county supervisors, mayors, and members of the California state legislature and Congress. Even President Obama and Rand Paul might find something worthwhile in the venture. Veterans' welfare organizations would be interested the potential jobs created.

Opponents of the plan would be those embedded in what President Eisenhower called the military-industrial-congressional complex. Indeed, a particularly annoying enemy of inventive negotiation in this area is the $40-million "Anti-Encroachment" budget used by the Department of Defense to defeat this kind of endeavor.

For the best outcome, the detractors would meet with the advocates.

Perhaps the old Russian approach of accumulating participants might work best. That is, A meets with B; when they agree, then both meet with C, and so on.

Personal relationships. Money and time would need to be invested here. In previous years, John Graham was able to spark a lively correspondence with the commander of the current Pendleton air station and was even cordially invited for a tour of the base. But no beers were tipped, and the former marine generals in the discussion continued to be firmly opposed. (You can track the discussions at www. PendletonX.org.)

Systems design. Once the initial team has been formed, it would be time to design the process. High on the list of tasks would be how to expand the discussion to include open-minded dissenters. Then you'd determine who should be included, what objective information sources could be tapped, and which potential meeting routines you'd use. The schedule should allow for relationship-building activities, technical sidebars, and creative sidebars. Of course, flexibility and an open systems channel must be built into the system.

People. Team makeup will be crucial. Particularly in a case like this, facilitation would be important. Selecting someone respected and approved by all would be essential. The material in chapter 6 regarding facilitators is particularly pertinent.

Diversity. Inventive processes work best in a context of diversity, no matter how it is defined. This would include military personnel from all branches and ranks, aerospace engineers, construction companies, architects, experts from other countries, green NGOs, government officials from local municipalities, men and women, union leaders, and management consultants.

Place/space/pace. Of course, related to systems design, choices about the environment for discussions must be made. Off-site locations will be essential. There is a wide and evolving variety of information-sharing software that would be appropriate for the group.

Changing roles. A key to creative thinking is trying to think like others. Walk a mile in my boots, so to speak. Marines with industry experience and politicians with military experience may be particularly helpful.

Stimulants. Coffee will be good. But the entire list from chapter 11 should be put on the table—small offers, celebrating small wins, changing chairs, surprises, breaks, sleeping on it, thinking backward, thinking big, and always using "yes and."

Crazy ideas. From applying principles of improvisation to clowning and play. Have fun.

Review and improve. Once an agreement has been reached, plan for periodic reviews and assessments of progress.

This is an ambitious plan. But billions of dollars could be generated and millions of people would benefit from developing a new international airport at Camp Pendleton. Just imagine the possibilities.

CHAPTER 14

Reviewing and Improving

The best way to predict your future is to create it.

—Abraham Lincoln

Once you have a verbal agreement, your negotiations can be even more inventive. In the United States, executives usually "conclude business deals." In many other countries, executives "establish business relationships." And these different attitudes influence postnegotiation procedures and eventual outcomes. So far, you may have the blueprints, but there are still important steps before you can build that pie factory.

Contracts

Contracts between American firms are often longer than 100 pages and include carefully worded clauses regarding every aspect of the agreement. American lawyers go to great lengths to protect their companies against all circumstances, contingencies, and actions of the other party. In a typical American commercial contract, conditional phrases such as, "if," "in the event," and "should," are often used more than fifty times. The best contracts are the ones so tightly written that the other party would not think of going to court to challenge any provision. Our adversarial system requires such contracts.

In most other countries, companies don't depend on legal systems to resolve disputes. Indeed, the term "disputes" doesn't reflect the way a business relationship should work. Each side should be concerned about the mutual benefits of the relationship, and therefore each should consider the interests of the other. Consequently, in many countries written contracts are very short, often only two to three pages. They are purposefully loosely written and primarily contain comments on principles of the relationship. Since contracts in other countries are designed to secure relationships, the American emphasis on tight contracts is tantamount to planning the divorce before the marriage.

Ironically, in Japan the government is currently ramping up legal training to better serve global (actually American) standards of commercial law. American/Japanese contracts now look much like American contracts, even in length. But appearances deceive. Even in Japan, the legal system doesn't have the capacity to play the commercial litigation game the way it's played in the litigious United States. Thus, contracts mean less and alternative dispute resolutions options are much more common (see exhibit 14.1).

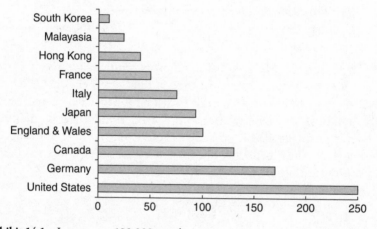

Exhibit 14.1 Lawyers per 100,000 people.
Source: Adapted from the University of Wisconsin, Institute for Legal Studies.

What form should a contract between a foreign and an American firm take? There is no simple answer—the form depends on the size and importance of the agreement and on the size and experiences of the firms involved. Generally, larger deals justify the extra expense of including legal review by both foreign and American lawyers. Large foreign firms with histories of American contracts will understand the Americans' need for detailed contracts. Some firms, recognizing the increasing frequency of litigation between US and foreign firms, will specify the American approach for their own protection. It is the executives of smaller foreign firms, inexperienced in the ways of Americans, who may become suspicious when faced with lengthy, fully detailed contracts. In these cases, it's particularly important to explain why you need the legal review and detailed contract. You should realize, however, that even with the most complete explanation not all foreign executives will understand.

An American-style contract will also cause considerable delays in signing. Foreign lawyers will painstakingly consider every detail. One rule of thumb suggests that every clause takes an entire day. Thus, something your legal counsel ordinarily reviews in three days may take three weeks in Bangkok or three months in Lagos. Recently, a firm in California was selling executive training services to First Auto Works, one of China's largest companies. All the prices, content, and terms and conditions were agreed upon, and the American firm sent the contract for signatures. Then the Chinese side balked. The Chinese delegates had never seen the standard "boilerplate" provisions in the contract. It took another frustrating month before things were finally straightened out.

Moreover, many American executives of even the largest firms have been satisfied with a "compromise" contract when strong, long-standing personal relationships are involved. Ford and Nissan designed and started production on a joint venture, and the minivans they produced were in customers' garages before the contract was actually signed. That's hundreds of millions of dollars invested without signatures. But each case is different. And only you and your legal counsel can determine what you need.

Remember that trust and harmony are more important to your relationship-oriented counterparts than any piece of paper. They'll actually be more interested in what James Sebenius and his colleagues call the "spirit of the deal."[1] In many countries, including China, Nigeria, Colombia, and Indonesia, contracts are for reference only and currently mean little. Yes, they are becoming increasingly important as countries have joined the WTO, but catching up to the American legal system will take decades. In the meantime, most of your foreign partners will continue to depend on interpersonal harmony.

Signing Ceremonies

Because informality is the norm in the United States, even the largest contracts between American firms are often sent through the mail for signature. Ceremony is considered a waste of time and money. But when a major agreement is reached with a foreign client or partner, your foreign counterparts will expect your top executives to meet with them and sign the contract with ceremony. It's wise to meet those expectations.

Headquarters' Assessment

Often US negotiators return to company headquarters with an agreement, only to receive a mixed welcome. Too often, executives say,

"The second half of the negotiation begins once I return to the home office." Headquarters, unaware of the requirements of international business negotiations, will ask, "What took so long?" Ordinarily, all compromises and concessions have to be explained and justified in detail. Then commitments requiring specific management actions must be delegated and ordered. All this can slow implementation and performance of the contract.

In the worst cases, when negotiator and home office communications have been poor, negotiators have to renege and start over. When this occurs, the foreign client or partner will either bypass this executive (who has lost face) and talk to someone who is a real decision maker, or decline further discussion and end the relationship.

The good news is that once the first deal has been struck with a foreign client or partner, successive negotiations tend to proceed more quickly. Often, it won't be necessary to send a complete negotiation team when new issues are to be considered. Clearly, then, it is best to start with a small, relatively simple, business proposal. Once the relationship has been established, even substantial and complex negotiations will proceed more smoothly. This is the approach used by most foreign firms entering the United States, and it's a sensible strategy when American firms court international business.

Follow-Up Communications

Just as personal considerations are more important during negotiations with relationship-oriented clients, they are also important after the negotiations are concluded. Obviously, you will be in touch with your overseas clients and partners regarding the business of the relationship. But it will be equally important to keep personal relationships warm.

Your top executive should send a formal letter to the other side's top executive, expressing happiness that the talks have been concluded successfully and confidence that the new relationship will be prosperous and long-lasting. Even more important are periodic personal visits—investing in what Americans call face time.

One final consideration is crucial when doing business internationally: Avoid switching the executives who manage those relationships. With American clients, this is not much of a problem—the economics of the business deal are more important than the personal relationships. Managers often shift positions within companies and between companies. But in almost all other countries, executives stay with their companies longer. And these executives are given longer-term responsibility for managing intercompany relationships. After all, they have invested in building the personal relations that make business work smoothly.

When American companies switch key managers, overseas clients get very nervous, so if you have to make a change, be prepared to engage in another round of nontask sounding and rapport building with all the proper introductions to make the new executive better accepted.

Dispute Resolution and Modifications

During the course of almost all business relationships, there will be changes in the environment or to the partners. In the United States, conflicts arising from the changing circumstance are settled through direct and confrontational legal channels or, more often, in arbitration.

In many other countries, given the same set of changing circumstances, companies will resolve the conflicts through conferral. Thus, local contracts often include phrases like, "All items not found in this contract will be deliberated and decided upon in a spirit of honesty and trust." When differences can't be ironed out through conversation, the next step is to express concerns through the all-important intermediaries, often the mutual contacts who made the original introductions. Only if they can't mediate a new understanding will they resort to confrontational and legal approaches. In relationship cultures, those tactics will destroy the harmony and trust required for continued business dealings. What's more, their fledgling legal systems are often plagued by favoritism and inefficiency, and even arbitration is viewed negatively in many countries.

The simplest solution is just to include an international arbitration clause in your contract for times when conflicts arise: "Any controversy or claim arising out of or relating to this contract shall be determined by arbitration in accordance with the rules of the International Chamber of Commerce's International Arbitration" or some other country-specific arbitration clause. But even with that, we suggest a Japanese approach to conflict resolution—that is, approach the dispute from a cooperative standpoint and talk with your international client or partner. If you've maintained the harmony and trust, and you have an honest mutual interest in the deal, problems can usually be resolved through simple conferral. And of course, you'll still have the option of personal mediation with a trusted mutual contact

You can also use a governance model or a shock absorber clause. In a governance model, people handle problems and developments, not just paper. With shock absorber clauses, you anticipate and allow changes in specific aspects of long-term relationships. These baby steps toward living agreements, however, won't really compare to strong personal relationships when you need to manage the inevitable shocks—positive or negative—the marketplace will deliver.

Conclusions

Even with a signed contract, negotiations are never really completed, and what Americans call "careful follow-up" is really just the continuing maintenance of an ever-evolving business relationship. A regularly scheduled semiannual or annual business relationship review is the best way to prevent disputes. If the business relationship is evolving and growing, you should make changes to contracts periodically. Even more important, you should add to the spirit of the relationship: "How can we make this relationship better?" and "What haven't we thought of?" The more you invest in your ongoing relationships, the better your pie factory will become.

Toy Story: A Story about Partners

To see how inventive negotiators build on relationships over time, let's finish the story we began in Chapter 2.[2]

Act one. About the same time young John Lasseter was falling in love with animation, Roy Disney was writing the scripts for *Zorro* on *The Wonderful World of Disney*. After a decade of writing, directing, and producing films for Uncle Walt's company, Roy was elected to the board of directors in 1967. His dreams, like Lasseter's, were controversial, and he soon resigned from the company and the board.

As the largest shareholder, though, Roy orchestrated a coup. First, he and his collaborators ousted the CEO and fended off a hostile takeover. Then they brought in Michael Eisner and Jeffrey Katzenberg from Paramount and Frank Wells from Warner Brothers. With this all-star team in place, Roy rejoined the board and became head of animation.

Just as Eisner landed his CEO position at Disney, Steve Jobs was losing his at Apple. And across town, *Star Wars* genius George Lucas was going through an ugly divorce. It was the mideighties and the world was about to change in ways that none of them could imagine.

Act two. Lucas had an odd asset, a tiny division that made the Pixar Image Computer, sold to government agencies and medical equipment companies. It was just the right size to sell for his divorce settlement, and the unemployed Steve Jobs was just the right buyer.

Unfortunately, hardware sales were tumbling. Pixar's management hired young Lasseter, freshly fired from Disney, to make short films to demonstrate the computer's capacity. Lasseter expanded his scope and began making successful commercials for outside clients, but sales of the hardware still fell. Katzenberg was now in charge at Disney and soon tried to lure Lasseter back, but Lasseter stayed at Pixar, grateful for the way Jobs had treated him and having fun working with CGI.

To protect his $10 million investment, Jobs liquidated the hardware division and laid off half of Pixar's 100 employees. Yet, Jobs was still in trouble. His other venture, the incredibly expensive NeXT computer, was circling the high-tech drain and his return to Apple was five years in the future not even he could foresee. Jobs needed a lifeline, and Katzenberg over at Disney had an offer: both the cash and the marketing creativity he needed so badly to save the fledgling Pixar. The deal was $26 million for Pixar to produce three CGI films for Disney to distribute.

In fact, Disney had all the advantages in this negotiation. Katzenberg had just had huge international success with *The Little Mermaid*, and *Beauty and the Beast* was ready for release. Disney had the reputation and the financial clout to set all the terms. And so they did.

Pixar would start by creating and producing *Toy Story*. After collecting 12.5 percent of the gross on theater, video, and DVD distribution, Disney would share the remaining profits with Pixar. Disney would also get *all* the rights to characters and sequels. And while Pixar was obligated to make the next two movies, Disney could kill them with only a small penalty.

What's more, Katzenberg could intervene in the production, and he did. He's the one who brought in Tim Allen for Buzz's voice when Billy Crystal dropped out. He even stopped production for two weeks to rewrite Woody's character, and his rants were legendary. Yet, between his creativity and Lasseter's at Pixar, the movie struggled on and kept getting better.

As Disney waffled on the release date, Jobs considered selling Pixar. It was hemorrhaging money. Meanwhile, over at Disney, major changes were taking place. Eisner and his president, Frank Wells, had increased the company's revenues from $1.5 billion to $8.5 billion and the stock price by 1,500 percent; clearly, they were a highly effective team. Then Wells died in a plane crash. Katzenberg expected Eisner to promote him to Wells's spot, and when he didn't, Katzenberg bolted for Dreamworks SKG, leaving behind a lawsuit.

Finally, Disney agreed to the lucrative late-November release date for *Toy Story*, and Jobs held on to Pixar just a little longer.

Act three. To everyone's astonishment, *Toy Story* was a huge hit. Box office revenues totaled $361 million. A critical success. Influenced by CGI's modest commercial success, Jobs had predicted, "If *Toy Story* is a modest hit—say $75 million at the box office—we'll both break even. If it gets $100 million, we'll both make money. But if it's a real blockbuster and earns $200 million or so at the box office, we'll make good money, and Disney will make a lot of money."

Eisner was blindsided too. "I don't think either side thought *Toy Story* would turn out as well as it has. The technology is brilliant, the casting is inspired, and I think the story will touch a nerve. Believe me, when we first agreed to work together, we never thought their first movie would be our 1995 holiday feature, or that they could go public on the strength of it."

Even famous toy experts at Mattel were blown away. Contacted originally to include Barbie in the film, they had refused: "Girls who play with Barbie dolls are projecting their personalities onto the doll. If you give the doll a voice and animate it, you're creating a persona that might not be every little girl's dream and desire." (They were, oddly enough, happy to license Barbie *and* Ken for the sequels.)

Of course, *Toy Story's* director and storyteller John Lasseter wasn't all that surprised. It's almost exactly what he had dreamed back in that darkened theater thirty years before.

Then, despite the four-year-old contract he'd signed, Jobs decided to ask for a new one. And here's where inventive negotiation comes in.

In the typical transaction model, the terms you write the first time are the ones you're stuck with. Even though no one could anticipate the billions of dollars from sequels, TV, toys, theme parks, and ice shows, Jobs knew he had a winner, and it was time to come back to the table.

To his surprise, Eisner agreed. Sure, there had been creative clashes, but the two firms had established trust in their collaboration, and they both knew that greater success would lie ahead if they continued that partnership.

Jobs offered a proposal: Pixar would make five new films—*A Bug's Life, Toy Story 2, Monsters, Inc., Finding Nemo,* and *The Incredibles.* Disney decided *Toy Story 2* was a sequel, originally slated as a video-only release, and wanted *Cars* instead. Because of the trust they'd established, they quickly forged a new deal.

Act four. Almost a decade later, by 2004, the balance of power had shifted. And the stage was set for an inventive negotiation that involved all the players in this story. Roles were changing fast.

At Pixar, Jobs was ready to make a change. His tenure at Apple was wildly successful; Pixar was making real money, and he was shopping for a new film distribution partner at Sony, Fox, and Warner Bros. He thought Pixar should get a greater percentage plus sequels and some of all that merchandising revenue. And he was also hoping Eisner would soon be replaced at Disney, which might give him a more inventive negotiation partner.

Over at Disney, Eisner was losing his grip. After Roy Disney's *Fantasia 2000* flopped, the board stacked by Eisner rejected Roy's request for an extension of his board term. His resignation letter cited Eisner's mismanagement, including the relationship with Pixar. Then, once again offstage but as largest shareholder, he stage-managed Eisner's ouster. Disney rejoined the board, and the board selected as its chairman former Senate majority leader George Mitchell, who had joined the board after successfully negotiating peace in Northern Ireland. A man who, as we learned in chapter 10, was a very skillful inventive negotiator.

Now Steve Jobs was known as a "my way or the highway" kind of guy. Yet, the reality was much different. According to Apple's former chairman Edgar Woolard, "If he has a good relationship with you, there is nobody better in the world to work with." Just one example: recall that master animator Lasseter had voted with his feet and stayed with Pixar back when Disney tried to woo him to return.

Jobs and Eisner hadn't agreed on much, but the board led by Mitchell had selected Robert Igers CEO, and Jobs figured he might be more creative. So Iger's first congratulatory call upon his appointment as CEO was from Jobs, who wished him well and hoped they could work together soon.

Soon occurred just two weeks later, when Iger stood on stage with Jobs to announce the new video iPOD, complete with two of ABC/Disney's most popular shows, *Lost* and *Desperate Housewives*.

Jobs believed in diversity of opinions and so did Iger. In short order, Iger established good relationships with Roy Disney and Chairman George Mitchell. Now the team was in place for the negotiation even Jobs hadn't anticipated—Pixar's sale to Disney.

The sale could have been a simple cash transaction, a decision to split the pie at a price all of them could agree on. But Jobs wanted more—a creative, long-term inventive relationship. So Jobs got Disney stock worth $7.4 billion (not a bad return on his $10 million), *and* put the Pixar creative team in control of Disney animation. And Lasseter finally returned to Disney, his boyhood dream, but this time as Disney's chief creative officer. He had, indeed, pulled his sword from the stone.

Disney, in turn, got more than it had bargained for. With Lasseter and Pixar's Ed Catmull as the new head of Disney's animation studios, both reporting directly to Iger, *Toy Story 3* quickly pulled in more than a billion dollars in international box office receipts alone. Disney's stock price jumped from $20 to $30 on news of the purchase, and Apple stock hasn't done badly either.

The key to this deal was actually an epiphany Iger had while he was watching the opening of Hong Kong Disneyland. In marched the company's most popular characters—nearly all of them from the early collaboration between Katzenberg and Jobs, Pixar and Disney. Most important, there wasn't a single character that had been created during the entire last decade Eisner had been in control. Despite Disney's financial gains, the creativity was gone, and Disney *needed* Pixar.

What made this an inventive negotiation is that Iger did something truly unexpected. He admitted that epiphany up front to Jobs. According to Jobs, "That's the dumbest thing you can do as you enter a negotiation, at least according to the traditional rule book. He just put his cards out on the table and said 'We're screwed.' I immediately liked the guy, because that's how I worked too."

The second element of this inventive negotiation was forged during long walks in Palo Alto and at a retreat in Sun Valley (note the walking in nature rule). The talks originally centered on simply revising the old contract. A new distribution deal would give Pixar all rights to the movies and characters it had already produced, and that would give Disney an equity stake in Pixar. Pixar would pay a simple fee to Disney for distribution. Iger, however, worried that this might set the two companies up as rivals.

"I want you to know that I am really thinking out of the box on this," Iger told Jobs, as he began to hint that the deal could actually be bigger. Jobs encouraged his advances, and he says, "It wasn't too long before it was clear to both of us that this discussion might lead to an acquisition."

It's no surprise that Jobs was inventive. What most people don't realize is what an inventive negotiator he was. With Eisner, a traditional, competitive guy, Jobs just negotiated the terms but also established a long-term relationship with others at Disney. On the strength of those relationships, when he needed a more creative approach, he got rid of that barrier—he helped Roy Disney oust Eisner by insisting that if he wasn't removed, the Pixar deal was dead. And animator Lasseter's long-term good relationship with Roy Disney helped in this stage. Finally, when the time was ripe and all the players were in place, Jobs listened to Iger in a creative setting.

Iger himself was no slouch. His recent acquisitions of LucasFilm and Marvel demonstrate both his ongoing quest for creativity and his abilities as an inventive negotiator. And his negotiation skills have resulted in another doubling of the stock price.

When people use inventive negotiation, it looks a lot like magic.

Appendix 1: Defining Inventive Negotiations in Technical Terms

W e offer a quick hypothetical example of the three approaches to negotiation: Bolter Turbines, Inc., is seeking to sell a $3.65 million gas-turbine power generator system to Maverick Offshore Co. for an oil platform in the Gulf of Mexico. Please see table A1. Columns A and B represent the (ballpark) goals for each company with respect to the sale/purchase of one Bolter CS2000 Gas Turbine Generation Set suitable for offshore use. You can see that Maverick is looking for a price reduction of about 20 percent and faster delivery, etc.

The agreement listed in Column I reflects a *competitive*, split-the-difference approach and coincides with one definition of "fair."

The agreement in Column II (striped) represents a series of trade-offs being made by the negotiators (sometimes called log-rolling) ideally based on differences in negotiators' interests, judgments about the future, risk tolerance, and time preferences as they are reflected in the negotiators' evaluations of products and terms. Maverick might have agreed to a higher price in return for a faster delivery, for example. This *integrative* approach depends on an honest exchange of information about preferences and cost/value calculations.

Finally, the agreement listed in Column III involves thinking outside the box. Rather than a simple buy/sell transaction, this agreement involves a long-term lease relationship that may be more appropriate for both parties. Indeed, for some time Solar Turbines, Inc. (the Caterpillar division that serves as a model for our hypothetical Bolter Turbines, Inc.), has gone beyond leasing to offering "power generation services" where customers buy kilowatts instead of

Table A1 Three types of agreements

	A	B	Agreement I	Agreement II	Agreement III
	Bolter Turbines *Price Quotation with Standard Terms*	**Maverick** *Purchasing Objectives*	**Competitive** *Negotiation (Split the Difference)*	**Integrative** *Negotiation (Log Rolling)*	**Inventive** *Negotiation (Outside the Box)*
CS2000 Generator Set	$2,500,000	$2,200,000	$2,350,000	$2,500,000	$3,000,000
Product Options					
Custom Built	400,000	300,000	350,000	300,000	lease machine
Marine Shelter	500,000	400,000	450,000	500,000	for 5 years with
Recuperator	100,000	60,000	80,000	60,000	full service and
Salt Spray Air Filter					warranty, including
Service Contract (normal maintenance, parts & labor)	150,000 (2 years)	90,000 (3 years)	120,000 (3 years)	150,000 (2 years)	labor
TOTAL PRICE	$3,650,000	$3,050,000	$3,350,500	$3,510,000	$3,000,000
Terms and Conditions					
Delivery	6 months	3 months	4.5 months	3 months	3 months
Penalty for late delivery	$10,000 /month	$75,000 / month	$42,500 /month	$10,000 / month	$10,000 / month
Cancellation charges	10% of contract price	2% of contract price	6% of contract price	2% of contract price	2% of contract price
Warranty	parts, one year	parts & labor, two years	parts & labor, one year	parts, one year	5 years, parts & labor
Terms of payment	COD	4 equal payments, 1st at delivery, 2nd at start-up, 3rd and 4th at 90-day intervals	3 equal payments, at delivery, start-up, after 30 days	4 payments	5 annual payments of $600,000
Inflation escalator	5% per year	3% per year	4% per year	5% per year	5% per year
3rd Party arbitration clause	no	yes	yes	yes	yes

machinery. Indeed, this latter definition of their business—services versus products—respects Ted Levitt's views so eloquently expressed in his classic article in the *Harvard Business Review*, "Marketing Myopia." The agreement in Column III also represents the result of an *inventive* approach to negotiations.

Appendix 2: 82 Ways to Generate More Ideas

All these recommendations are supported by empirical evidence, some of it very strong. We include the citations for the supporting studies for each of the 82 on our website www.InventiveNegtotiation.com/82ways.

Get Physical

1. Go offsite to a neutral environment
2. Paint the room blue
3. Stretch the visual space with a high ceiling
4. Stock the room with toys and tools
5. Even make it a little messy
6. Keep the room warm
7. Make sure there are scenic views
8. Add plants and flowers
9. Hang some modern art
10. Infuse a lavender scent
11. Get people in close physical proximity
12. Encourage them to lie down and lounge around
13. Arrange soft chairs and sofas
14. Make it just about as noisy as a coffee shop
15. Build group identity by assigning colors to teams
16. Make sure teams touch
17. Add physical movement
18. And sing or dance together
19. Ask them to create something with their hands
20. Or show ideas with their hands
21. Or just squeeze rubber balls with their left hands
22. Feed them candy to make them happy

23. Give them a glass of wine or a couple of beers
24. Take a walk in the park to refresh. And walk in step.

Get the Right People in the Room

1. Reduce the size of the group—at least five but no more than 12
2. Add more women
3. Add more extroverts
4. Add older people
5. Add people with diverse personality profiles
6. Add people with diverse experience
7. Add cultural diversity
8. Add experts
9. Add nonexperts
10. Add people with wide social networks
11. Add creative consultants such as painters, musicians, writers, or poets
12. Throw in a handful of narcissists
13. Change group members for each exercise

Time Matters

1. Set real deadlines
2. Hold the session in the evening
3. Reduce the brainstorming time to five minutes
4. Let people take a nap or sleep on the problem

Teach Them Well

1. Teach people how to brainstorm
2. Train people longer in the techniques, for fifteen minutes
3. Use well-trained facilitators
4. Give them background information
5. Jump-start them with ideas from a previous group
6. Play a tape of others working on the same problem
7. Tell participants that you expect more ideas and set performance standards

Rules of Engagement

1. Open with a personal element
2. Help people get to know each other

3. Add two new rules to the four standard Osborne rules: relax, play, have fun, and silence is OK
4. Add humor
5. Add music and art
6. Remind people of their own loving relationships
7. Direct them to think like a kid
8. Ask them to question their ability to create
9. Encourage them to contribute unique ideas only they can bring
10. Start by having them do something ordinary in an unusual order
11. Challenge participants to write as many ideas as possible in a very short time
12. Alternate nominal and interactive periods of brainstorming on the same project
13. Break problem solving into stages
14. Suggest participants imagine objects as component parts, like wax and string instead of candles
15. Share the task
16. Hand out surprise rewards
17. Ask participants to solve creative problems for someone else
18. Tell them they are solving problems for a distant client
19. Get them to imagine they are solving problems in the future
20. Give a brief time for reflection or incubation
21. Lead participants through visualization
22. Give them more stimuli
23. Give them more disparate stimuli
24. Show Apple logos
25. Shift participants' assumptions
26. Get people to think about love, but not sex
27. Challenge them to paint, build, or sing and act silly
28. Use metaphors
29. Allow some debate
30. Take a break within the session. Do a totally unrelated activity
31. Compare participants with other groups
32. Let them know that their ideas will be used
33. Reinforce participants' own feelings of being a creative team
34. Tell participants a story about creativity

About the Authors

John L. Graham is professor emeritus of international business at the University of California, Irvine. He was a founding director of both the Center for Citizen Peacebuilding and the John & Marilyn Long U.S./China Institute for Business & Law at UCI. Graham has provided expert advice and training on international negotiations to executive groups at Fortune 500 companies for three decades. In 2009 he was selected as International Trade Educator of the Year by NASBITE International. A Berkeley PhD, Graham has published more than 60 articles in journals such as the *Harvard Business Review* (2), the *Negotiation Journal*, the *Journal of Marketing*, and *Management Science*. His five books with partners (see just below) have all been best sellers on their respective topics. He has also written articles for the *New York Times*, the *Los Angeles Times*, *USAToday*, the *Christian Science Monitor,* the *Orange County Register, and La Opinion*. His research has been the subject of articles in *Smithsonian* and the *Chronicle of Higher Education* and coverage on the NBC Nightly News, ABC Good Morning America, and Fox News. Graham is a veteran having served for nine years as an officer in the US Navy UDT/SEAL Teams. His works include:

with William Hernández Requejo, *Global Negotiation: The New Rules* (2008).

with N. Mark Lam, *China Now: Doing Business in the World's Most Dynamic Marketplace* (2007).

with Sharon Graham Niederhaus, *All in the Family: A Practical Guide to Successful Multigenerational Living*, 2nd edition (2013).

with Ambassador James Day Hodgson and Yoshiro Sano, *Doing Business in the New Japan,* 4th edition (2008).

with Philip R. Cateora and Mary C. Gilly, *International Marketing*, 16th edition (2013).

Lynda Lawrence is chief idea officer at Ideaworks Consulting and teaches innovation management at the Merage School of Business at the University of California, Irvine. She has more than 30 years of experience fostering creativity in many industries as well as in trade groups, nonprofits, and government agencies, and she has won more than 500 awards for creativity and public service. Her work has appeared in publications as diverse as *Creativity*, *the Journal of Philanthropy*, and *Qualitative Market Research: An International Journal*. She is an advisor to the Beall Center for Innovation and Entrepreneurship, a founding director of UCI Citizen Peacebuilding and the Olive Tree Initiative, and she has served on several boards of directors for more than two decades.

As a graduate of the Executive Program in Innovation and Organizational Change from the JFK School of Government at Harvard University and with a master's degree in organizational development, she combines hands-on knowledge of creativity and organizational dynamics to guide groups to more inventive and profitable relationships.

William Hernández Requejo is president and senior advisor at Requejo Consulting, a boutique advisory firm specializing in the area of international management, international strategic development, international negotiations, and advanced projects. He has worked with numerous multinational corporations on a wide variety of sophisticated matters. Requejo is also adjunct faculty in international business negotiations, international business transactions, international joint ventures and strategic alliances, and international marketing at different universities in the United States and Europe. He is coauthor of *Global Negotiation: The New Rules* (2008) and *Global Business Today*, Global Edition (2011). He was the founding director of the Asturias Business School in Spain. Requejo has a Juris Doctor from Georgetown University Law Center specializing in International Law.

Notes

Introduction: Bought a Car Lately?

1. Harvey Mackay, author of no 1 *New York Times* best seller *Swim with the Sharks without Being Eaten Alive* (New York: HarperBusiness, 2005).
2. Daniel H. Pink, *To Sell Is Human* (New York: Riverhead Books, 2012).
3. Stephen Denning, *The Leader's Guide to Storytelling: Mastering the Art and Discipline of Business Narrative* (San Francisco: Jossey-Bass, 2011).
4. F. Heider and M.Simmel, "An Experimental Study of Apparent Behavior," *American Journal of Psychology* 57 (1944): 243–259.

1 Going Forward to the Past: A Brief History of Negotiation

1. Jared Diamond, *Guns, Germs, and Steel: The Fate of Human Societies* (New York: Norton), 1999.
2. Amy Chozick, "Jared Diamond: 'New Guinean Kids Are Not Brats,'" *New York Times Magazine*, January 10, 2014.
3. But then why war? Why violence? Among the remaining modern hunter-gatherer groups around the world today violence is mostly a consequence of competition for women or climatically caused resource scarcity. Indeed, it is estimated that 40 percent of Yanomami tribesmen living deep in the Amazonian jungle have killed a human over such issues. But everyday life, even for the Yanomami, is filled with collaboration within and between the tribes. Also see Steven Pinker's *The Better Angels of Our Nature: Why Violence Has Declined* (New York: Viking, 2011); *The Economist*, "The Origins of War: Old Soldiers?" July 20, 2013, pages 69–70; and David B. Barash, "Are We Hard-Wired for Violence?" *New York Times*, September 29, 2013, page 12.
4. Spencer Wells, *The Pandora's Seed: The Unforeseen Cost of Civilization* (New York: Random House, 2010).
5. Richard Nisbett, *The Geography of Thought* (London: Nicholas Brealey, 2005).

6. We think this is the most often forgotten word in his sentence. He says "frequently," not "always" or even "most of the time." Through his use of the term "frequently" Smith granted that competitive behavior can have negative consequences for society and organizations, and cooperative behavior can be a good thing. This subtlety in his lesson is most often missed (ignored?) by our colleagues in the finance departments of our business schools and on Wall Street. Gordon Gecko actually should have said, "Greed is *frequently* good."

7. Actually, we may have all been better off if Thomas Jefferson and the founding fathers had used the more accurate terms, "Declaration of Political Sovereignty." Globalization has taught us that nations, even the "most powerful country on the planet," are still *inter*dependent.

8. John L. Graham and Roy A. Herberger, "Negotiators Abroad: Don't Shoot from the Hip," *Harvard Business Review*, July–August 1983, pages 160–168.

9. We note that many US medical schools have gone to a pass/fail grading system because the competition between the high-achieving students over grades did damage to the learning process.

10. We laud James Sebenius and his colleagues at the Harvard Business School for making a course on negotiation a requirement in their MBA program. Most schools offer courses on negotiation as a popular elective, but Harvard has rightly recognized that negotiation is a fundamental aspect of commercial activity by giving these courses prominence in its curriculum.

11. Richard Boudreaux, "Putin Urges Using Dialogue, Not 'Truncheons,'" *Wall Street Journal*, September 24, 2011, page A9.

12. Jeffrey Z. Rubin and Bert R. Brown, *The Social Psychology of Bargaining and Negotiation* (New York: Academic Press, 1975).

13. Jeffrey Z. Rubin, "Editor's Introduction to the First Issue," *Negotiation Journal* 1 no. 1 (1984): 5–9.

14. Roger Fisher, William Ury, and Bruce Patton, *Getting to Yes: Negotiating Agreement without Giving In* (New York: Penguin, 2011).

15. Howard Raiffa with John Richardson and David Metcalfe, *Negotiation Analysis: The Science and Art of Collaborative Decision Making* (Cambridge: Belknap/Harvard University Press, 2002), page 196.

16. David A. Lax and James K. Sebenius, *3-D Negotiation: Powerful Tools to Change the Game in Your Most Important Deals* (Boston: Harvard Business School Press, 2006).

17. Lawrence Susskind, Sarah McKearnan, and Jennifer Thomas-Larmer, *The Consensus-Building Handbook: A Comprehensive Guide to Reaching Agreement* (Thousand Oaks, CA: Sage, 1999).

18. J. William Breslin, "Negotiation Journal Editor Jeffrey Z. Rubin Dies in Accident," *Negotiation Journal*, July 1995, pages 195–199.

19. Tom Kelley and Jonathan Littman, *The Ten Faces of Innovation: IDEO's Strategies for Defeating the Devil's Advocate and Driving Creativity throughout the Organization* (New York: Currency Doubleday, 2005); Tom Kelley,

Jonathan Littman, and Tom Peters, *The Art of Innovation from IDEO, Americas Leading Design Firm* (New York: Crown Books, 2001).

20. Henry Chesbrough, *Open Innovation: The New Imperative for Creating and Profiting from Technology* (Boston: Harvard Business School Press, 2006).

21. John Hagel III, John Seely Brown, and Lang Davison, *The Power of Pull: How Small Moves, Smartly Made, Can Set Big Things in Motion* (New York: Basic Books, 2012).

22. David Obstfeld, "Social Networks, the *Tertius Iungens* Orientation, and Involvement in Innovation," *Administrative Science Quarterly* 50 no. 1 (March 2005): 100–130.

23. James D. Hodgson, Yoshihiro Sano, and John L. Graham, *Doing Business with the New Japan,* 4th ed. (Boulder: Rowman & Littlefield, 2008).

24. We note that the field of social psychology is currently under attack again, this time for different reasons—sloppy methods, fraudulent reporting of findings, and an academic culture of questionable ethics. See Christopher Shea, "Fraud Scandal Fuels Debate over Practices of Social Psychology," *Chronicle of Higher Education,* November 13, 2011; and Martin Enserink, "Final Report: Stapel Affair Points to Bigger Problems in Social Psychology," *Science Insider,* November 28, 2012, online.

2   Spotting a Glimmer of Opportunity

1. See Stephen Denning, *The Leader's Guide to Storytelling: Mastering the Art and Discipline of Business Narrative* (San Francisco: Jossey-Bass, 2011) for more detail.

2. Kirk Johnson and Nick Wingfield, "As Amazon Stretches, Seattle's Downtown is Reshaped," *New York Times,* August 25, 2013, online.

3. Edmund Sanders, "Mideast Peace Poll Stirs Worries," *Los Angeles Times,* August 7, 2013, page A3.

4. Paul Israel, *Edison: A Life of Invention* (New York: Wiley, 1998); Randall Stross, *The Wizard of Menlo Park* (New York: Three Rivers Press, 2007); Francis Jehl, *Menlo Park Reminiscences,* vols. 1–3 (Dearborne, MI: The Edison Institute, 1936, 1938, and 1941).

3   Identifying and Creating Partners

1. Paul Israel, *Edison: A Life of Invention* (New York: Wiley, 1998); Randall Stross, *The Wizard of Menlo Park* (New York: Three Rivers Press, 2007); Francis Jehl, *Menlo Park Reminiscences,* vols. 1–3 (Dearborne, MI: The Edison Institute, 1936, 1938, and 1941).

2. The evidence for team-based invention is stacking up quite high. Please see Jonah Lehrer, "Sunset of the Solo Scientist," *Wall Street Journal,* February 5, 2011, online; and Michael Nielsen, "The New Einsteins Will Be Scientists Who Share," *New York Times,* October 29–30, 2011, page C3.

3. Matt Ridley, "From Phoenicia to Hayek to the 'Cloud,'" *Wall Street Journal*, September 24, 2011, A15.

4. R. Bruce Money, Mary C. Gilly, and John L. Graham, "Explorations of National Culture and Word-of-Mouth Referral Behavior in the Purchase of Industrial Services in the United States and Japan," *Journal of Marketing* 62 (October 1998): 76–87.

5. For more detail please see Steven D. Levitt and Stephen J. Dubner, *Freakonomics: A Rogue Economist Explores the Hidden Side of Everything* (New York: William Morrow, 2009).

6. Josh Fischman, "International Teams, Papers Draw More Citations than Works by U.S.-Only Authors," *Chronicle of Higher Education*, March 10, 2011, online.

4 Building Personal Relationships

1. Richard Norton-Taylor, "When Winston Churchill Met Joseph Staling: Suckling Pigs and Savage Brews," *The Guardian*, May 22, 2013, online.

2. Fareed Zakaria, "Hail, President. Well Met," *Time Magazine*, June 12, 3013, online.

3. We classify English-speaking and Northern European countries as "information-oriented" cultures. Asian, African, and Latin American cultures tend to be "relationship-oriented," that is, valuing personal relationships over rules, laws, etc. For much more on this topic see William Hernández Requejo and John L. Graham, *Global Negotiation: The New Rules* (New York: Palgrave Macmillan, 2008).

4. Mary Robinson, *Everybody Matters: My Life Giving Voice* (London: Walker, 2013).

5. This material was gleaned from William T. Graham, "The Effectiveness of Consensus Building in Renewable Energy Project Development," unpublished MA thesis in Environmental Management, Harvard University, 2008.

6. This principle was pioneered by Nazi interrogator Hanns Joachim Scharff—see Raymond F. Toliver, *The Interrogator* (Atglen, PA: Schiffer Military History, 1997).

7. Matthew Alexander with John R. Bruing, *How to Break a Terrorist* (New York: Free Press, 2008).

5 Designing Systems for Success

1. David A. Lax and James K. Sebenius, *3-D Negotiation: Powerful Tools to Change the Game in Your Most Important Deals* (Boston: Harvard Business School Press, 2006); and Lax and Sebenius, "3-D Negotiations: Playing the Whole Game," *Harvard Business Review*, November 2003, pages 1–8.

2. David A. Lax and James K. Sebenius, "Deal Making 2.0: A Guide to Complex Negotiations," *Harvard Business Review*, November 2012, pages 92–100.

3. *Research Brief,* "Face up to Innovation," March 1, 2013, online, http://www.imex-frankfurt.com/documents/MeetologyLabIMEX-FinalReport.pdf.

6 Getting the Team Right

1. N. Mark Lam and John L. Graham, *China Now: Doing Business in the World's Most Dynamic Market* (New York: McGraw-Hill, 2007).
2. Daniel Goleman, *Social Intellignece: The New Science of Human Relationships* (New York: Bantam, 2006) 84.
3. Daniel H. Pink, *To Sell is Human: The Surprising Truth about Moving Others* (New York: Riverhead Books, 2012).
4. Daniel Goleman, *Emotional Intelligence: Why It Can Matter More than IQ* (New York: Bantam, 1995).
5. Kal Bishop, "Beyond Brainstorming, Large Groups," retrieved April 1, 2005, from http://www.ezinearticles.com; Rena Manning, "Idea Generation in Brainstorming and Turn-Taking Groups: Differences in Idea Quantity, Quality, and Task Perceptions," PhD dissertation, Texas Tech University, 1996.
6. Margaret Kolkena, "Remembering to Jump: Innovation in Comedy Improvisation Teams and Business Process Reengineering Teams," MA thesis, Pepperdine University, 1995; Lu Hong and Scott E. Page, "Groups of Diverse Problems Solvers Can Outperform Groups of High Ability Problem Solvers," *Proceedings of the National Academy of Sciences,* September 17, 2004, online; Tracy Kidder, *The Soul of a New Machine* (New York: Little Brown, 1981); William W. Maddux and Adam D. Galinshy, "Cultural Borders and Mental Barriers: The Relationship between Living Abroad and Creativity," *Journal of Personality and Social Psychology* 6, no. 5 (2009): 1047–1061; Aron Bolin, "The Relationships among Personality, Process, and Performance in Interactive Brainstorming Groups," PhD dissertation, Northern Illinois University, 2002.
7. Warren E. Watson, Kamalesh Kumar, and Larry K. Michaelson, "Cultural Diversity's Impact on Interaction Process and Performance: Comparing Homogeneous and Diverse Task Groups," *Academy of Management Journal* 6, no. 3 (1993): 590–602; Angela Ka-yee Leung, William W. Maddux, Adam D. Galinshy, and Chiyue Chiu, "Multicultural Experience Enhances Creativity: The When and How," *American Psychologist* 63, no. 3 (2008): 169–181; Anita Woolley, Cristopher Chabris, Alex Pentland, Nada Hashni, and Tomas W. Malone, "Evidence for a Collective Intelligence Factor in the Performance of Human Groups," *Science* 330, no. 6004 (October 29, 2010): 696–698.
8. Melba Burns, "A Comparison of Three Creative Problems-Solving Methodologies (Brainstorming, Personal Analogy, Forced Relationship)," unpublished PhD dissertation, University of Denver, 1983; Woolley et. al. 2010.

9. Malcolm Gladwell, *Blink: The Power of Thinking without Thinking* (New York: Little Brown, 2005).

10. Katherine Wiley, "Expertise as Mental Set: The Effects of Domain Knowledge in Creative Problems Solving," *Memory and Cognition* 26, no. 4 1998: 716–730.

11. Theresa Amabile, "How to Kill Creativity," *Harvard Business Review*, September/October 1998, pages 76–78.

12. Marc G. Berman, John Jonides, and Stephen Kaplan, "The Cognitive Benefits of Interaction with Nature," *Psychological Science* 19, no. 12 (2008): 1207–1212; Alice M. Isen, "An Influence of Positive Affect on Decision Making in Complex Situations: Theoretical Issues with Practical Implications," *Journal of Consumer Psychology* 11, no. 2 (2001): 75–85.

13. Ullrich Wagner, Steffen Gais, Hilda Haider, Rolf Verleger, and Jan Bern, "Sleep Inspires Insight," *Nature* 427 (January 22, 2004): 352–355; Erin J. Wamsley, Matthew Tucker, Jessica Payne, Joseph A. Benavides, Robert Stickgold, "Dreaming of Learning Task is Associated with Enhanced Sleep-Dependent Memory Consolidation," *Current Biology* 20, no. 9 (May 2010): 850–855.

14. David Obstfeld, "Social Networks, the *Tertius Iungens* Orientation, and Involvement in Innovation," *Administrative Science Quarterly* 50, no. 1 (2005): 100–130.

15. Malcolm Gladwell, *The Tipping Point: How Little Things Can Make a Big Difference* (New York: Little Brown, 2000).

16. James Day Hodgson, Yoshihiro Sano, and John L. Graham, *Doing Business with the New Japan,* 4th ed. (Boulder, CO: Rowman & Littlefield, 2008).

17. Lam and Graham, *China Now,* op. cit.

18. William T. Graham, *The Effectiveness of Consensus Building in Renewable Energy Project Development: A Thesis in the Field of Environmental Management,* (Cambridge: Harvard University, 2008).

19. Lawrence Susskind and Jeffrey Cruikshank, *Breaking the Impasse: Consensual Approaches to Resolving Public Disputes* (New York: Basic Books,1987); Lawrence Susskind, Sarah McKearnan, and Jennifer Thomas-Larmer, *The Consensus-Building Handbook: A Comprehensive Guide to Reaching Agreement* (Thousand Oaks, CA: Sage, 1999).

7 Leveraging Diversity

1. Geert Hofstede, *Culture's Consequences,* 2nd ed. (Thousand Oaks, CA: Sage, 2001).

2. Warren E. Watson, Kamalesh Kumar, and Larry K. Michaelsen, "Cultural Diversity's Impact on Interaction Process and Performance: Comparing Homogeneous and Diverse Task Groups," *Academy of Management Journal* 36, no. 3 (1993): 590–602.

3. The following institutions and people have provided crucial support for the research upon which this material is based: US Department of Education; Toyota Motor Sales USA, Inc.; Solar Turbines, Inc. (a division of Caterpillar Tractors Co.); the Faculty Research and Innovation Fund and the International Business Educational Research (IBEAR) Program at the University of Southern California; Ford Motor Company; The Marketing Science Institute; Madrid Business School; and Professors Nancy J. Adler (McGill University), Nigel Campbell (Manchester Business School), A. Gabriel Esteban (University of Houston, Victoria), Leonid I. Evenko (Russian Academy of the National Economy), Richard H. Holton (University of California, Berkeley), Alain Jolibert (Université des Sciences Sociales de Grenoble), Dong Ki Kim (Korea University), C. Y. Lin (National Sun-Yat Sen University), Hans-Gunther Meissner (Dortmund University), Alena Ockova (Czech Management Center), Sara Tang (Mass Transit Railway Corporation, Hong Kong), Kam-hon Lee (The Chinese University of Hong Kong), and Theodore Schwarz (Monterrey Institute of Technology).

4. For additional details see John L. Graham, "Culture and Human Resources Management," in Alan M. Rugman and Thomas L. Brewer (eds.), *The Oxford Handbook of International Business* (Oxford: Oxford University Press, 2001), pp. 503–536. For a more in-depth discussion of the influences of culture on negotiation see Michele J. Gelfand and Jeanne M. Brett (eds.), *The Handbook of Negotiation and Culture* (Sanford, CA: Stanford Business Books, 2004).

5. Roger O. Crockett, "The 21st Century Meeting," *BusinessWeek*, February 26, 2007, pages 72–80.

6. Albert Mehrabian, *Silent Messages: Implicit Communication of Emotions and Attitudes,* 2nd ed. (Belmont, CA: Wadsworth, 1980).

7. Geert Hofstede, *Culture's Consequences*, 2nd ed. (Thousand Oaks, CA: Sage, 2001); Susan P. Douglas, "Exploring New Worlds: The Challenge of Global Marketing," *Journal of Marketing*, January 2001, pp. 103–109.

8. Edward T. Hall, *The Silent Language* (New York: Doubleday, 1959), p. 26.

9. Harry C. Triandis, *Individualism and Collectivism* (Boulder, CO: Westview Press, 1995).

10. Joel West and John L. Graham, "A Linguistic-based Measure of Cultural Distance and Its Relationship to Managerial Values," *Management International Review* 44, no.3 (2004): 239–260.

11. N. Mark Lam and John L. Graham, *China Now: Doing Business in the World's Most Dynamic Market* (New York: McGraw-Hill, 2007).

12. Richard E. Davis, "Compatibility in Corporate Marriages," *Harvard Business Review*, July–August 1968, pages 87–93.

13. Scarlet Pruitt, "AOLTW Board May Attempt to Oust Case," *InfoWorld Daily News*, September 17, 2002.

14. William L. Cron, Mary C. Gilly, John L. Graham, and John W. Slocum, "Gender Differences in the Pricing of Professional Services: Implications for Income and Customer Relationships," *Organizational Behavior and Group Decision Processes* 109, no. 1 (2009): 93–105.

15. Deborah Tannen, *You Just Don't Understand: Men and Women in Conversation* (New York: William Morrow, 1990).

16. Jay Newton-Small, "Women Are the Only Adults Left in Washington," *Time*, October 16, 2013, online.

17. For more ways of inventing options for the United States government debt problem see John's comments on the *Harvard Business Review* blog network, "The Debt Ceiling Debate Needs a Moderator," July 19, 2011, see http://blogs.hbr.org/2011/07/the-debt-ceiling-debate-needs/.

18. Steven Pinker, *The Better Angels of Our Nature: Why Violence Has Declined* (New York: Viking, 2011), pages 684–685.

19. Joyce Neu, John L. Graham, and Mary C. Gilly, "The Influence of Gender on Behaviors and Outcomes in a Retail Buyer-Seller Negotiation," *Journal of Retailing* 64, no. 4 (Winter 1988): 427–438.

20. For a summary of the recent research see "Sex and Brains: Vive la Difference," *The Economist*, December 7, 2013, 81–82.

21. Samantha N. N. Cross and Mary C. Gilly, "The Creolization of Family and Society: When Tradition Meets Innovation," working paper, The Paul Merage School of Business, University of California, Irvine, 2014.

8 Exploring Place/Space/Pace

1. Larry Berman, *No Peace, No Honor: Nixon, Kissinger, and Betrayal in Vietnam* (New York: Touchstone, 2001).

2. Alison Stein Wellner, "A Perfect Brainstorm," *Inc.* 25, no. 10 (October 2003): 31.

3. Ravi Mehta and Rui Zhu, "Red or Blue: Discovering the Effect of Color on Cognitive Task Performances," *Science Magazine Online*, February 5, 2009.

4. Joan Meyers-Levy and Rui Zhu, "The Influence of Ceiling Height: The Effect of Priming on the Type of Processing that People Use," *Journal of Consumer Research* 34, no. 2 (August 2007): 174–186.

5. Paul Kelly, *The Seven Slide Solution: Telling Your Business Story Effectively in Seven Slides or Less* (Westport, CT: Silvermine Press, 2005).

6. John A. Bargh and Idit Shalev, "The Substitutability of Physical and Social Warmth in Daily Life," *Emotion* 12, no. 1 (February 2012): 154–162.

7. Stephen Kellert and Edward Wilson, *The Biophilia Hypothesis* (Washington, DC: Island Press, 1995).

8. Nancy Etcoff, "21st Century Well Being, Commitment, and Productivity," *Havard Medical School and Massachusetts General Hospital Study*, fall/winter 2006; Seiji Shibata and Naoto Suzuki, "Effects of an Indoor Plant on Creative Task Performance and Mood," *Scandinavian*

Journal of Psychology 45 (2004): 373–381; Roger Ulrich, "The Impact of Flowers and Plants on Workplace Productivity," *Texas A&M University, The Center for Health Systems and Design Study* (spring/summer 2003), 49–59.

9. Ronald S. Friedman and Jens Forster, "Effects of Motivational Cues on Perceptual Asymmetry: Implications Creative and Analytical Problem Solving," *Journal of Personality and Social Psychology* 88, no. 2 (February 2005): 263–275.

10. J. Degel and E. E. Koster, "Odors: Implicit Memory and Performance Effects," *Chemical Senses* 24 (1999): 317–325.

11. Heinrich Pierer and Bolko V. Oetinger, *A Passion for Ideas: How Innovators Create the New and Shape Our World* (West Lafayette, IN: Purdue University Press, 2002); Mandy Wechsler Segal, "Alphabet and Attraction: An Unobtrusive Measure of the Effect of Propinquity in a Field Setting," *Journal of Personality and Social Psychology* 30 (1974): 254–257.

12. Joshua Ackerman, Christopher C. Nocera, and John A. Bargh, "Incidental Haptic Sensations Influence Social Judgements and Decisions," *Science* 328, no. 5986 (June 25, 2010): 1712–1715.

13. Darrin M. Lipnicki and Don G. Byrne, "Thinking on Your Back: Solving Anagrams Faster When Supine than When Standing," *Cognitive Brain Research* 24, no. 3 (August 2005): 719–722.

14. Ravi Mehta, Rui Zhu, and Amar Cheema, "Is Noise Always Bad? Exploring the Effect of Ambient Noise on Creative Cognition," *Journal of Consumer Research* 39, no. 4 (December 2012): 784–799.

15. Martha C. White, "Business Meetings Move Poolside (Don't Overdress)," *New York Times*, August 19, 2013, online.

16. Edward T. Hall, "The Silent Language in Overseas Business," *Harvard Business Review*, May–June 1960, pages 87–96.

17. James D. Hodgson, Yoshihiro Sano, and John L. Graham, *Doing Business in the New Japan*, 4th ed. (Boulder, CO: Rowman & Littlefield, 2008).

18. Gregory Boyle, *Tattoos on the Heart: The Power of Boundless Compassion* (New York: Free Press, 2010), pages 76–77 and 111–115.

9 Preparing for Emotions/Power/Corruption

1. Christian McEwen, "Don't Just Do Something; Stand There," *Los Angeles Times*, August 14, 2011, page A20.

2. Paul Ekman and W. V. Friesen, *Facial Action Coding System: A Technique for the Measurement of Facial Movement* (Palo Alto, CA: Consulting Psychologist Press, 1978).

3. John L. Graham, "An Exploratory Study of the Process of Marketing Negotiations Using a Cross-Cultural Perspective," chapter 14 in Robin C. Scracella, Elaine S. Anderson, and Stephen D. Krashen, (eds.) *Developing Communicative Competence in a Second Language* (Boston: Heinle & Heinle Publishers, 1990).

4. Paul Ekman, *Emotions Revealed: Recognizing Faces and Feelings to Improve Communication and Emotional Life,* 2nd ed. (New York: Holt, 2003).
5. John R. P. French and Bertram Raven, "Bases of Social Power," in Dorwin Cartwright (ed.), *Studies in Social Power* (Ann Arbor: University of Michigan, 1959).
6. Paul Ekman, *Emotions Revealed, op. cit.*
7. James Day Hodgson, Yoshihiro Sano, and John L. Graham, *Doing Business in the New Japan,* 4th ed. (Boulder, CO: Rowman & Littlefield, 2008).
8. See http://www.haaretz.com/print-edition/opinion/thou-shalt-not-be-a-freier-1.211247 for an extended discussion.

10 Changing Roles

1. George J. Mitchell, *Making Peace: The Behind-the-Scenes Story of the Negotiations that Culminated in the Signing of the Northern Ireland Peace Accord* (Berkeley: University of California Press, 1999).
2. For copious details on this subject see Sharon Graham Niederhaus and John L. Graham, *All in the Family: A Practical Guide to Successful Multigenerational Living,* 2nd ed. (Lanham, MD: Taylor Trade, 2013).
3. E. S. Browning, "Debt Hobbles Older Americans," *Wall Street Journal,* September 7, 2011; Catey Hill, "Coming Soon: Smaller Raises for Seniors?" *SmartMoney.com,* July 13, 2011; Mark Whitehouse, "Another Threat to the Economy: Boomers Cutting Back," *Wall Street Journal,* August 16, 2010; and *The Economist,* "Demand for Equities May Drop," January 9, 2012.
4. Kathleen McGarry and Robert F. Schoeni, "Social Security, Economic Growth, and the Rise of Independence of Elderly Widows in the 20th Century," *NBER Working Paper No. 6511,* April 1998.
5. Judy Richter, "A Full Table," *San Francisco Chronicle,* September 10, 2005, sec. F. Used with permission.
6. Niederhaus and Graham, *All in the Family,* op. cit.

11 Creating Surprises

1. For more detail about many of the ideas listed here please see Steve Johnson, *Where Good Ideas Come From: The Natural History of Innovation* (New York: Riverhead Books, 2010).
2. Nicole Oxley and Mary Dzindolet, "The Effects of Facilitators on the Performance of Brainstorming Groups," *Journal of Social Behavior and Personality* 11, no. 4 (December 1996): 633–647;Thomas Krammer, Gerard Fleming, and Scott Mannis, "Improving Face-to-Face Brainstorming through Modeling and Facilitation," *Small Group Research* 32, no. 5 (October 2001): 533–541; and Lawrence Susskind and Jeffrey Cruikshank, *Breaking the Impasse: Consensual Approaches to Resolving Public Disputes* (New York: Basic Books, 1987); Lawrence

Susskind, Sarah McKearnan, and Jennifer Thomas-Larmer, *The Consensus-Building Handbook: A Comprehensive Guide to Reaching Agreement* (Thousand Oaks, CA: Sage, 1999).

3. Hoon-Seok Choi and Leigh Thompson, "Old Wine in a New Bottle: Impact of Membership Change on Group Creativity," *Organizational Behavior and Human Decision Processes* 98, no. 2 (November 2005): 121–132; Charlan Jeanne Nemeth and Margaret Omiston, "Creative Idea Generation: Harmony versus Stimulation," *European Journal of Social Psychology* 37, no. 3 (2006): 525–535.

4. Pavan Singh, "An Empirical Study of the Idea Generation Productivity of Decision-Making Groups: Implications for GDSS Research Design and Practice," PhD dissertation, York University, 2000; and Aybuke Aurum, "Solo Brainstorming: Behavioral Analysis of Decision Makers," PhD dissertation, University of New South Wales, 1997.

5. Michael Diehl and Wolfgang Stroebe, "Productivity Loss in Idea Generating Groups," *Journal of Personality and Social Psychology* 61, no. 3 (September 1991): 392–401; Emily Pronin and Elana Jacobs, "Thought Speed, Mood, and the Experience of Mental Motion," *Perspectives on Psychological Science* 6, no. 3 (2008): 461–486.

6. Timothy Kochery, "IGP Brainstorming: Investigating a Methodology that Accommodates to Personal Characteristics in Idea-generating Groups," PhD dissertation, University of Minnesota, 2003; Alison Stein Wellner, "A Perfect Brainstorm," *Inc.* 25, no. 10 (April 2009): 31; Hami Koskun, "The Effects of Problem Presentation in Nominal and Interactive Groups (Brainstorming)," MA thesis, University of Texas at Arlington, 1996; Dennis Brophy, "The Initial Testing of a Tri-level Matching Theory of Creative Problem Solving," PhD dissertation, Texas A&M University, 1995.

7. Susan Campbell, "The Influence of Group Communication on Open-ended Problem Solving among Undergraduate Engineering Students," PhD dissertation, Pennsylvania State University, 2001.

8. Robyn Porterfield, "The Effects of Incubation and Attention on Brainstorming Productivity," MA thesis, University of Texas at Arlington, 2000; Josie Glausiusz, "Devoted to Distraction," *Psychology Today*, March/April 2009, online; Ap Dijksterhuis, "Think Different: The Merits of Unconscious Thought in Preference Development and Decision Making," *Journal of Personality and Social Psychology* 87, no. 5 (2004): 586–598.

9. Marc G. Berman, John Jonides, and Stephen Kaplan, "The Cognitive Benefits of Interacting with Nature," *Psychological Science* 19, no. 12 (2008): 1207–1212.

10. Stephen Kellert and Edward Wilson, *The Biophilia Hypothesis* (Washington, DC: Island Press, 1995).

11. Nira Liberman and Y. Trope, "The Psychology of Transcending the Here and Now," *Science* 322 (2008): 527–534.

12. Ullrich Wagner, Steffen Gais, Hilda Haider, Rolf Verleger, and Jan Bern, "Sleep Inspires Insight," *Nature* 427, January 22, 2004, pages 352–355; Jeffrey M. Ellenbogen, Peter T. Hu, Jessica Payne, Debra Titone, and Matthew Walker, "Human Relational Memory Requires Time and Sleep," *Proceedings of the National Academy of Sciences* 104, no. 18 (May 1, 2007): 7723–7728; Erin J. Wamsley, Matthew Tucker, Jessica Payne, Joseph A. Benavides, and Robert Stickgold, "Dreaming of a Learning Task is Associated with Enhanced Sleep-Dependent Memory Consolidation," *Current Biology* 20, no. 9 (May 2010): 850–855.

13. Denise J. Cai, Sarnoff A. Mednick, Elizabeth M. Harrison, Jennifer C. Kanady, and Sara C. Mednick, "REM, Not Incubation, Improves Creativity by Priming Associative Networks," *Proceedings of the National Academy of Sciences*, June 8, 2009, online.

14. Alice M. Isen, "An Influence of Positive Affect on Decision Making in Complex Situations: Theoretical Issues with Practical Implications," *Journal of Consumer Psychology* 11, no. 2 (2001): 75–85.

15. David H. Krantz, Howard Kunreuther, and Elke Weber, *Group Identity, Context, and Social Goals*, Center for Research on Environmental Decisions. Cited in "Why Isn't the Brain Green?" *New York Times Magazine*, April 19, 2009, pages 36–43.

16. Tanya Chartran and John A. Bargh, "The Chameleon Effect: The Perception-Behavior Link and Social Interaction," *Journal of Personality and Social Psychology* 76, no. 6 (1999): 893–910; S. S. Wiltermuth and C. Heath, "Synchrony and Cooperation," *Psychological Science* 20 (2009): 1–5.

17. Adam Blattner, "Using Creativity to Explore in Psychotherapy," *Psychiatric Times*, June 1, 2003, online; Melinda Wenner, "The Serious Need for Play," *Scientific American Mind*, March/April 2009, pages 21–29.

18. An adaptation of Ralph Linton, *The Study of Man* (New York: Appleton-Century-Crofts, 1936), page 327.

19. Ann Hulbert, "Re-Education," *New York Times Magazine*, April 1, 2007, pages 36–43.

20. Lawrence Susskind and Jeffrey Cruikshank, *Breaking the Impasse: Consensual Approaches to Resolving Public Disputes* (New York: Basic Books, 1987).

21. Henry Chesbrough, *Open Innovation: The New Imperative for Creating and Profiting from Technology* (Cambridge: Harvard Business School Press, 2006).

12   Improvising

1. Gwendolyn Oxenham, *Finding the Game: Three Years, Twenty-five Countries, and the Search for Pickup Soccer* (New York: St. Martin's Press, 2012)., see pages 108–119.

2. Apama Labroo with V. M. Patrick, "Psychological Distancing: Why Happiness Helps You See the Big Picture," *Journal of Consumer Research* 35, no. 5 (2009): 800–809; Floyd Hunt, "Better Brainstorming," *Training & Development* 48, no. 11 (1994): 57; Edward DeBono, *Serious Creativity: Using the Power of Lateral Thinking to Create New Ideas* (New York: Harper Business, 1992); Roger von Oech, *A Whack on the Side of the Head: How You Can Be More Creative* (New York: Business Plus, 2008).

3. John L. Graham, Jennifer P. Hite, and Joyce Neu, "Explorations of the Effects of Conversational Behaviors on Interpersonal Attraction in a Work Setting, Face-to-Face Business Negotiations," a working paper, The Paul Merage School of Business, University of California, Irvine, 2014.

4. Eli Simon, *The Art of Clowning: More Paths to Your Inner Clown,* 2nd ed. (New York: Palgrave Macmillan, 2012).

5. Daniel H. Pink, *To Sell is Human: The Surprising Truth about Moving Others* (New York: Riverhead Books, 2012).

13 Playing Together Nicely

1. Robert Cohen, *Working in Theater: Collaboration and Leadership* (New York: Palgrave Macmillan, 2011).

2. Steven Pinker, *The Better Nature of Our Angels: Why Violence Has Declined* (New York: Viking, 2011).

14 Reviewing and Improving

1. Ron S. Fortgang, David A. Lax, and James K. Sebenius, "Negotiating the Spirit of the Deal," *Harvard Business Review*, February 2003, pages 66–73.

2. The material here is based on many sources including Walter Isaacson, *Steve Jobs* (New York: Simon & Schuster, 2011); Leander Kahney, *Inside Steve's Brain* (New York: Portfolio, 2008); "Charlie Rose Talks to Bob Iger," *Bloomberg Businessweek*, March 14–20, 2011, page 26; Eva Dou, "Apple Shifts Supply Chain away from Foxconn to Pegatron," *Wall Street Journal*, May 29, 2013, online.

Index